SUPPORTING K–12 ENGLISH LANGUAGE LEARNERS IN SCIENCE

The contribution of this book is to synthesize important common themes and highlight the unique features, findings, and lessons learned from three systematic, ongoing research and professional learning projects for supporting English learners in science. Each project, based in a different region of the U.S. and focused on different age ranges and target populations, actively grapples with the linguistic implications of the three-dimensional learning required by the Framework for K–12 Science Education and the Next Generation Science Standards. Each chapter provides research-based recommendations for improving the teaching of science to English learners. Offering insights into teacher professional learning as well as strategies for measuring and monitoring how well English learners are learning science and language, this book tells a compelling and inclusive story of the challenges and the opportunities of teaching science to English learners.

Cory A. Buxton is Athletic Association Professor of Education, Department of Educational Theory and Practice, University of Georgia, USA.

Martha Allexsaht-Snider is Associate Professor, Department of Educational Theory and Practice, University of Georgia, USA.

TEACHING AND LEARNING IN SCIENCE SERIES
Norman G. Lederman, Series Editor

Responsive Teaching in Science and Mathematics
Robertson/Scherr/Hammer (Eds.)

Reconceptualizing STEM Education
Duschl/Bismack (Eds.)

Re-examining Pedagogical Content Knowledge in Science Education
Berry/Friedrichsen/Loughran (Eds.)

Student Thinking and Learning in Science: Perspectives on the Nature and Development of Learners' Ideas
Taber

Integrating Science, Technology, Engineering, and Mathematics: Issues, Reflections, and Ways Forward
Rennie/Venville/Wallace (Eds.)

Rethinking the Way We Teach Science: The Interplay of Content, Pedagogy, and the Nature of Science
Rosenblatt

Exploring the Landscape of Scientific Literacy
Linder/Östman/Roberts/Wickman/Erickson/MacKinnon (Eds.)

Designing and Teaching the Elementary Science Methods Course
Abell/Appleton/Hanuscin

Interdisciplinary Language Arts and Science Instruction in Elementary Classrooms: Applying Research to Practice
Akerson (Ed.)

Aesthetic Experience in Science Education: Learning and Meaning-Making as Situated Talk and Action
Wickman

Visit **www.routledge.com/education** for additional information on titles in the Teaching and Learning in Science Series

SUPPORTING K–12 ENGLISH LANGUAGE LEARNERS IN SCIENCE

Putting Research into Teaching Practice

Edited by
Cory A. Buxton and
Martha Allexsaht-Snider

NEW YORK AND LONDON

First published 2017
by Routledge
711 Third Avenue, New York, NY 10017

and by Routledge
2 Park Square, Milton Park, Abingdon, Oxon, OX14 4RN

Routledge is an imprint of the Taylor & Francis Group, an informa business

© 2017 Taylor & Francis

The right of Cory A. Buxton and Martha Allexsaht-Snider to be identified as the authors of the editorial material of this work, and of the authors for their individual chapters, has been asserted by them in accordance with sections 77 and 78 of the Copyright, Designs and Patents Act 1988.

All rights reserved. No part of this book may be reprinted or reproduced or utilised in any form or by any electronic, mechanical, or other means, now known or hereafter invented, including photocopying and recording, or in any information storage or retrieval system, without permission in writing from the publishers.

Trademark notice: Product or corporate names may be trademarks or registered trademarks, and are used only for identification and explanation without intent to infringe.

Library of Congress Cataloguing in Publication Data
Names: Buxton, Cory A., editor. | Allexsaht-Snider, Martha, editor.
Title: Supporting K-12 English language learners in science : putting research into teaching practice / edited by Cory A. Buxton and Martha Allexsaht-Snider.
Description: New York : Routledge, 2017. | Series: Teaching and learning in science series
Identifiers: LCCN 2016025187| ISBN 9781138961180 (hardback) | ISBN 9781138961197 (pbk.) | ISBN 9781315659930 (ebk.)
Subjects: LCSH: Science—Study and teaching (Elementary) | Science—Study and teaching (Secondary) | English language—Study and teaching (Elementary)—Foreign speakers. | English language—Study and teaching (Secondary)—Foreign speakers.
Classification: LCC LB1585 .S885 2017 | DDC 372.35/044—dc23
LC record available at https://lccn.loc.gov/2016025187

ISBN: 978-1-138-96118-0 (hbk)
ISBN: 978-1-138-96119-7 (pbk)
ISBN: 978-1-315-65993-0 (ebk)

Typeset in Bembo
by diacriTech, Chennai

To all the teachers, students, families, and colleagues who taught and learned along with us.

CONTENTS

Preface   *xi*
Acknowledgments   *xv*

1. Introduction – Teaching Science to Emergent Bilingual Learners: Research and Practice at the Intersection of Science and Language Learning   1
   Cory A. Buxton & Martha Allexsaht-Snider

PART I
P-SELL: PROMOTING SCIENCE AMONG ENGLISH LANGUAGE LEARNERS   13

2. Promoting Science among English Language Learners (P-SELL) Model: Curricular and Professional Development Intervention in Elementary Science Instruction with a Focus on English Language Learners   15
   Okhee Lee, Corey O'Connor, & Alison Haas

3. Measures and Outcomes for Students and Teachers in the Promoting Science among English Language Learners (P-SELL) Project   31
   Jaime Maerten-Rivera, Lorena Llosa, & Okhee Lee

4 Challenges in Implementing and Evaluating a Large-Scale Science Intervention: The Case of the Promoting Science among English Language Learners (P-SELL) Project   52
Lorena Llosa, Jaime Maerten-Rivera, & Christopher D. Van Booven

PART II
LISELL-B: LANGUAGE-RICH INQUIRY SCIENCE WITH ENGLISH LANGUAGE LEARNERS THROUGH BIOTECHNOLOGY   67

5 Reassembling Science Teacher Educator Professional Learning in the LISELL-B Project   69
Cory A. Buxton, Martha Allexsaht-Snider, Regina Suriel, Shakhnoza Kayumova, Elif Karsli, & Rouhollah Aghasaleh

6 Using Teacher Logs to Study Project Enactment and Support Professional Learning in the LISELL-B project   93
Linda Caswell, Gabe Schwartz, Daphne Minner, Martha Allexsaht-Snider, & Cory A. Buxton

7 The Value of Theory and Practice in the Context of the LISELL-B Project: Examples of Plug-ins   119
Shakhnoza Kayumova, Rouhollah Aghasaleh, & Max Vazquez Dominguez

PART III
ESTELL: EFFECTIVE SCIENCE TEACHING FOR ENGLISH LANGUAGE LEARNERS   139

8 Promoting English Language Learner Pedagogy in Science with Elementary School Teachers: The ESTELL Model of Pre-Service Teacher Education   141
Trish Stoddart

9 Capturing Pre-Service Teachers' Enactment of Amplified Science Instruction for English Language Learners   156
Marco A. Bravo, Jorge L. Solís, & Eduardo Mosqueda

10 Capitalizing on the Synergistic Possibilities
between Language, Culture, and Science 180
Jorge L. Solís, Marco A. Bravo, & Eduardo Mosqueda

**PART IV
CONCLUSIONS** **209**

11 Crosscutting Findings and Recommendations for
Research and Practice in Teaching Science with
Emergent Bilingual Learners 211
*Martha Allexsaht-Snider, Cory A. Buxton,
Yainitza Hernández Rodríguez, Lourdes Cardozo-Gaibisso,
Allan Cohen, & Zhenqiu Lu*

Contributors *243*
Index *244*

PREFACE

This book, *Supporting K–12 English Language Learners in Science: Putting Research into Teaching Practice*, is our attempt to summarize the lessons learned from three systematic, ongoing, research and development projects that have engaged in the work of supporting emergent bilingual learners and their teachers in science learning over multiple years. Each of these projects has done its work in a distinct and important region of the United States in terms of educating emergent bilinguals – students who speak a home language other than the primary language of instruction in school – and each has focused on different age ranges and target populations. Each project has also received ongoing federal funding over multiple years and multiple project iterations. Further, each project is actively grappling with the linguistic as well as the science learning implications of the three-dimensional learning framework put forward in the Framework for K–12 Science Education (2011), the Next Generation Science Standards (2013), and other current reform initiatives. Together, the three projects tell a compelling and inclusive story of the challenges and the opportunities in teaching science to emergent bilinguals.

We have compiled the experiences of these three projects with the aim of supporting teacher educators, professional developers who engage in teacher professional learning, and researchers who do work directly or indirectly with emergent bilinguals and science learning. We also intend this book to be of practical help to classroom teachers and school leaders who are looking for research-based recommendations for improving the teaching of science to emergent bilinguals and other students who are underserved by current approaches to science teaching.

Given the needs of these varied audiences, we have highlighted in-depth explorations of research-based pedagogical practices at the intersection of the teaching and learning of science and the teaching and learning of language. In light of evolving standards, curriculum, and assessment frameworks, the role of language used to communicate and interpret scientific ideas is of increasing importance for all students, and especially for emergent bilingual learners. This is not a book of ready-to-use instructional strategies or teaching methods, and there are other existing resources that may better serve that need. That said, there is still much practical classroom advice to be gained from the work of the projects described here. The findings that emerge from these large-scale research and development efforts to better understand the complexities and nuances of science teaching and learning with emergent bilinguals have explicit implications for daily classroom practices. Grappling with these issues is not easy, and we have tried to be honest and open about the challenges that each project encountered, and how the project teams attempted to manage and overcome those challenges. Here, too, there are many applicable lessons for multiple audiences.

Whether you are a teacher, teacher educator, school leader, researcher, or simply someone with an interest in better understanding science teaching and learning in multilingual and multicultural classrooms, we hope you will find the work of the projects described here to be useful. As we will elaborate in the introduction, each of the projects was given the general task of writing three chapters that highlight both the research and the development aspects of their effort with an eye toward providing practical lessons that will be of use to the various stakeholders who engage in or support the teaching of science with emergent bilingual learners. Within those broad guidelines, each project team was given the freedom to share those facets of their project that they felt would be most compelling for readers of this volume. The chapter authors took up this challenge and described project features ranging from student and teacher learning outcomes, to innovative methods of data collection, to the application of new theories for analyzing classroom practices. Despite the different emphases that resulted from this approach, the reader will also note a number of shared qualities that run across the three sections. These include:

1. Each of the three teams of researchers has been at the forefront of studying the teaching of science to emergent bilinguals for more than a decade.
2. Each of the projects has been working in distinct regions of the country and with different age ranges and target populations, but addressing common challenges with regional variations.
3. Each project has received ongoing federal funding, allowing the work to occur at a larger scale than much of the other published research on this topic.
4. Each project has used carefully selected theoretical, analytical, and methodological approaches to the research and has developed innovative research instruments and approaches to better understand the complexities and nuances of teaching science to emergent bilinguals.
5. Each project offers insights for innovative teacher learning as well as strategies for monitoring how well emergent bilinguals are learning science and language.

6. Each project brings together expertise in science education and language education in varied ways to better understand the possibilities for science teaching and learning and the linguistic implications of the current science education reforms.
7. Each project team discusses various challenges they encountered and how they managed and responded to those challenges, rather than representing the project as if everything had always gone smoothly, which, as every educator knows, is an unrealistic expectation.

We hope that, whatever your reason for reading this book, these distinctive features, and the quality of the projects themselves, will ensure that you find something of value.

ACKNOWLEDGMENTS

We would like to acknowledge the many people who have helped to create this book. First and foremost are our spouses, Jean-Marie and Don, who are always supportive of our passion for this work and the long hours that it requires. Special thanks go to our colleagues in the University of Georgia College of Education, the Department of Educational Theory and Practice, and especially the LISELL-B project team, who continually push us to think in new ways about the assets and opportunities, as well as the challenges, of working in multilingual and multicultural contexts.

This book is the work of three project teams, and each project is only as successful as the teamwork that develops among faculty, graduate students, research assistants, teachers, students, and other project participants. Thus, we wish to acknowledge all members of each of the project teams, and especially the leadership of Okhee Lee on the P-SELL project and Trish Stoddart on the ESTELL project. On the LISELL-B project team, we would especially like to acknowledge our project manager, Yainitza Hernández Rodríguez, for helping us keep this (and so many other projects) running smoothly.

We wish to acknowledge that the work of each of these projects has been supported with federal funding. The P-SELL efficacy study was supported by the Institute of Education Sciences, U.S. Department of Education, through Grant R305A090281. The P-SELL effectiveness study was supported by the National Science Foundation (NSF Grant DRL-1209309). The LISELL project was supported by the National Science Foundation under grant DRL-1019236 and the LISELL-B project under grant DRL-1316398. The ESTELL project has been supported by the National Science Foundation Discovery Research K–12 Program under grant DRL-0822402004. The opinions, findings, conclusions, and recommendations expressed in this book are those of the authors and do not necessarily reflect the positions, policies, or endorsements of the funding agencies.

We would like to thank Norm Lederman, the series editor, for the invitation to write this book. Naomi Silverman, our editor at Routledge, was patient and insightful. Her input throughout the planning and writing of this book made it a much better product. Our sincere thanks also go to Editorial Assistant Brianna Pennella, Production Editor Hélène Feest, and Project Manager Susie Foresman for their help in finalizing the many details that go into finishing a project of this kind.

This book was much improved by the suggestions of its reviewers. We would specifically like to thank Teaching and Learning in Science Series Editor Norman G. Lederman and peer reviewers Nazan Bautista and Alberto Rodriquez for their thoughtful comments and suggestions as we initially conceptualized this project. Numerous chapter authors served as reviewers for chapters in other sections of the book, and their knowledgeable feedback improved those chapters substantially. A number of our colleagues and doctoral students at the University of Georgia also conducted valuable chapter reviews and deserve our thanks: Ajay Sharma, Mardi Schmeichel, Allan Cohen, Susan Harper, Amanda Latimer, Christina Hylton, Lourdes Cardoso-Gaibisso, and Yainitza Hernández Rodríguez.

It was both fun and rewarding to pull together and synthesize the work of these projects, and we hope that our enthusiasm for this work comes across to you, the reader.

Cory A. Buxton
Martha Allexsaht-Snider
Athens, GA, 2016

1
INTRODUCTION – TEACHING SCIENCE TO EMERGENT BILINGUAL LEARNERS

Research and Practice at the Intersection of Science and Language Learning

Cory A. Buxton & Martha Allexsaht-Snider

In the second decade of the twenty-first century, when the vast majority of Americans readily access information with the touch of a screen on a computer, tablet, or smartphone, the need to memorize factual information has decreased sharply, while the need for skills to help us use information thoughtfully and productively has gained new urgency (Jacobs, 2014). How, where, and when we support students in becoming critical consumers of information and social problem solvers who can put that information to work for their own ends will be a driving question that shapes fundamental educational reforms over the next few decades. No less importantly, we need to grapple with the question of who receives access to new models of teaching that benefit from this information revolution, and who continues to receive traditional learning experiences rooted in outdated learning goals. Schools, classrooms, out-of-school learning contexts, virtual learning environments, student–teacher interactions, teacher–parent interactions, and student–student interactions, among others, are all being changed in substantive ways by rapid shifts in technology, in academic and occupational pathways, and in human demographics. Despite more than fifteen years of rhetoric of No Child Left Behind and Race to the Top, we continue to run the risk of leaving large portions of our population behind economically and socially if we fail to equip them with the thinking, communicating, and problem-solving skills needed to address the challenges and embrace the opportunities of the coming decades (Lockman & Schwartz, 2014). To this end, we see the ability to apply scientific understanding to everyday contexts and decision-making as increasingly important.

While the shift in science education from learning as acquiring information to learning as applying information is challenging for everyone, there are additional obstacles, as well as unique resources, for individuals who must engage in these learning expectations in a non-native language that they are still working to acquire. The challenges for emergent bilingual learners – those students who are learning in English at school while speaking a different home language – include making sense of the unique grammar, academic vocabulary, and communication patterns of science, resolving possible discrepancies between the norms and world views of science and those norms and world views brought from home, and learning to communicate their own scientific ideas, explanations, and arguments in both written and oral form (Buxton & Lee, 2014). While these challenges are substantial, emergent bilingual learners also bring various assets and resources, such as the multiple perspectives and perceptions that multilingualism provides, potentially useful cognates from their home language, and in many cases, practical experiences with applied science and engineering skills (Gándara, 2015). Often, however, these assets go unrecognized and underutilized in the science classroom, as many teachers and school leaders have not received the preparation for how to get the most out of these kinds of student resources (Samson & Collins, 2012). Regardless of their background or preparation, however, all students can gradually take ownership of their science learning, and all teachers can learn to support their emergent bilingual students in becoming proficient with the practices of scientific thinking and communicating.

Changing Occupational Landscapes and Changing Student Demographics

The work described in this book occurs at the intersection of rapidly shifting demographic trends that are altering the population of American students and workers at the same time that changing employment trends are shifting the jobs, skills, and technologies for which today's students must be prepared. According to the U.S. Department of Labor (USDoL, 2015), the most critical employment needs for the decade of 2015–2025 are linked to a mid-level STEM career gap. A report from the Brookings Institution (Rothwell, 2013) found that nearly half of all current STEM jobs require less than a four-year college degree at the entry point, while still paying an average salary of $53,000. Many of these jobs are in manufacturing, health care, and construction industries, fields that in the past would not have been considered as STEM occupations. However, the changing nature of these jobs now requires workers to have STEM skills to perform them. Another interesting finding of this report is that while STEM jobs that do require a bachelor's degree or higher are disproportionally clustered in only a few metropolitan areas, such as San Jose, CA, and Washington, DC, sub-bachelor's STEM jobs are much more widely dispersed. For example, Baton Rouge, LA, Birmingham, AL, and Wichita, KS, have among the highest percentages of STEM jobs in fields that do not require four-year college degrees. In short, sub-bachelor's STEM jobs are geographically dispersed, pay relatively high wages, and cut across a range of traditional and emerging sectors of manufacturing, service, and knowledge economies.

In Baltimore, for example, a city with a rich manufacturing history and local leaders who have continually tried to adapt to changing manufacturing conditions, a study by the Greater Baltimore Committee (Seals, 2016) found that workers in middle-skill STEM jobs were earning 61 percent more than workers in non-STEM occupations with the same education level. These middle-skill STEM careers included jobs in energy, manufacturing, technology, design, construction, health care, and bioscience. The biggest share of these jobs is in health care, in positions such as medical records technician, radiology specialist, surgical technician, and paramedic. The second largest sector is in technology, in positions such as network specialist, security analyst, data base administrator, and web designer. A third major growth area is in the energy sector, including positions both in manufacturing and in installation and servicing. In short, middle-skill STEM jobs have moderate education requirements, good salary, geographic flexibility, high job satisfaction, and continued growth potential. We wish to be clear that we are not implying that emergent bilingual learners can or should only aspire to middle-skill STEM jobs. Rather, we claim that these are high-growth occupational pathways in which emergent bilinguals are greatly underrepresented and to which many students might be attracted.

While STEM occupational pathways are rapidly evolving and expanding, so too are the demographics of the U.S. population. At one end of the spectrum, Americans are living longer, resulting in increasing numbers of senior citizens, and a corresponding range of challenges unique to an aging population (Whelehan & Gwynne, 2014). At the other end of the continuum, the 2015–2016 school year was the first time that the number of Latino/a, African-American, and Asian-American students in public K–12 classrooms in the U.S. surpassed the number of non-Hispanic, white students (Maxwell, 2015). This tipping point occurred at least a decade earlier than had been anticipated only a few years ago, due to accelerating shifts both in birth rates and in parents' school choice decisions (Roda & Wells, 2013). Simultaneously, for the first time since the 1950s, the majority of our public school students now come from low-income families (Southern Education Foundation, 2015). While the levels of poverty of today's public school students are not unprecedented in American educational history, the return to student poverty levels not seen since prior to the civil rights movement is a clear marker of the dramatic income inequality that characterizes post-recession America in 2016.

Among the various implications of these shifting student demographics, schools and teachers in many regions of the U.S. that have historically had limited experience educating emergent bilingual learners are now confronted with classes that may be composed of one-half or more emergent bilinguals, including significant numbers of first- and second-generation immigrant students. Regardless of their home languages or their English proficiency, the vast majority of students in U.S. schools experience English monolingualism as the instructional norm. In these classrooms, instructional practices continue to reproduce a monolingual view of academic language and literacy (Hornberger & Link, 2012). There are, however, currently more than 460 home languages spoken by students in U.S. public schools, with Spanish accounting for over 75 percent of these cases (Ryan, 2013). A recent study by Dabach (2015) investigated the ways in which differentiated instruction for emergent bilingual learners, while attempting to be supportive, actually hindered many students' opportunities to access a rigorous education. As one striking example, Kanno and Kangas (2014) documented how a school district in Pennsylvania placed all students classified as English language learners in low-level sheltered science and math classes during their freshman year of high school, regardless of their past academic performance in middle school. There was no subsequent course-taking path for these students that would allow them to take advanced placement science or math classes by their senior year. In effect, this language-based policy limited emergent bilingual students' college options by prohibiting them from taking the most rigorous science and math courses available, an admissions criterion at most selective universities.

Barring major changes in how schools prioritize staffing decisions, it will never be possible for trained ESOL teachers to "push in" to general education classes as co-teachers in sufficient numbers to provide adequate language support for all the emergent bilinguals in our schools. This leaves as the most viable option the enhancement of professional learning for general education teachers in how to support emergent bilinguals in their content area, combined with the limited support that English for speakers of other languages (ESOL) teachers and bilingual paraprofessionals can provide (Lyon, Tolbert, Solís, Stoddart, & Bunch, 2016). With the exception of a few states (e.g., California, Florida) where ESOL endorsement is a required component of all teacher preparation programs, the vast majority of U.S. teachers have received little or no preparation in ESOL instruction (Bunch, 2013). In the science classroom, there are many basic but effective strategies that teachers can use to support their emergent bilingual students, and these strategies begin with an assumption of students' linguistic competence.

Changing Science Standards

The shifts in occupational opportunities and student demographics are occurring at a time when science education is also undergoing its first major reform in two decades. Driven by rapidly changing scientific and technological discoveries, as well as evolving understandings of how people learn, the field of science education has been engaged in a substantive reformulation of science content and pedagogy for preK–12 education. The three-dimensional model of disciplinary core ideas, science and engineering practices, and crosscutting concepts has been promoted in the Framework for K–12 Science Education (NRC, 2011) and the Next Generation Science Standards (NGSS) (NGSS Lead States, 2013) as a more accurate representation of what science is and how it is practiced.

The experiences of the projects represented in this book, while supportive of the goals of these latest science education reforms, point to the need for more explicit teaching of the language of science as part of this effort. There are a number of new initiatives focused on the language demands inherent in NGSS that need to be considered if all students and especially emergent bilinguals are to succeed in acquiring and applying scientific literacy and problem-solving skills. First, NGSS Appendix F provides lists of specific skills needed to engage in the science and engineering practices, with embedded language demands, while Appendix D presents cases, including a focus on English learners, meant to demonstrate how all students can meet the goals of NGSS. Second, the Council of Chief State School Officers (Pimentel, Castro, Cook, Kibler, Lee, Pook, Stack, Valdés, & Walqui, 2012) has published a framework for the development of English language proficiency standards meant to outline the language requirements and strategies that support the explicit disciplinary knowledge and skills relevant for NGSS as well as for the Common Core. Third, the Understanding Language Initiative at Stanford University and the resulting work of the ELPA21 Consortium have undertaken the development and assessment of English language proficiency standards aligned with NGSS science and engineering practices (Linquanti & Hakuta, 2012). The work of the projects described in this book implicitly and sometimes explicitly builds on and tests assumptions of these initiatives. A common theme is that language skills should be taught as they are needed by students, while they engage in, make sense of, and communicate meaningfully about science concepts and practices.

Acquiring and Using the Language in Science

The linguist M. A. K. Halliday (2004) has argued that the language of science can be traced back to Greek philosophy and the philosophers' desire to create and describe abstract objects that were more persistent, and therefore easier to categorize and debate, than were transient happenings. These transformations of linguistic classes became even more important for the purposes of science during the Enlightenment. Galileo, Newton, and others embraced the power of these linguistic transformations to create our modern discipline-based organization of technical knowledge, and along with it, our modern language of science (Chomsky, 2002). The language of science habitually transforms the names of happenings (verbs) into things (nouns), such that *create* becomes *creation* and *measure* becomes *measurement*. These more stable and persistent linguistic classes facilitate the creation of technical taxonomies. While we may not routinely think about the language of science in terms of its grammatical functions, we can easily distinguish the results of these grammatical functions when the language we encounter sounds more or less "scientific" to our ear.

While some students grow up in homes where the academic language of science is commonplace, for many students, school science classes are the first settings where they are consistently exposed to this language. Students are suddenly asked to interpret and express their experiences and ideas about the natural world through the language of science, which may seem quite foreign to many of them.

Gaining competence and confidence using this language in speaking, reading, and writing is critical for success in school science because it allows for the development of sustained scientific discourse that is needed to engage, for example, in arguing from evidence and the other science and engineering practices that are central to the NGSS.

The technical nature and unique qualities of the language of science are challenging for most students, but can be especially challenging for emergent bilingual learners who must confront this discourse while still gaining fluency in an additional language. Teachers who either take for granted students' familiarity with scientific language, or those who assume that some students, such as emergent bilinguals, must certainly lack such familiarity, are neglecting the important tasks of explicitly evaluating their students' competences for using scientific language and of explicitly teaching what makes the language of science unique. Insights from classroom experience and from research are needed to support teachers in guiding all of their students, including emergent bilinguals, to better express their scientific thinking through the language of science. Elsewhere, we have written more extensively about how perspectives from linguistically diverse classrooms can help all students to unlock the language of science (Buxton, Cardozo Gaibisso, Xia, & Li, in press).

The purpose of any language is to reflect, describe, and explain the world in which people live. Thus, a primary role of language is to clarify how new things we experience fit in with our prior understandings (Halliday, 2004). As children learn language, that language both shapes and is shaped by their growing experience with the world around them. As children move toward school age, and their language skills continue to develop, they begin to interact with language in new ways, through speaking, reading, and writing and a host of new media technologies.

Parents and other family members, peers and playmates, and eventually teachers and classmates all play important roles in how children acquire and use language for meaningful communication and for personal sense making. Many research-based strategies have been shown to promote both first and second language acquisition in school settings, in and beyond science. These include:

- Creating an authentic need for individuals to meaningfully interact using the language;
- Ensuring that everyone's ideas are sought and valued;
- Supporting students in understanding and reflecting each other's ideas rather than just the teacher trying to understand what a student means;
- Using visual representations to contextualize and focus language;
- Using successive approximations towards more complex conceptual knowledge and linguistic abilities;
- Using high interest and linguistically accessible topical reading material;

- Providing writing opportunities that have a clear purpose and audience beyond evaluation by the teacher;
- Promoting paired reading/thinking/talking/writing;
- Encouraging students to use all the languages and linguistic resources they have access to in order to make meaning;
- Using the first language to support and develop skills in the second language and vice versa, acknowledging that maintenance of the first language is an asset for content learning in the second language;
- Strengthening home–school connections by sending home bilingual discussion prompts and class updates to engage families and build cultural connections;
- Valuing everyday conversational language for explaining science ideas rather than moving too fast to replace everyday with academic language; and
- Structuring conversations to construct, share, and debate ideas.

The use of these and various other strategies for simultaneously developing science and language skills and applying these skills to meaningful science learning opportunities will be seen throughout the work of the projects described in this book.

Thinking Beyond the U.S. Context

While each of the projects described in this book is set in a U.S. context, we believe that there are many lessons here that are applicable for an international audience. The increase in large-scale immigration from less developed to more developed nations has been global news in recent years. Many European countries, as well as a range of non-European, English-speaking countries including Canada, Australia, and New Zealand, have been receiving large numbers of immigrants. In all of these countries, parallel conversations are taking place about policies and practices for supporting students who come to school speaking a language that is not the primary language of instruction. In response, educators and researchers are seeking means of supporting immigrant students in achieving school success in and beyond science and are learning lessons about how to do so (Allexsaht-Snider, Harman, & Buxton, 2012). We hope that this book can contribute to discussions in these other contexts, as well as the debates occurring in the U.S.

In addition to the findings of the projects that are reported in this volume, each of the projects has undertaken innovative and effective approaches to the research that was used to reach their conclusions. Many of these research approaches, whether tracking curriculum implementation in the P-SELL project, using teacher logs and constructed response assessments in the LISELL-B project, or rethinking classroom observation instruments in the ESTELL project, can be adopted or adapted by researchers in other contexts to better understand the science teaching and learning processes in which they are engaged. Further, the teams of researchers represented in this volume are multinational, multilingual, and multicultural and have, in many cases, taken ideas from this work and transported it to projects in other parts of the world. As one example, the Turkish National Science Foundation recently funded a project that has its roots in the LISELL-B project to support the teaching of mathematics to Syrian refugees who are now living and going to school in Turkey.

Organization of the Book

This book is divided into three sections – one for each of the three research projects that are discussed. Each project team has written three chapters for their section, highlighting unique features, findings, and lessons learned from that project, as well as addressing important common themes, such as integrating science and language learning and addressing the three-dimensional science learning model of the Framework for K–12 Science Education and the NGSS. A concluding chapter ties together the lessons learned across the projects and provides a comprehensive set of recommendations for research and practice in science teaching, learning, and teacher education that focuses on the needs and assets of emergent bilingual learners. The three sections have been arranged to follow an increase in age of the students who are the focus of the project: elementary grades students and their teachers in the P-SELL project, secondary grades students and their teachers in the LISELL-B project, and university pre-service teachers in the ESTELL project. Each of the three projects also works in a different geographical context within the U.S., with the P-SELL project working in the geographic context of Florida, the LISELL-B project working in the context of Georgia, and the ESTELL project working in the context of California. Here we provide brief conceptual overviews of each project.

P-SELL

Promoting Science among English Language Learners (P-SELL) is a fifth-grade curricular and professional development (PD) intervention aimed at improving the science achievement of all students, with particular focus on English language learners (ELLs). P-SELL consists of a comprehensive, stand-alone, yearlong curriculum for fifth-grade students and teachers, as well as PD workshops for teachers focusing on curriculum implementation. The P-SELL model employs a standards-based, inquiry-oriented, and language-focused approach delivered through educative curriculum materials and effective professional development. Through a decade of research (2004–2015), P-SELL has evolved over three distinct stages of development, efficacy testing, and effectiveness testing. The three stages of P-SELL took place across multiple school districts in Florida where the fifth-grade state science assessment counted toward school accountability. After P-SELL concluded, two of the participating school districts continued implementation of the curriculum and PD through either district funding or external funding.

The three chapters about the P-SELL project in this volume describe the project's teacher professional development model, the outcomes of the project for students and teachers, and some of the challenges that the project faced as it scaled up to include increasing numbers of schools and districts over time. The P-SELL project team has published widely about many other aspects of the project as well. Additional key references that may be of interest to readers who wish to learn more about the P-SELL project are listed in Chapter 11.

LISELL-B

The Language-rich Inquiry Science with English Language Learners (LISELL) project and subsequent Language-rich Inquiry Science with English Language Learners through Biotechnology (LISELL-B) project (hereafter collectively referred to as LISELL-B) has worked since 2010 to support all students, and especially emergent bilinguals, in gaining proficiency in using the language of science and scientific problem-solving skills, both in the context of school science learning and in their daily lives beyond the science classroom. The project has developed, implemented, tested, and refined a pedagogical model for structuring the teaching of the language of science investigation practices, with a particular focus on the needs and resources of emergent bilingual learners. This pedagogical model is aligned with the three-dimensional learning framework of the NGSS, and focuses on the simultaneous development of conceptual science knowledge, science investigation practices, and the language of science. The LISELL-B project has also developed and refined a professional learning framework that provides multiple, intentionally structured contexts within which the project team, teachers, students, and families come together to learn about and engage in the project practices.

The three chapters in this volume highlight diverse aspects of the project, including the preparation of the next generation of science teacher educators to support emergent bilinguals, how online teacher logs can be used to study project enactment and support professional learning, and how theoretical frameworks that are rarely applied to scaled, mixed methods research, such as post-structural and new materialist theories, can be used to examine the situated experiences of the LISELL-B researchers and participants. The LISELL-B project team has also published about a number of other aspects of the project. Additional key references that may be of interest to readers who wish to learn more about the LISELL-B project are listed in Chapter 11.

ESTELL

The Effective Science Teaching for English Language Learners (ESTELL) project offers a model for promoting English learner pedagogy in science with pre-service teachers. This model is meant to enhance pre-service teachers' knowledge about amplifying science instruction to make science content accessible to English learners. The model includes systematic and explicit attention to the language needed to do science as well as the cultural connections possible with science teaching and learning. Project researchers introduced pedagogical modifications to the faculty who teach science methods courses to K–12 pre-service teachers, as well as to the master teachers who supervise the teacher candidates in their teaching placements. The project research examines the impact of the ESTELL strategies on the knowledge, beliefs, and practices of novice teachers who participated in the ESTELL project compared to those in a comparison group in the "business as usual" teacher education programs at the same institutions.

The three chapters in this volume highlight the conceptual framework for ESTELL pedagogy, design of the ESTELL pre-service teacher education program, the development and application of an innovative ESTELL observation instrument to understand pre-service teachers' enactment of science instruction with the infused project pedagogy, and a self-study by the science teacher educators who restructured and then implemented a new science methods course framework. As with the other two projects, the ESTELL project team has published about multiple other aspects of the project. Additional key references that may be of interest to readers who wish to learn more about the ESTELL project are listed in Chapter 11.

Conclusion

The final chapter by the editors provides crosscutting findings and recommendations for research and practice based on the collective work represented in this volume. The chapter discusses contributions, challenges, and recommendations that emerge from this work in relation to classroom practice, teacher preparation, and teacher professional learning designed to improve the science learning experiences and opportunities for emergent bilingual learners. The chapter also explores the topic of how the next generation of measurement and testing of students' science learning needs to be responsive to the needs and assets of emergent bilinguals. Finally, the concluding chapter discusses other important topics that were not central to the work described in this book but that also need to be considered when designing culturally and linguistically responsive science learning opportunities for emergent bilinguals. These topics include the role of families, academic and occupational pathways, understanding student learning, and the role of school leadership and partnership building to support sustainability of reform practices.

Note about Word Choices

Due to both project preferences and regional differences, the three projects represented in this book sometimes use different labels for similar concepts. Rather than make changes to be consistent throughout the entire book, we have, instead, opted to retain the terms used by each project. So, for example, students who are learning English as an additional language in school are referred to as English learners or ELs in one project, as emergent bilingual learners in the second project, and as English language learners, or ELLs, in the third project. Similarly, people living in the Americas who have a mix of Spanish and indigenous American ancestry are referred to as Hispanic in one project and as Latino/a in the other two projects. As a third example, the professional education of teachers is referred to as professional development, or PD, in one project and as professional learning in another project. As a final example, we note that the projects use the terms inquiry, investigations, and practices in similar ways to refer to students engaging in doing science. The reader may notice additional differences in word choice across projects as well. Each project has attempted to define its use of terms clearly, to make distinctions when needed, and to be internally consistent within its own section.

References

Allexsaht-Snider, M., Buxton, C., & Harman, R. (Eds.). (2012). *International Journal of Multicultural Education: Theme Issue on Challenging Anti Immigration Discourses in School and Community Contexts*, 14(2).

Bunch, G. C. (2013). Pedagogical language knowledge preparing mainstream teachers for English learners in the new standards era. *Review of Research in Education*, 37, 298–341.

Buxton, C., Cardozo Gaibisso, L., Xia, Y., & Li, J. (in press). How perspectives from linguistically diverse classrooms can help all students unlock the language of science. In L. Bryan & K. Tobin (Eds.). *13 questions: Reframing education's conversation: Science*. New York, NY: Peter Lang.

Buxton, C., & Lee, O. (2014). English language learners in science education. In N. Lederman & S. Abell (Eds.). *Handbook of Research on Science Education, Vol. 2* (pp. 204–222). New York, NY: Routledge.

Chomsky, N. (2002). *On nature and language*. Cambridge, UK: Cambridge University Press.

Dabach, D. B. (2015). Teacher placement into immigrant English learner classrooms limiting access in comprehensive high schools. *American Educational Research Journal*, 52, 243–274.

Gándara, P. (2015). Charting the relationship of English learners and the ESEA: One step forward, two steps back. *RSF: The Russell Sage Foundation Journal of the Social Sciences*, 1(3), 112–128.

Halliday, M. A. K. (2004). *The language of science*. London, UK: Continuum.

Hornberger, N. H., & Link, H. (2012). Translanguaging and transnational literacies in multilingual classrooms: A biliteracy lens. *International Journal of Bilingual Education and Bilingualism*, 15(3), 261–278.

Jacobs, G. (2014). Towards a new paradigm in education: Role of the World University Consortium. *Cadum*, *2*(2), 116–125.

Kanno, Y., & Kangas, S. N. (2014). "I'm not going to be, like, for the AP": English language learners' limited access to advanced college-preparatory courses in high school. *American Educational Research Journal*, *51*, 848–878.

Linquanti, R., & Hakuta, K. (2012). How Next-Generation Standards can foster success for California's English learners. West Ed Policy Brief. Retrieved April 27, 2016 from www.wested.org/online_pubs/resource1264.pdf.

Lockman, J. L., & Schwartz, A. J. (2014). Learn it – Memorize it! Better yet – Open your smartphone and use the information! *The Journal of the American Society of Anesthesiologists*, *120*(6), 1309–1310.

Lyon, L., Tolbert, S., Solís, J., Stoddart, P., & Bunch, G. (2016). *Secondary science teaching for English learners: Developing supportive and responsive learning contexts for sense-making and language development*. New York, NY: Roman & Littlefield.

Maxwell, L. (2015). U.S. schools become "majority minority." *Education Week*, *34*(1), 12–15.

National Research Council (NRC). (2011). *A framework for K–12 science education: Practices, crosscutting themes, and core ideas*. Washington, DC: The National Academies Press.

NGSS Lead States. (2013). *Next Generation Science Standards: For states, by states*. Washington, DC: The National Academies Press.

Pimentel, S., Castro, M., Cook, G., Kibler, A., Lee, O., Pook, D., Stack, L., Valdés, G., & Walqui, A. (2012). *Framework for English Language Proficiency Development Standards corresponding to the Common Core State Standards and the Next Generation Science Standards*. Washington, DC: CCSSO.

Roda, A., & Wells, A. S. (2013). School choice policies and racial segregation: Where white parents' good intentions, anxiety, and privilege collide. *American Journal of Education*, *119*(2), 261–293.

Rothwell, J. (2013). *The hidden STEM economy*. Washington, DC: Brookings Institution.

Ryan, C. (2013). Language use in the United States: 2011. *American Community Survey Reports*, 3. Retrieved April 27, 2016 from www.census.gov/prod/2013pubs/acs-22.pdf.

Samson, J. F., & Collins, B. A. (2012). Preparing all teachers to meet the needs of English language learners: Applying research to policy and practice for teacher effectiveness. *Center for American Progress*. Retrieved April 27, 2016 from http://files.eric.ed.gov/fulltext/ED535608.pdf.

Seals, C. (2016). *STEM middle-skill career pathways in the Baltimore region*. Baltimore, MD: Greater Baltimore Committee. Retrieved April 27, 2016 from www.abc-md.org/wp-content/uploads/2016/01/STEM-Study-2_v8.pdf.

Southern Education Foundation. (2015). *A new majority: Low income students now a majority in the nation's public schools*. Atlanta, GA: Author.

U.S. Department of Labor (USDoL). (2015). *Occupational outlook handbook*. Retrieved April 27, 2016 from www.bls.gov/ooh/.

Whelehan, I., & Gwynne, J. (2014). Introduction: Popular culture's "silver Tsunami." In *Ageing, popular culture and contemporary feminism* (pp. 1–13). London, UK: Palgrave Macmillan.

PART I
P-SELL
Promoting Science among English Language Learners

2
PROMOTING SCIENCE AMONG ENGLISH LANGUAGE LEARNERS (P-SELL) MODEL

Curricular and Professional Development Intervention in Elementary Science Instruction with a Focus on English Language Learners

Okhee Lee, Corey O'Connor, & Alison Haas

Promoting Science among English Language Learners (P-SELL) is a fifth-grade curricular and professional development (PD) intervention aimed at improving the science achievement of all students, with particular focus on English language learners (ELLs). P-SELL consists of a comprehensive, stand-alone, yearlong curriculum for fifth-grade students and teachers, as well as PD workshops for teachers focusing on curriculum implementation. The P-SELL model employs a standards-based, inquiry-oriented, and language-focused approach delivered through educative curriculum materials and effective PD. Through a decade of research (2004–2015), P-SELL has evolved over three distinct stages of development, efficacy testing, and effectiveness testing. The three stages of P-SELL took place across multiple school districts in Florida where the fifth-grade state science assessment counted toward school accountability. After P-SELL concluded, two of the participating school districts continued its implementation through either district funding or external funding.

This chapter focuses on the P-SELL model and theory of change. It starts with a historical perspective on our research to contextualize how the three sequential versions of P-SELL addressed the need for effective science instruction for ELLs. Then, it describes the design and implementation of the student and teacher components of the P-SELL model based on its theory of change. The chapter concludes with implications for science education interventions for ELLs as the Next Generation Science Standards (NGSS; NGSS Lead States, 2013) present new learning opportunities and demands for all students and ELLs in particular. The second chapter of this book describes the student and teacher measures and outcomes from our P-SELL efficacy and effectiveness studies. The third chapter describes challenges in large-scale implementation (e.g., changing district leadership and policies) and large-scale evaluation (e.g., magnitude and complexities of data collection and analysis) of the intervention.

Context

This section describes the national context that attests to the need for effective science education interventions with ELLs and the historical research context for the three sequential versions of P-SELL that were developed.

National Context

The imperative that all students, especially ELLs, achieve high academic standards in science is becoming more urgent as a result of four key factors: (a) the growing diversity of the U.S. student population, (b) the persistent science achievement gaps affecting non-dominant student groups, (c) the increased focus on high-stakes testing and accountability policy in science education, and (d) new learning opportunities and demands introduced with the creation of the NGSS.

First, while student diversity has been rapidly increasing, ELLs make up the fastest growing student population in the United States. According to the 2010 U.S. Census (U.S. Census Bureau, 2012), 21 percent of children 5 to 17 years old spoke a language other than English at home. During the 2011–2012 school year, students with "limited English proficiency" (the term used by the federal government), or ELLs, constituted 9 percent of public school students, or an estimated 4.4 million students (National Center for Education Statistics [NCES], 2014). In addition, many students who have exited English for Speakers of Other Languages (ESOL) or English as a Second Language (ESL) programs still have unique language learning needs and require appropriate resources during (and even after) the monitoring period. Despite increased student diversity, few teachers report feeling prepared to provide science instruction for diverse student groups, especially ELLs (Banilower, Smith, Weiss, Malzahn, Campbell, & Weis, 2013). Thus, preparing teachers to meet the academic needs of ELLs should be a major concern of educators, researchers, and policymakers.

Second, science achievement gaps persist among demographic subgroups. On the National Assessment of Educational Progress (NAEP) between 1996 and 2011, science achievement gaps between ELLs and non-ELLs remained consistently wide (NCES, 2011, 2012). Thus, given these gaps between ELL and non-ELL populations in science, as well as other subjects, one of the fundamental questions of U.S. education reform in the twenty-first century will be how to best attend to ELLs' educational needs.

Third, since the 2007–2008 school year, each state administers science assessments at least one time during grades 3–5, grades 6–9, and grades 10–12. In some states, such as Florida where our research took place, science counts toward a school's annual evaluation. Thus, in the context of high-stakes testing and accountability policy, an intervention to promote science achievement of all students, including ELLs, is necessary.

Finally, the changing student demographics, the persistent science achievement gaps, and science accountability policy intersect with new learning opportunities and demands that arise with the release of the NGSS. While "science inquiry" has been emphasized as essential for science teaching and learning since the publication of the National Science Education Standards (National Research Council [NRC], 1996, 2000), its meaning has been refined and deepened by the explicit definition of a set of science and engineering practices in A Framework for K–12 Science Education: Practices, Crosscutting Concepts, and Core Ideas (NRC, 2012), upon which the NGSS are based. Engagement in these practices is language intensive, which presents new language demands and language learning opportunities for students, especially ELLs. Thus, an important role of science teachers will be to support students' language use and development (Lee, Quinn, & Valdés, 2013; Quinn, Lee, & Valdés, 2012).

Research Context

Here we describe the progression of the three sequential P-SELL studies: (a) the development study, (b) the efficacy study, and (c) the effectiveness study. We made the distinction between the efficacy and effectiveness studies according to Common Guidelines for Education Research and Development (U.S. Department of Education and National Science Foundation, 2013). The distinction is made in terms of two main criteria for implementation of an intervention or strategy: (a) involvement of the developer in the implementation of the intervention and (b) its implementation under "ideal" conditions or under conditions of routine practice. In the development study, the research team developed, field-tested, and implemented the curriculum units. In the efficacy study, the research team facilitated PD workshops and provided support for teachers. In the effectiveness study, in collaboration with the research team, the school district personnel primarily facilitated PD workshops and provided support for teachers. The evolution of these three studies reflects the changing knowledge base on teaching science to ELLs and the shifting policies regarding science education.

The P-SELL development study (2004–2009) took place as science became a part of Florida accountability policy during the 2006–2007 school year. A series of nine curriculum units for students and teachers was developed for grades 3 through 5 based on the Florida science standards and focusing on science inquiry and language development. The curriculum units for third grade comprised measurement, changes of states of matter, and water cycle and weather systems, all serving as the foundation for subsequent fourth- and fifth-grade units.

The fourth-grade units included energy, force and motion, and processes of life. The fifth-grade units included nature of matter, Earth systems, and a synthesis of the fourth- and fifth-grade units.

This comprehensive curriculum replaced the district science curriculum in schools that participated in the intervention. The research employed a quasi-experimental design involving six schools in the treatment group and six matched schools in the comparison group from one large, urban, and culturally and linguistically diverse school district in Florida. All the selected schools enrolled high proportions of ELLs and students from low socioeconomic status backgrounds and had traditionally performed poorly according to the state's accountability plan. The intervention was conceptualized as responses to a series of competing tensions in three categories: (a) balancing science content and inquiry, (b) supporting English language through science, and (c) recognizing contextual features common to urban settings and policies involving science education and ELLs (Buxton, Lee, & Santau, 2008).

The P-SELL efficacy study (2009–2013) focused on fifth-grade science only for two primary reasons. First, scaling up required a larger number of schools based on power analysis. Second, we chose fifth grade because in Florida grade 5 is the only elementary grade tested in which science assessments count toward school accountability. In response to this accountability policy, science was taught regularly and extensively in the fifth grade. As fifth-grade science assessment covered the science standards from grades 3 through 5, the third through fifth-grade curriculum from the previous P-SELL development study was condensed and revised into a comprehensive, stand-alone, yearlong curriculum for fifth-grade students and teachers. The efficacy study took place in the same large urban school district as in the previous development study. This efficacy study used a cluster randomized controlled trial involving 64 randomly selected schools: 32 schools randomly assigned to the treatment group and 32 schools randomly assigned to the control group. After the first year of implementation, one treatment school withdrew. Thus, a total of 31 treatment schools and 32 control schools participated over the 3-year implementation. The research examined the impact of the intervention on students' science achievement and teachers' science content knowledge and instructional practices. The intervention had beneficial impacts on students (Maerten-Rivera, Ahn, Lanier, Diaz, & Lee, in press) and teachers (Diamond, Maerten-Rivera, & Lee, 2015; Diamond, Maerten-Rivera, Rohrer, & Lee, 2014).

The P-SELL effectiveness study (2011–2015) was extended to three geographically dispersed and demographically diverse school districts across the state of Florida. Again, the study focused on fifth-grade science in response to the state science assessment being part of school accountability. The effectiveness study left the school district that had been the site of successful implementation and positive effects at a large number of participating schools from the previous two P-SELL studies and expanded to three new Florida districts with no prior collaboration with the research team. In each of the three school districts, 22 elementary schools were randomly selected, yielding a total of 66 schools. Using a cluster randomized controlled trial within each district, half of the selected schools were randomly assigned to the treatment group and half to the control group, yielding a total of 33 treatment schools and 33 control schools across the three districts. As in the efficacy study, this effectiveness study examined the impact of the intervention on students' science achievement and teachers' science content knowledge and instructional practices across the three participating school districts. After the first year of the intervention, the results indicated positive outcomes with students (Llosa, Lee, Jiang, Haas, O'Connor, Van Booven, & Kieffer, in press) and teachers (Lee, Llosa, Jiang, Haas, O'Connor, & Van Booven, in press).

Theory of Change for the P-SELL Model

The P-SELL model uses a standards-based, inquiry-oriented, and language-focused approach delivered through educative curriculum materials (Davis & Krajcik, 2005; Drake, Land, & Tyminski, 2014) and core and structural features of effective teacher professional development (Desimone, 2009; Garet, Porter, Desimone, Birman, & Yoon, 2001). The theory of change for the model involves student components and teacher components in the intervention, which result in teacher intermediate outcomes and student outcomes (see Figure 2.1). In this section, we provide theoretical justifications and empirical evidence to guide the design and implementation of the student and teacher components in the intervention. Teacher intermediate outcomes and student outcomes in the intervention based on our efficacy and effectiveness studies are presented in Maerten-Rivera et al. (this volume).

Student Components of the P-SELL Intervention

The first major component of the P-SELL intervention involves curriculum materials for students based on the emerging literature on effective science instruction with ELLs. In recent years, research on interventions to promote science achievement of ELLs indicates that hands-on, inquiry-based science provides opportunities for ELLs to develop scientific understanding and engage in inquiry while learning English (see the literature reviews by Buxton & Lee, 2014; Janzen, 2008; Lee, 2005). Scientific understanding involves deep and complex understanding of science concepts, making connections among concepts, and applying concepts in explaining natural phenomena and real world situations (Kennedy, 1998; NRC, 2007). To enable students to develop scientific understanding, teachers should be aware of how students' prior knowledge relates to their learning. To foster student engagement in science inquiry, teachers should engage students in the practices of science as students ask questions about natural phenomena,

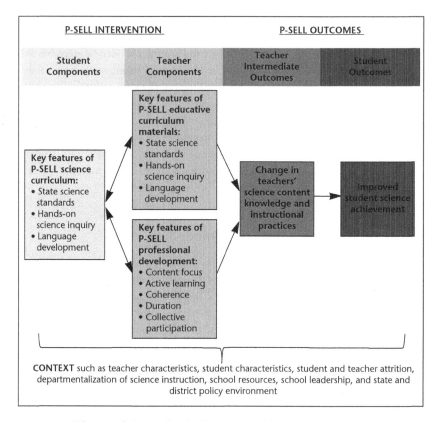

FIGURE 2.1 Theory of change for the P-SELL model.

construct explanations, argue from evidence based on observations or data, and communicate findings using multiple forms of representation (NRC, 2000, 2012).

The student components of the P-SELL curriculum consist of the following materials: (a) consumable student books to be replaced each year and (b) science supplies to perform the inquiry activities. The P-SELL curriculum encompasses the nature of science, Earth and space science, life science, and physical science. For the purpose of describing the P-SELL student book, we use a typical chapter to serve as an example. We have selected the chapter framed around the "Big Idea" of Properties of Matter to provide structural features that are representative of the other chapters.

Student book. The student book features the standards-based, inquiry-oriented, and language-focused approach of the P-SELL model. First, P-SELL uses a standards-based approach by aligning with state science standards and high-stakes science assessment administered in fifth grade. In the state of Florida, the science standards consist of 18 "Big Ideas" according to four bodies of knowledge including the nature of science, Earth and space science, life science, and physical science. These standards are assessed using the Florida Comprehensive Assessment

Test (FCAT) 2.0 Science, and student performance on this test is part of the state's accountability system. The P-SELL curriculum is organized around these Big Ideas. Each chapter of the student book represents a Big Idea and starts with identification of the science content standards and benchmarks addressed. Furthermore, each hands-on inquiry activity, reading passage, and writing section designates the science content standard(s) and benchmark(s) addressed. The curriculum embeds all tested standards from grades 3 through 5.

The "Properties of Matter" chapter begins by identifying the two science standards that correspond to this Big Idea: SC.5.P.8.1 (to compare and contrast the basic properties of solids, liquids, and gases, such as mass, volume, color, texture, and temperature) and SC.5.P.8.3 (to demonstrate and explain that mixtures of solids can be separated based on observable properties of their parts, such as particle size, shape, color, and magnetic attraction).

Second, the P-SELL curriculum uses an inquiry-oriented approach. Science inquiry is emphasized both as a goal of science learning and as a means through which students develop scientific understanding of the Big Ideas. Each Big Idea presented in a chapter centers around a minimum of one inquiry activity and a couple of hands-on activities. P-SELL uses a scaffolded inquiry framework to engage students in investigations. The inquiry framework involves several processes including questioning, planning, implementing, concluding, reporting, and applying. The student book is designed to move progressively from teacher-directed instruction to student-directed inquiry. By providing more structure in earlier chapters, and a more open-ended approach in later chapters, the curriculum encourages student initiative and exploration. For example, in the earlier chapters, students make predictions by selecting one of three provided choices. As the year progresses, this scaffold is released, and students write their own predictions. At the completion of inquiry activities, students are encouraged to design their own extension inquiry activities and apply key science concepts to everyday events or phenomena in home and community contexts.

For example, the Properties of Matter chapter starts with several hands-on activities that address the first aforementioned standard concerning the student's ability to compare and contrast basic properties of matter. The activities begin by engaging students with the world around them. They are asked to write out types of matter they observed that day; where they observed each one; which senses were used to observe each example of matter; whether each type was in solid, liquid, or gas form; and which properties were attributed to each type of matter. A series of measurement activities (on measuring length, mass, volume, and temperature) follows the introductory activity, and in between, sections of text are interspersed that explain those properties investigated in the activities. These activities culminate with the understanding that matter has mass, takes up space, and exists in one of three states. Then, the inquiry activity addresses the second standard, wherein students must demonstrate and explain the separation of different types of granular matter (salt, sand, and iron filings) based on dissolving and magnetism.

Finally, the P-SELL curriculum addresses the learning needs of ELLs by providing guidance and scaffolding for English language development. Each chapter starts with key science terms, pertinent to the contents of that chapter, in English, Spanish, and Haitian Creole, the three primary languages spoken by students of the participating school districts. For example, in the beginning of the Properties of Matter chapter, the relevant vocabulary words are introduced in English, Spanish, and Haitian Creole, including centimeter, gram, ruler, mixture, measure, matter, mass, volume, solid, liquid, gas, and states of matter. Then, the chapter introduces key science concepts by relating them to students' prior knowledge or experiences in their home and community contexts, as well as their knowledge from previous chapters. Students learn key science terms and concepts by engaging in inquiry activities described above. The curriculum uses multiple modes of representation in textual and graphic formats (e.g., students write their responses, develop models, and draw graphs and charts in the student book) and oral and aural forms (e.g., students discuss in small and whole groups). Each chapter concludes with an expository text summarizing key science concepts, with Spanish and Haitian Creole translations available on the project website. Additional language development activities for beginning level ELLs and a complete Spanish translation of the curriculum are available on the project website.

Science supplies. In addition to consumable books, each classroom is provided with all the science supplies necessary to complete the inquiry activities. Supplies vary from more traditional science supplies (e.g., graduated cylinders and balances) to simpler supplies (e.g., pencils and rulers). While durable supplies are reused, consumable supplies are replenished each year.

Teacher Components of the P-SELL Intervention

Teacher components to support effective science instruction with ELLs include (a) the teacher guide, (b) supplementary teacher resources on the project website, and (c) teacher PD workshops. The literature highlights that "curriculum materials play a defining role in classrooms, affecting both what and how teachers teach" (Taylor, Getty, Kowalski, Wilson, Carlson, & Scotter, in press; see Ball & Cohen, 1996, for extensive discussions). In addition to providing teachers with educative curriculum materials, integrating these materials with "face-to-face PD could be the most effective approach to enhancing teachers' understanding of the philosophy and key features of curriculum materials" (Taylor et al., in press).

Teacher guide. The P-SELL curriculum is developed based on the notion of educative curriculum materials by Davis and Krajcik (2005; Davis, Palincsar, Arias, Bismack, Marulis, & Iwashyna, 2014; Drake et al., 2014). To support teachers' capacity to implement and enact curriculum materials, "educative curriculum materials should help to increase teachers' knowledge in specific instances of instructional decision making but also help them develop more general knowledge that they can apply flexibly in new situations" (Davis & Krajcik, 2005, p. 3).

In the P-SELL intervention, the teacher guide is designed to assist teachers with curriculum implementation. The front matter of the teacher guide offers explanations on how the curriculum is designed to enable students to master the state science standards, why science inquiry is key to enabling students to understand the Big Ideas in the state science standards, how teachers can guide students toward student-initiated inquiry, and how teachers can support language development of ELLs.

For each chapter, following the science inquiry activities, the teacher guide provides science background information and explanations for the questions under investigation and related natural phenomena, with an emphasis on students' common learning difficulties. In addition, the teacher guide provides content-specific teaching strategies for each chapter. For example, it offers suggestions about how to set up and implement hands-on activities, along with cautions about potential problems and how a teacher might respond to such situations. It offers suggestions for different levels of guidance and scaffolding by using additional activities for students who need support for content mastery as well as enrichment activities for students who need challenge beyond content mastery.

The growing literature offers instructional approaches to science and language integration (for instructional strategies, see Fathman & Crowther, 2006; Rosebery & Warren, 2008) and key findings (for literature reviews, see Buxton & Lee, 2014; Janzen, 2008; Lee, 2005). The literature indicates four domains of strategies to integrate content and language for ELLs across subject areas, including science (see Lee & Buxton, 2013, for detailed descriptions). First, effective teachers incorporate experientially oriented strategies, including hands-on and purposeful activities, and multiple examples of language in various contexts. Second, effective teachers facilitate ELLs' participation in classroom discourse to help the students understand academic content. Effective teachers are aware of and adaptive to variation in their students' levels of English proficiency and use multiple modes of representation (gestural, oral, pictorial, graphic, and textual). Third, effective teachers focus on students' home language as an instructional support (Goldenberg, 2013). Finally, effective teachers capitalize on students' "funds of knowledge" (Moll, Amanti, Neff, & González, 1992) by incorporating students' cultural artifacts and community resources in ways that are both academically meaningful and culturally relevant.

To incorporate the four strategic domains for integrating language development and science content, the P-SELL teacher guide considers student language needs. The teacher guide directs teachers to language development activities on the P-SELL website (see the description below) whenever it is relevant to the current activity. Embedded literacy components (e.g., literacy-based Post-its weaved throughout the text, vocabulary terms listed in three languages, graphic representation throughout each inquiry) appear frequently to enable teachers to focus on language development strategies during pivotal points of science instruction. Although most of the teachers in our intervention were monolingual

English speakers, a majority of them had training (commonly in the form of endorsement) in English for Speakers of Other Languages (ESOL) and were skillful at using the language development strategies and resources provided by the teacher guide and project website.

Supplementary teacher resources on the project website. The P-SELL research team created and maintains the project website. Teachers receiving the intervention are provided the password-protected access to the teacher portal within the website, which is updated every year for security. For each Big Idea chapter, the teacher portal contains the image file of the student book, so that teachers can project, modify, print, or present the curriculum in various modes, and the teacher guide files for easy access. Teachers can also access additional, high-difficulty assessment items that require critical thinking and multiple steps, a series of projectables (enlarged graphics and charts for teachers to project on a smart board, etc.), home learning and practice activities, additional lesson ideas (intended for students who need remediation or additional practice), translated Big Idea chapter summaries in Spanish and Haitian Creole, various language development activities (science language for beginning ELLs, word walls, reading text-to-self connections, writing science books with children, and semantic maps), and online games.

Teacher professional development workshops. The P-SELL teacher workshops incorporate core features of effective teacher PD: (a) focus on science content knowledge and how students learn that content, (b) opportunities for teachers to engage in active learning by doing the same inquiry activities their students will do, and (c) coherence with other activities for teacher learning and development. In addition, the teacher workshops have built-in structural features of effective PD: (d) sufficient duration including number of contact hours and span across the calendar year and (e) collective participation of teachers from the same school, department, or grade level (Desimone, 2009; Garet et al., 2001; Penuel, Fishman, Yamaguchi, & Gallagher, 2007). Below, each core and structural feature is described as it is presented in the P-SELL teacher workshops.

First, the workshops focus on teachers' science content knowledge as specified in the state science standards and content limits of these standards, so that the intervention is coherent with expectations for science instruction and assessment. We address how the standards relate to content instruction and afford teachers the opportunity to think about how they can incorporate standards into their science content knowledge. For example, the standards for the Properties of Matter chapter are communicated explicitly with teachers at the introduction of the chapter during the workshop, as the standards similarly appear at the top of the chapter in the teacher guide.

Second, a primary goal of the P-SELL teacher workshops is to promote inquiry-based science. During the workshops, teachers perform every hands-on inquiry activity in the curriculum, as their students are expected to throughout the year. By engaging in the inquiry activities, teachers have opportunities to use science content to explain the results of the activities, apply the content to new situations, and ask questions for extension activities. They discuss components of the activities that may go wrong in the classroom, possible errors to avoid, and common mistakes their students should experience as potential learning opportunities. Through this process, teachers experience firsthand what classroom discourse might look like during inquiry activities and discuss how they could facilitate classroom discourse before/during/after the inquiry process. With ELLs, teachers discuss how to utilize second language pedagogies (ESOL strategies) and strategies typical of contextualized experiential approaches, classroom discourse strategies, students' home language as an instructional support (Goldenberg, 2013), and "funds of knowledge" (González, Moll, & Amanti, 2005). For example, teachers explore science terms in students' home language and cognates between English and the home language. Teachers also explore how bilingual students could assist less English proficient students in their home language. The supplemental language development activities on the P-SELL website are introduced to support monolingual teachers who do not speak a student's home language. These language activity resources, such as Science Language for Beginning ELLs, Word Walls, and Semantic Maps, embed home languages themselves, so the monolingual teacher doesn't have to.

For example, during the PD related to the Properties of Matter chapter, to initiate teachers' active learning, they assemble in small groups and complete the inquiry activity to separate salt, sand, and iron filings. As the teachers work in their groups, they are pressed to consider various issues that might arise when they implement this activity in their classrooms. They discuss how to ensure that students understand the purpose of this activity using the inquiry framework as a guide, with particular attention paid to application of science content and questions for extension inquiry activities. Engaging in the activity allows teachers to become familiar with the science supplies provided in the science supply bin. For the activity to proceed smoothly, teachers discuss how to unpack the magnets included in the science supply bin, how to save time regarding measuring out the amounts of materials (salt, sand, and iron filings), a reminder of using safety goggles, and several other idiosyncratic features.

Third, teachers become familiar with the state science standards and content limits of these standards, so that the intervention is coherent with expectations for science instruction in accordance with Florida accountability policy. In addition, the workshops account for district initiatives by ensuring that these initiatives are addressed during workshop hours and embedded in the delivery of workshop content. For example, one district attempted to integrate their literacy and science block, so the teacher workshops in this district invested time to explore ways that teachers could use the language development strategies and resources (available on the project website) to effectively integrate these two subjects. When another district implemented a district-wide professional learning community initiative, this initiative was incorporated in the workshops.

Fourth, to ensure sufficient duration, teacher workshops are offered across the calendar year over the 3-year implementation. During the first year of implementation, all teachers participate in four full-day workshops during the summer and throughout the school year and one full-day year-end meeting for data collection, feedback, and planning for the following year. During the second year and third year of implementation, workshops are provided separately for those teachers who are new to the intervention (i.e., new teachers) and those who implemented the intervention the previous year(s) and will continue their participation (i.e., returning teachers). Thus, the contact hours and contents of the workshops differ between new and returning teachers. The workshops, after starting at 5 days in the first year of implementation, move down to 4 days during the second year and 1 day during the third year, and are designed for sustainability of the intervention after completion of the project. Teachers are given a stipend for attending the summer workshops, and schools receive payments for substitutes during school days.

Finally, the workshops promote collective participation of all fifth-grade science teachers within each school and each school district. Teachers are given time for collaborative planning to develop common goals, share resources, and exchange ideas and experiences arising from the common context of the intervention. The networks generated during the workshops give teachers opportunities to build social capital that otherwise would not be afforded them. In addition, science coaches, school administrators, and district administrators attend some of the workshops and provide additional support to engender collective participation.

Implications

Across the three studies of the P-SELL intervention, positive results were consistently observed with respect to teachers' science content knowledge and instructional practices and students' science achievement. We believe its success is largely due to the features upon which the P-SELL model is founded: (a) alignment with state science standards, (b) progression from teacher-directed instruction to student-directed inquiry, and (c) focus on language by supporting language development of all students including ELLs while engaging in science inquiry and developing scientific understanding. These three features are embedded in the science curriculum for students, educative teacher materials, and teacher PD of the P-SELL intervention (see Figure 2.1).

The literature on science curriculum development has shown significant progress in meeting the needs of ELLs. While the early history of curricular modifications for ELLs often amounted to little more than conceptually and linguistically simplified versions of existing curricula, the current generation of curricular development for supporting the learning needs of ELLs has held curricular rigor as a fundamental goal (Lee & Buxton, 2008).

Science has a rich language base; thus, the teaching of science and the teaching of language are integrally related (Lee et al., 2013). Researchers have long pointed to the utility of hands-on activities as a concrete and experiential context for learning science and developing language (Chamot & O'Malley, 1994). More recently, while hands-on activities continue to be important in science instruction for ELLs, researchers have emphasized the need to integrate cognitively demanding science inquiry as scientists engage in the practices of science with an explicit focus on language development (Buxton & Lee, 2014; Fathman & Crowther, 2006; Janzen, 2008; Lee, 2005; Rosebery & Warren, 2008).

With the arrival of the NGSS, a new generation of science education interventions will need to be developed, and teachers will likewise need a new generation of PD to implement these interventions with all students, including ELLs. As the science and engineering practices in the NGSS represent refinement and deepening of science inquiry, these practices raise the bar for academic rigor and intensive language and call for a high level of classroom discourse (Lee et al., 2013; Quinn et al., 2012). Because the NGSS are academically rigorous, teachers should make instructional shifts to enable students to explain phenomena and design solutions to problems by blending the three dimensions of science and engineering practices, crosscutting concepts, and disciplinary core ideas. At the same time, because the science and engineering practices are language intensive, teachers should meet increased language demands while capitalizing on language learning opportunities for all students and ELLs in particular. Furthermore, teachers should engage all students, including ELLs, in rich classroom discourse in oral and written forms. In the classrooms where the NGSS are implemented, students will engage in science talk (i.e., speaking and listening) and science text (i.e., reading and writing) through receptive and productive language functions.

Design, implementation, and testing of science education interventions for teachers and students will become increasingly important as the NGSS become partially or fully adopted and implemented in more states. Even in those states that may not adopt or adapt the NGSS, the knowledge base on effective science instruction in A Framework for K–12 Science Education (NRC, 2012), from which the NGSS were developed, is likely to have an influence.

Teachers are integral to education innovations and improvements, and the success of any intervention relies on enabling them to effectively adopt and implement reform-oriented practices. As the nation's schools become increasingly diverse culturally and linguistically, there is a growing awareness that today's teachers need a broader array of knowledge, skills, and dispositions to provide equitable learning opportunities for all students, including ELLs. Rapidly changing student demographics are accompanied by the arrival of the NGSS, presenting both new opportunities and demands for science and language learning for ELLs. Greater attention to increased academic and linguistic rigor with growing student diversity should lead to new opportunities for teacher professional learning focused on the needs of ELLs.

References

Ball, D. L., & Cohen, D. K. (1996). Reform by the book: What is – or might be – the role of curriculum materials in teacher learning and instructional reform? *Educational Researcher, 24*(9), 6–8, 14.

Banilower, E. R., Smith, P. S., Weiss, I. R., Malzahn, K. A., Campbell, K. M., & Weis, A. M. (2013). *Report of the 2012 national survey of science and mathematics education*. Chapel Hill, NC: Horizon Research.

Buxton, C. A., & Lee, O. (2014). English language learners in science education. In N. G. Lederman & S. K. Abell (Eds.), *Handbook of research in science education* (2nd ed., pp. 204–222). Mahwah, NJ: Erlbaum Associates.

Buxton, C. A., Lee, O., & Santau, A. (2008). Promoting science among English language learners: Professional development for today's culturally and linguistically diverse classrooms. *Journal of Science Teacher Education, 19*(5), 495–511.

Chamot, A. U., & O'Malley, J. M. (1994). *The CALLA handbook: Implementing the cognitive academic language learning approach*. Reading, MA: Addison-Wesley.

Davis, E. A., & Krajcik, J. S. (2005). Designing educative curriculum materials to promote teacher learning. *Educational Researcher, 34*(3), 3–14.

Davis, E. A., Palincsar, A. S., Arias, A. M., Bismack, A. S., Marulis, L., & Iwashyna, S. (2014). Designing educative curriculum materials: A theoretically and empirically driven process. *Harvard Educational Review, 84*(1), 24–52.

Desimone, L. M. (2009). Improving impact studies of teachers' professional development: Toward better conceptualizations and measures. *Educational Researcher, 38*(3), 181–199.

Diamond, B. S., Maerten-Rivera, J., & Lee, O. (2015). Effects of a multi-year curricular and professional development intervention on elementary teachers' science content knowledge. Manuscript submitted for publication.

Diamond, B. S., Maerten-Rivera, J., Rohrer, R. E., & Lee, O. (2014). Effectiveness of a curricular and professional development intervention at improving elementary teachers' science content knowledge and student achievement outcomes: Year 1 results. *Journal of Research in Science Teaching, 51*(5), 635–658.

Drake, C., Land, T. J., & Tyminski, A. M. (2014). Using educative curriculum materials to support the development of prospective teachers' knowledge. *Educational Researcher, 43*(3), 154–162.

Fathman, A. K., & Crowther, D. T. (2006). *Science for English language learners: K–12 classroom strategies*. Arlington, VA: NSTA Press.

Garet, M. S., Porter, A. C., Desimone, L., Birman, B. F., & Yoon, K. S. (2001). What makes professional development effective? Results from a national sample of teachers. *American Educational Research Journal, 38*(4), 915–945.

Goldenberg, C. (2013). Unlocking the research on English learners: What we know – and don't yet know – about effective instruction. *American Educator, 37*(2), 4–11, 38.

González, N., Moll, L. C., & Amanti, C. (2005). *Funds of knowledge: Theorizing practices in households, communities, and classrooms*. Mahwah, NJ: L. Erlbaum Associates.

Janzen, J. (2008). Teaching English language learners in the content areas. *Review of Educational Research, 78*(4), 1010–1038.

Kennedy, M. M. (1998). Education reform and subject matter knowledge. *Journal of Research in Science Teaching, 35*(3), 249–263.

Lee, O. (2005). Science education with English language learners: Synthesis and research agenda. *Review of Educational Research, 75*(4), 491–530.
Lee, O., & Buxton, C. (2008). Science curriculum and student diversity: A framework for equitable learning opportunities. *The Elementary School Journal, 109*(2), 123–137.
Lee, O., & Buxton, C. (2013). Integrating science and English proficiency for English language learners. *Theory into Practice, 52*(1), 36–42.
Lee, O., Llosa, L., Jiang, F., Haas, A., O'Connor, C., & Van Booven, C. (in press). Teachers' science knowledge and practices with English language learners. *Journal of Research in Science Teaching.*
Lee, O., Quinn, H., & Valdés, G. (2013). Science and language for English language learners in relation to Next Generation Science Standards and with implications for Common Core State Standards for English language arts and mathematics. *Educational Researcher, 42*(4), 223–233.
Llosa, L., Lee, O., Jiang, F., Haas, A., O'Connor, C., Van Booven, C., & Kieffer, M. (in press). Science achievement of English language learners. *American Educational Research Journal.*
Maerten-Rivera, J., Ahn, S., Lanier, K., Diaz, J., & Lee, O. (in press). Science achievement over a three-year curricular and professional development intervention with English language learners in urban elementary schools. *The Elementary School Journal.*
Moll, L. C., Amanti, C., Neff, D., & González, N. (1992). Funds of knowledge for teaching: Using a qualitative approach to connect homes and classrooms. *Theory Into Practice, 31*(2), 132–141.
National Center for Education Statistics (NCES). (2011). *Science 2009: National Assessment of Educational Progress at grades 4, 8, and 12* (NCES 2011-451). Washington, DC: U.S. Department of Education.
National Center for Education Statistics. (2012). *Science 2011: National Assessment of Educational Progress at grade 8* (NCES 2012-465). Washington, DC: U.S. Department of Education.
National Center for Education Statistics. (2014). *The condition of education 2011* (NCES 2014-083). Washington, DC: U.S. Department of Education.
National Research Council (NRC). (1996). *National science education standards.* Washington, DC: National Academy Press.
National Research Council. (2000). *Inquiry and the national science education standards: A guide for teaching and learning.* Washington, DC: National Academy Press.
National Research Council. (2007). *Taking science to school.* Washington, DC: National Academies Press.
National Research Council. (2012). *A framework for K–12 science education: Practices, crosscutting concepts, and core ideas.* Washington, DC: National Academies Press.
Next Generation Science Standards Lead States. (2013). *Next Generation Science Standards: For states, by states.* Washington, DC: National Academies Press.
Penuel, W. R., Fishman, B. J., Yamaguchi, R., & Gallagher, L. P. (2007). What makes professional development effective? Strategies that foster curriculum implementation. *American Educational Research Journal, 44*(4), 921–958.
Quinn, H., Lee, O., & Valdés, G. (2012). *Language demands and opportunities in relation to Next Generation Science Standards for English language learners: What teachers need to know.* Retrieved September 1, 2015 from http://ell.stanford.edu/publication/language-demands-and-opportunities-relation-next-generation-science-standards-ells.

Rosebery, A.S., & Warren, B. (Eds.). (2008). *Teaching science to English language learners: Building on students' strengths.* Arlington, VA: NSTA.

Taylor, J. A., Getty, S. R., Kowalski, S. M., Wilson, C. D., Carlson, J., & Scotter, P.V. (in press). An efficacy trial of research-based curriculum materials with curriculum-based professional development. *American Educational Research Journal.*

U.S. Census Bureau. (2012). *Statistical abstract of the United States, 2012.* Washington, DC: U.S. Government Printing Office.

U.S. Department of Education and the National Science Foundation. (2013). *Common guidelines for education research and development.* Retrieved September 8, 2015 from www.nsf.gov/pubs/2013/Nsf13126/nsf13126.pdf.

3
MEASURES AND OUTCOMES FOR STUDENTS AND TEACHERS IN THE PROMOTING SCIENCE AMONG ENGLISH LANGUAGE LEARNERS (P-SELL) PROJECT

Jaime Maerten-Rivera, Lorena Llosa, & Okhee Lee

Recognizing the potential importance of professional development (PD) in improving teachers' knowledge and practice and student outcomes, scholars have identified elements of effective PD including core and structural features (Garet, Porter, Desimone, Birman, & Yoon, 2001; Penuel, Fishman, Yamaguchi, & Gallagher, 2007; Wayne, Yoon, Zhu, Cronen, & Garet, 2008) and have developed a causal model for evaluating PD programs (Desimone, 2009). The Promoting Science among English Language Learners (P-SELL) model's theory of change (see details in Lee, O'Connor, & Haas, previous chapter in this volume) was developed based on the elements of effective PD and the call for a causal model for evaluating PD.

To build a stronger knowledge base about links among PD, teacher knowledge and practice, and student achievement, researchers have called for more rigorous study designs (Borko, 2004; Desimone, 2009; Wayne et al., 2008), including the use of randomized experiments (Wayne et al., 2008). In addition, it has been noted that conducting rigorous studies of PD is a challenge due to the lack of adequate measures, particularly in regard to teacher learning and change (Desimone, 2009). This is in part due to few standardized measures existing for both students and teachers in science classrooms (Liu, 2009, 2012). The P-SELL project developed over time in terms of study design and measures to provide a stronger research base about PD interventions for science instruction focused on English language learners (ELLs).

In this chapter, we describe the three sequential studies of the P-SELL intervention, focusing specifically on measures and outcomes with students and teachers. We start with contextual information regarding the role of science accountability in the state in which the P-SELL project was developed and tested.

Then, we describe the design of the three P-SELL studies – the development study (2004–2009), the efficacy study (2009–2013), and the effectiveness study (2011–2015). Table 3.1 displays the key characteristics of each of these projects. Next, we discuss how measures of both student and teacher outcomes evolved throughout the three projects. Finally, we provide an overview of the outcomes along with information on where to find more detailed descriptions of the data analyses and results.

TABLE 3.1 Characteristics of P-SELL Projects

	P-SELL Development Study	*P-SELL Efficacy Study*	*P-SELL Effectiveness Study*
Number of years	5 years (2004–2008)	4 years (2009–2013)	4 years (2011–2015)
Planning	None	1 year	1 year
Implementation	5 years	3 years	3 years
Study design	Quasi-experimental	Randomized controlled trial	Randomized controlled trial
Number of schools	6 treatment	31 treatment 32 control	33 treatment 33 control
Number of teacher participants	198	359	447
Grades	3, 4, 5	5	5
Number of student participants	~2,500	~10,000 treatment ~10,000 control	~10,000 treatment ~10,000 control
Student measures	1. Researcher-developed science assessments for grades 3, 4, and 5 (pre and post) 2. State standardized science assessment at grade 5 (post only)	1. State standardized science assessment (post only)	1. Researcher-developed science assessment (pre and post) 2. State standardized science assessment (post only)

(continued)

TABLE 3.1 Characteristics of P-SELL Projects (*continued*)

	P-SELL Development Study	P-SELL Efficacy Study	P-SELL Effectiveness Study
Teacher measures	1. Teacher questionnaire (pre and post)	1. Teacher questionnaire (pre and post) 2. Science content knowledge assessment (pre and post)	1. Teacher questionnaire (pre and post) 2. Science content knowledge assessment (pre and post)

Overview of P-SELL Projects

All of the P-SELL projects took place in Florida and implemented a curricular and PD intervention for elementary school. The projects aimed at improving science achievement of all students with a focus on ELLs within the context of accountability.

The state's school accountability system originated in 1999 and has been revised periodically. All public schools are assigned a "school grade" (A, B, C, D, or F) based on state high-stakes assessments. At the elementary level, students are assessed on reading and mathematics in grades 3 through 5, writing in grade 4, and science in grade 5. In the 2011–2012 school year, the state science assessment was changed to cover the areas of the nature of science, Earth and space science, life science, and physical science. Prior to that, the state science assessment covered the topics of physical and chemical science, Earth and space science, life and environmental science, and scientific thinking. Based on scale scores, students are assigned achievement levels ranging from 1 to 5. For the purpose of accountability, students classified as level 3, 4, or 5 are considered proficient. The percent of students scoring proficient on the fifth-grade state science assessment counts for one-eighth of the overall school grade.

Beginning in the 2011–2012 school year, ELLs with 1 full year of instruction in the United States at the time of testing were included in school performance calculations. In previous years, the date of entry to English for Speakers of Other Languages (ESOL), which came after being admitted to the school, was used as the means of inclusion of ELLs in school performance calculations. This change led to ELLs being assessed, and their results counting toward school grades, when students were at a lower level of English language proficiency. Additionally, students with disabilities are required to take state assessments, and their results are included in the school grade calculations for proficiency in reading, math, writing, and science.

The Development Study

For the development study (2004–2009), a science curriculum was developed for grades 3 through 5 based on the state's science standards (see details in Lee, O'Connor, & Haas in this volume). The development study took place in one large, diverse school district in Florida and involved six treatment schools that were selected based on three criteria: (a) percentage of ELLs above the district average at the elementary school level (24 percent), (b) percentage of students on free or reduced price lunch programs above the district average at the elementary school level (72 percent), and (c) academically low performing schools according to the state's accountability plan. Based on the same criteria, six comparison schools were selected from the pool of remaining elementary schools in the district. The intervention was implemented with a small group of schools that met specific criteria; thus, the participating schools were not randomly selected, nor were the selected schools randomly assigned to conditions (i.e., treatment and control).

The development study established the foundation for the efficacy and effectiveness studies that were larger in scale and used randomized controlled trial designs. The efficacy and effectiveness studies focused on fifth grade only for a number of reasons. First, due to the increase in the number of schools participating in the intervention there was a need to downsize the scope from that of the development study that involved grades 3 through 5. Second, the teachers and schools felt a greater push to focus on fifth grade when implementing science instruction because state science assessment in fifth grade counted toward accountability. Finally, the results of the development study demonstrated that fifth-grade teachers gained the most from the intervention, probably due to the pressure of accountability at this grade when the state science assessment counts toward the school grade (Lee & Maerten-Rivera, 2012).

The Efficacy Study

The efficacy study (2009–2013) took place in the same large, urban, and culturally and linguistically diverse school district as the development study. The P-SELL intervention was implemented for 3 years from the 2010–2011 school year through the 2012–2013 school year. During the first year of implementation, the K–12 student demographic composition was 24 percent Black, 65 percent Hispanic, 9 percent White non-Hispanic, and 2 percent Other; 72 percent received free or reduced price lunch (FRL); and 19 percent were designated as limited English language proficient (LEP, the federal term) or ELLs.

A cluster randomized controlled trial was conducted. At the time when schools were randomly selected to participate, there were 238 elementary schools in the district. Initially, 23 schools were removed from the pool due to participation in alternate district interventions, and nine schools were removed because they had participated in our previous development study. This resulted in a final pool of 206 eligible schools. From this pool, 64 schools were randomly selected to participate in the study. The 64 schools were then randomly assigned, 32 to the treatment group and 32 to the control group. One treatment school dropped from the project after the first year, leaving 31 schools in the treatment group. All fifth-grade teachers in the selected schools participated in the study. Each year of the study there were about 100 teachers in each group. Due to teacher attrition (e.g., teachers leaving the school, moving to a different grade within the same school), new fifth-grade teachers were added to the study each year. Thus, across the three years, approximately 175 teachers participated in the treatment group and a similar number participated in the control group. Each year approximately 6,500 students participated in the study, with half of those in the treatment group and the other half in the control group. In the study sample, 16 percent of the students were ELLs (also referred to as ESOL levels 1–4 by the state), while an additional 36 percent were former ELLs who were being monitored after they had exited out of ELL status within the past two years (referred to as ESOL level 5 by the state).

Control schools were comparable to the intervention schools in terms of student demographics, academic achievement from previous years, and school size. The teachers in the control schools did not receive the intervention and implemented science instruction as directed by the district using the district-adopted curriculum.

The Effectiveness Study

The effectiveness study (2011–2015) took place in three school districts in Florida, not including the district that participated in the development and efficacy studies. During the first year of implementation (2012–2013), District A, located in the northeastern part of the state, had a K–12 student demographic composition of 45 percent Black, 8 percent Hispanic, 40 percent White non-Hispanic, and 7 percent Other; 52 percent received FRL; and 3 percent were designated as ELLs. District B was located in the southwestern part of the state with a K–12 student demographic composition of 28 percent Black, 15 percent Hispanic, 51 percent White non-Hispanic, and 6 percent Other; 52 percent received FRL; and 8 percent were designated as ELLs. District C was located in the central part of the state with a K–12 student demographic composition of 30 percent Black, 34 percent Hispanic, 28 percent White non-Hispanic, and 8 percent Other; 60 percent received FRL; and 14 percent were designated as ELLs.

A randomized control trial was conducted. During the 2012–2013 school year, District A had 103 elementary schools, District B had 44 elementary schools, and District C had 125 elementary schools. Within each of the three school districts, 22 schools were randomly selected to participate, yielding a total of 66 participating schools. Within each district, half of the selected schools were randomly assigned to the treatment group and half to the control group, yielding a total of 33 schools in the treatment group and 33 schools in the control group across the three districts. There were no significant differences in demographic school characteristics between the two groups at the beginning of the first year of implementation. All fifth-grade teachers in the 66 selected schools participated in the study. Each year of the study there were about 125 teachers in each group, but throughout the 3 years, there was teacher attrition. By the third year of implementation, about 40 percent of the teachers had participated in the study for all 3 years of implementation, 20 percent had participated for 2 years, and about 40 percent of the teachers were new to the study. Each year approximately 6,500 students participated in the study, with half of those in the treatment group and the other half in the control group. In the first year of implementation, 8 percent of students were ELLs (ESOL 1–4), 4 percent were recently reclassified ELLs (ESOL 5), 12 percent were former ELLs, and 77 percent were non-ELLs. The teachers and students in the 33 control schools implemented the district-adopted science curriculum ("business as usual").

Student Measures and Outcomes

All of the P-SELL studies took place in the context of standardized testing. Thus throughout all studies one of the student outcomes was performance on the state standardized science test, which provided a distal assessment (National Research Council, 2014; Ruiz-Primo, Shavelson, Hamilton, & Klein, 2002). Distal assessments are external to the intervention, usually more distant in time and content from the instruction guided by the intervention. They are typically designed or selected by states and are used to monitor learning. However, even in the development study, we recognized the need for another measure that was more closely related to the intervention, a proximal assessment. Proximal assessments, also known as "close assessments," are closely tied to instructional activities. They can include formal classroom exams that cover material from one or more units and are often created by curriculum developers. An important reason to include a researcher-developed measure was to have a premeasure of science achievement. The state science assessment is only administered at the end of fifth grade. Also, given that state assessment only includes multiple-choice items and a major focus of the intervention was language development, we wanted a measure that included open-ended questions and elicited student-produced language. The sections below describe how each study utilized both distal and proximal assessments to evaluate the impact of the P-SELL intervention, along with how the measures, particularly the researcher-developed measure, evolved.

The Development Study

In the development study a researcher-developed student test was given at each grade level (3, 4, 5) to determine whether the P-SELL intervention showed promise of effectiveness. This test assessed science topics that were covered throughout the curriculum at the grade level. Some test questions at each grade level were selected from the public release items from the National Assessment of Educational Progress (NAEP), and Trends in International Mathematics and Science Study (TIMSS), so that comparisons could be made between the study sample (which only included a treatment group but no control) and both national and international samples of students (Lee, Maerten-Rivera, Penfield, LeRoy, & Secada, 2008; Santau, Maerten-Rivera, & Huggins, 2011).

In addition to the researcher-developed science assessment, which served as a proximal measure, the state science assessment scores for the fifth grade were used as a distal measure (National Research Council, 2014; Ruiz-Primo et al., 2002). In addition, the results from the state math assessment at grade 3 were analyzed since a significant portion of the grade 3 science curriculum covered measurement, which was a topic on the state math test (Adamson, Secada, Maerten-Rivera, & Lee, 2011).

Both the researcher-developed assessment and the state science assessment provided useful information in the development study. As researchers, we had more control and knowledge of what was tested on the researcher-developed assessment, whereas we did not have access to the questions used in the state science assessment. Thus, at each grade level, we could assess whether the students were learning the content and if there were areas of weakness that should be addressed again before the fifth-grade state science assessment. The state science assessment scores for the fifth grade were the greatest concern of the school district due to the accountability policy.

The Efficacy Study

In the planning stages of the efficacy study, a considerable amount of time and resources were spent developing a fifth-grade student science assessment that was to be administered as a pretest and posttest and would serve as a proximal measure of student achievement. This assessment was different from that of the development study, because in the development study assessments were given at grades 3, 4, and 5. The science assessment developed for the efficacy study focused on the more challenging material across all topics that students would be expected to know by the time the state science assessment was administered at the end of fifth grade. Again, the assessment consisted of some questions selected from the public release items from NAEP and TIMSS so that comparisons could be made between the study sample and both national and international samples of students.

Unfortunately, due to requirements of the University Institutional Review Board (IRB), as well as concerns raised by the collaborating school district over requiring students to participate in an additional test on top of extensive state- and district-mandated testing, we were unable to administer the researcher-developed student assessment.

Thus, in the efficacy study, the fifth-grade state science assessment was the only measure of student science achievement that was used to assess the impact of the intervention. As stated previously in the chapter, in the 2011–2012 school year, the topics covered on the state science assessment were changed. In Year 1 of the efficacy study, the state science assessment covered physical and chemical science, Earth and space science, life and environmental science, and scientific thinking. In Year 2 and subsequent years, the state science assessment was changed to cover the nature of science, Earth and space science, life science, and physical science. In addition, there were changes made in the scale scores for the state science assessment during the efficacy study implementation. In Years 1 and 2, the science scale ranged from 100 to 500. Based on scale scores, students were assigned achievement levels ranging from 1 to 5. For the purpose of accountability, students classified as level 3, 4, or 5 were considered proficient. In Year 3, the science scale was changed to range from 140 to 260. Again, students classified as level 3, 4, or 5 were considered proficient.

Given all of these changes, when analyzing the student science achievement data, we used science proficiency (i.e., students classified as level 1 or 2 versus students classified as level 3, 4, or 5), instead of science scale scores, to examine the intervention effect. This is consistent with other intervention studies that evaluated outcomes based on the percent of students deemed "passing" state tests (Silverstein, Dubner, Jon, Glied, & Loike, 2009; Weaver & Dick, 2009). Also, because accountability policies were based on percent proficient as opposed to scale scores, district and school administrators were much more interested in examining intervention effects in terms of percent proficient.

The general descriptive data showed trends in differences between the treatment and control groups. Across all 3 years, the percent of proficient students was greater in the treatment group than the control group, with the difference in the percent proficient being the greatest in Year 3 (T = 54 percent, C = 47 percent) as compared to Year 2 (T = 50 percent, C = 45 percent) and Year 1 (T = 50 percent, C = 45 percent). There were some differences in the percent of proficient students classified as ESOL between the treatment and control groups, with the treatment group having a higher percent of proficient students in both ESOL categories (i.e., ESOL levels 1 to 4 and ESOL level 5) across all 3 years. In the group of students classified as ESOL levels 1 to 4, in Year 1 there was a 1 percent difference between the treatment and control groups (T = 13 percent, C = 12 percent), while in Year 2 there was a 4 percent difference (T = 18 percent, C = 14 percent), and in Year 3 there was an 8 percent difference (T = 21 percent, C = 13 percent). To evaluate whether the odds of being proficient on state science assessment differed between students in the treatment group and those in the control group, a series of hierarchical generalized linear models, also referred to as hierarchical logistic models, was examined for each year of the intervention separately, which included both demographic and control variables (for details of the analysis and results, see Maerten-Rivera, Ahn, Lanier, Diaz, & Lee, 2016).

Overall, the trends in differences between the treatment and control groups across the 3 years indicated that there was no significant difference in Year 1, the difference approached statistical significance in Year 2 (in which case, it may be more meaningful to examine the effect size), and there was a statistically significant difference in Year 3. Based on the odds ratio estimates – a measure of effect size – in both Year 2 and Year 3, the effect size was small and increased slightly from Year 2 to Year 3, indicating a positive effect of the intervention on student achievement in the treatment group. According to Lipsey, Puzio, Yun, Hebert, Steinka-Fry, Cole, Roberts, Anthony, and Busick (2012), a small effect size is practically meaningful for an educational intervention that implements a school-based curriculum and uses a standardized test as an outcome measure. The finding of the efficacy study suggests that there was a lag in the impact of the intervention on student achievement, which is consistent with other studies indicating a delayed effect of PD on student outcomes (Kreider & Bouffard, 2006; Silverstein et al., 2009).

The Effectiveness Study

In the effectiveness study, we were able to use two outcome measures of science achievement: (a) a revised version of the researcher-developed assessment that had been developed for the efficacy study but was not used and (b) the state science assessment. Unlike the state science assessment, which is only administered at the end of each school year in fifth grade, the researcher-developed assessment was administered at the beginning (pre) and at the end (post) of each school year during the 3 years of the study. The administration of the researcher-developed assessment at the beginning of the year served as a measure of initial science achievement that was used as a covariate in the statistical analyses of the intervention effect. In addition, because the two assessments varied with regard to their degree of alignment to the intervention, we were able to examine whether the intervention produced results that were robust enough to have an effect on the state science assessment as well as the researcher-developed assessment (i.e., proximal versus distal assessment) (National Research Council, 2014; Ruiz-Primo et al., 2002). For example, in addition to multiple-choice items, the researcher-developed assessment included open-ended items to reflect the intervention's focus on language.

Multilevel modeling was used to examine the impact of the intervention on students' science achievement as measured by the researcher-developed assessment and the state science assessment scale scores. We decided to use scale scores in our analyses since, unlike during the efficacy study, the scale scores had remained consistent throughout the duration of the effectiveness study. Scale scores allow for more variability in the data that makes it possible to identify finer distinctions in the differences between groups, which is especially important when looking at subgroups. We were able to look at students according to four language proficiency categories: ELLs (ESOL 1–4), recently reclassified ELLs (ESOL 5), former ELLs, and non-ELLs. For details of the analyses and results of the first year see Llosa, Lee, Jiang, Haas, O'Connor, Van Booven, and Kieffer (2016).

There was a significant and meaningfully sized average intervention effect on the researcher-developed science assessment scores ($d = 0.25$, $p < .001$) and the state science assessment scale scores ($d = 0.15$, $p = .003$), indicating that students in the treatment group outperformed students in the control group on both measures of science achievement. According to Lipsey et al. (2012), the mean effect size of interventions that focus on curriculum or broad instructional programs is 0.13 and the median effect size is 0.08. Thus, effect sizes of 0.15 on the state science assessment and 0.25 on the researcher-developed assessment are of practical importance.

Subgroup analyses by language classification revealed that the intervention had significant and meaningfully sized effects for ELLs, recently reclassified ELLs, former ELLs, and non-ELLs on the researcher-developed assessment. This finding indicates that each subgroup in the treatment group outperformed that subgroup in the control group on the researcher-developed assessment. Significant intervention effects were found on the state science assessment for non-ELLs and former ELLs. However, the intervention effects on the state science assessment were positive, but not statistically significant, for recently reclassified ELLs or ELLs.

One explanation for these findings might be that, unlike the state science assessment, the researcher-developed assessment included open-ended items. Some researchers have argued that open-ended responses might be less affected by student background variables, including ELL status, than those on multiple-choice tests (Abedi, 2010; Buxton, Allexsaht-Snider, Aghasaleh, Kayumova, Kim, Choi, & Cohen, 2014; Goldschmidt, Martinez, Niemi, and Baker, 2007). Also, even though the researcher-developed assessment was composed of existing NAEP and TIMMS items, care was taken to avoid including items with less frequently occurring vocabulary words that were unrelated to the science content being assessed and could be unfamiliar to ELLs (e.g., "cupboard").

Overall, the fact that a significant main effect of practical importance was found in the effectiveness study is noteworthy considering that P-SELL was implemented large-scale across three school districts and under routine conditions.

Conclusions on Student Achievement

The positive effects of the P-SELL intervention on student science achievement demonstrated in both the efficacy and the effectiveness study can be attributed to the three key features of the intervention – standards-based, inquiry-oriented, and ELL-focused. The curriculum materials (i.e., student books, teachers' guide, and supplies) were designed to be educative for teacher learning (Davis, Palincsar, Arias, Bismack, Marulis, & Iwashyna, 2014; Davis & Krajcik, 2005; Drake, Land, & Tyminski, 2014) and emphasized these key features throughout. In addition, the teacher workshops followed the core and structural features of effective PD (Desimone, 2009; Garet et al., 2001) and emphasized these key features.

Teacher Measures and Outcomes

In the P-SELL projects, a main goal has always been to improve teacher knowledge of science content and their teaching practices. In all three studies of the P-SELL intervention, a teacher questionnaire was used to collect information directly from the teachers regarding how knowledgeable they felt and how often they used specific practices (e.g., teaching for understanding, inquiry, and language development). The main development over the course of these studies was a teachers' science content knowledge measure for the efficacy study based on the limitations encountered in the development study. The measure was then refined for the effectiveness study. A challenge of PD research in examining the influence of teachers on students is determining how to measure the various components of teacher change, with teachers' knowledge being one of the most difficult components to measure (Desimone, 2009). Therefore, the focus of this section is on the teacher knowledge test (Maerten-Rivera, Huggins-Manley, Adamson, Lee, & Llosa, 2015).

The Development Study

The development study first began addressing how to change teachers' science content knowledge. Findings from the development study, based on a knowledge scale administered to the teachers, suggested that teachers felt their knowledge had improved, particularly for fifth-grade teachers (Lee & Maerten-Rivera, 2012). However, the study used a self-report measure and the scale allowed only limited variability.

As we moved from the development study to the efficacy study, more researchers had begun to develop direct tests of teachers' content knowledge as opposed to using indirect measures such as number of courses taken and self-report knowledge scales. Though most of this research developed out of mathematics education (Baumert, Kunter, Blum, Brunner, Voss, Jordan, & Tsai, 2010; Hill, Ball, & Schilling, 2008), later research in science, like ours, began utilizing direct tests of science content knowledge (Heller, Daehler, Wong, Shinohara, & Miratrix, 2012; Jüttner, Boone, Park, & Neuhaus, 2013). Since a main goal of the project was to improve teachers' science content knowledge, it was imperative that this was directly measured, and not just teachers' perceptions that may not have been accurate.

The Efficacy Study

For the efficacy study, we recognized the need and opportunity to develop a measure of teachers' science content knowledge that could be used to measure the change in teachers' knowledge that resulted from participating in the intervention. In the planning stages of the efficacy study, we created the researcher-developed student assessment. As stated earlier, we did not use this assessment due to difficulties with the University IRB and the school district with which we were collaborating. However, as we developed the student assessment, a pool of unused fifth-grade science items was created, and these were then used on a science content knowledge test for teachers.

The teacher content knowledge test for the efficacy study was aligned with the fifth-grade science content standards in Florida, at the time of developing the measure. Two researchers took the lead in searching for test items that mapped onto these topics from two main sources: (a) publicly released items at fourth and eighth grades in NAEP 2000 and 2005 (https://nces.ed.gov/nationsreportcard/itmrlsx/landing.aspx) and (b) publicly released items at fourth and eighth grades in TIMSS 1995, 1999, and 2003 (https://nces.ed.gov/timss/educators.asp). In addition, previously researcher-developed test items were included in the pool of possible items; these items had been developed and used on one of the fifth-grade student tests in the development study. NAEP reports the difficulty level of each item as easy, medium, or hard, along with the percentage of national student respondents answering each item correctly. TIMSS reports the cognitive domain as factual knowledge, conceptual knowledge, or reasoning and analysis, along with the percentage of national and international student respondents answering each item correctly. The two researchers reviewed items along with the information provided about each item and ranked each item as easy, medium, or hard in terms of difficulty for the fifth-grade student level. We chose to rank the items at the fifth-grade difficulty level because this was the grade level being taught. At this time we felt that the test should be based upon the knowledge needed at the grade level they were teaching. Most items were of medium or hard difficulty (at the fifth-grade level) with fewer items of easy difficulty.

The final version of the test contained 30 items that mapped onto the science topics assessed at fifth grade, which included 24 multiple-choice and 6 constructed response items. Only 30 items were selected because we wanted the test to take about 30 minutes to complete. Each multiple-choice item was worth 1 point, one constructed response item was worth 1 point, two were worth 2 points each, and three were worth 3 points each. Appendix A displays two items from the test. In addition, the full test is available in our previously published paper (Maerten-Rivera et al., 2015; see supplementary material).

During the efficacy study, the test was administered to teachers prior to the beginning of the intervention and at the end of each school year. At each data collection, most teachers completed the test, with fewer than 6 percent not completing due to a variety of reasons (e.g., refusal, teacher absent or on leave). Time was coded as baseline (T0) when a teacher completed the test prior to beginning the intervention, Time 1 (T1) at the end of the first year, Time 2 (T2) at the end of the second year, and Time 3 (T3) at the end of the third year. A teacher could start participation during any time of the 3-year intervention. If a teacher started teaching fifth-grade science at a school during Year 3 of the intervention, when the teacher completed the test at the beginning of the year the time would be coded as T0, and at the end of the year the time would be coded as T1 since it was his/her first year of participating in the intervention.

Since the test was in development for the efficacy study, much of the analyses focused on examining the psychometric properties of the test using the Rasch framework. In addition, the measure was examined for its ability to detect changes in the treatment group compared to the control group. For details of the analysis and results see Maerten-Rivera et al. (2015).

The test developed for the efficacy study had acceptable reliability at T0, but was below the threshold considered acceptable at T1, T2, and T3, in part because some of the items on the test were not a good measure of teachers' science content knowledge, particularly at the later time points. At T0 the test matched the ability level of respondents fairly well, but at T1, T2, and T3 the test became easy for respondents and some items were too easy to be useful at measuring science content knowledge. There was a pattern that measurements closer together in time were more highly correlated, which provides evidence of test validity.

In the efficacy study, the test ability estimates at T0 were not related to group, but they were at T1. This finding indicated that the test ability estimates by group were changing over time based on the effect of the intervention. We were not able to examine the differences at T2 and T3 because the reliability estimates for these time points were too low. The test was able to detect some change over time (between T0 and T1) in the teachers and some difference between the treatment and control group at T1. These findings suggested that the test might be useful in evaluating the effects of the intervention on teachers' science content knowledge, but that some modifications were needed. These modifications were made for the effectiveness study.

The Effectiveness Study

The teacher test used in the effectiveness study differed from that used in the efficacy study in three main ways. First, the state adopted new science standards with 18 "Big Ideas" in 4 strands: the nature of science, Earth and space science, life science, and physical science. Thus, the test for the effectiveness study was developed around these strands, and the content differed somewhat from the science topics covered in the previous test. Second, results of the analyses conducted during the efficacy study suggested that the test was too easy for the teacher sample, as it was developed to measure science content knowledge at the fifth-grade level. For the effectiveness study, the overall difficulty level of the test was increased. Third, in the efficacy study, the test might have been too easy for teachers over time since they were taking the same test repeatedly. For the effectiveness study, two equated forms of the test were developed with approximately 10 percent of the items being linking items (i.e., appearing on both forms to link the scores from the two forms). A schedule was set up such that teachers who participated in the full 3 years of the study took Form A at T0, Form B at T1, Form A again at T2, and Form B again at T3. Although they took each form twice, it was nearly 2 years in between answering the same form. This schedule of test administration should have reduced memory effects, where teachers retaking the same form might have recalled their answers to the previous form or have discussed answers with others prior to retaking the test.

The same two researchers who worked for the efficacy study took the lead in searching for NAEP and TIMSS public release items that mapped onto the new science standards in the state. They focused on more difficult items that were typically administered at the middle and high school levels. This added some challenge to finding appropriate items because it was hard to find more difficult items that covered the more basic content areas at the elementary school level. We did not include any researcher-developed items on the teacher test for the effectiveness study; rather, if an item on a topic covered by the standards was not found in NAEP or TIMSS, we searched public release items from other states' assessments. The items considered for the pool were rated as being of easy, medium, or hard difficulty for a fifth-grade teacher (as opposed to at the fifth-grade level as we had done in the efficacy study) with consideration of information from the original sources.

Two final forms of the test were developed for the effectiveness study. For each form, 33 items were chosen that mapped onto the topics assessed at fifth grade, and each included 30 multiple-choice and 3 constructed response items. There were nine linking items, including all three of the constructed response items. Appendix B displays two items from the test. In addition, the full test is available in our previously published paper (Maerten-Rivera, Huggins-Manley, Adamson, Lee, & Llosa, 2015; see supplementary material).

The data collection and coding of time points was the same as those in the efficacy study. The exception was that for the effectiveness study the analyses included only the first year of data, and thus the maximum number of time points that a teacher could have was two, in which case the teacher completed a baseline test, participated in 1 year of the study, and completed the test at the end of the year.

By analyzing data from the first year of the effectiveness study, we were able to examine the internal and external structure of the test along with evidence of validity and whether we had addressed some of the weaknesses of the test in the efficacy study. The results from the effectiveness study indicated that the reliability was acceptable at both times, which was an improvement over the efficacy study. Further analyses indicated that all items were good at measuring teachers' science content knowledge. Finally, the results indicated that the test ability estimates for teachers were higher than the items, yet ability level and items were fairly well matched. The effectiveness study created a balance in that the test had stronger psychometric properties, yet it was not so difficult that it was not able to accurately measure teachers' science content knowledge (Maerten-Rivera et al., 2015).

In the effectiveness study the test ability estimates were not related to group at T0, suggesting that there was no difference in science knowledge prior to the intervention. However, the test ability estimates were related to group at T1, suggesting that there was a difference between the groups after the first year of the intervention. ANOVA results suggested small differences between the groups in the change found between the two time points. Thus, the test was able to detect some change over time (between T0 and T1) in the teachers and some difference between the treatment and control groups at T1 (Maerten-Rivera et al., 2015). Multilevel analyses to examine the impact of the intervention on teachers' science content knowledge revealed that the intervention had a positive impact on teachers' knowledge: the treatment effect was statistically significant ($p = .005$) and the effect size was 0.24, a small effect size (Lee, Llosa, Jiang, Haas, O'Connor, & Van Booven, 2016).

Conclusions on Teacher Outcomes

The P-SELL intervention is longitudinal in design, as the same teachers participate over multiple years. In both the efficacy and effectiveness studies, the test was able to detect some change over time in the treatment group compared to the control group. Developing a teacher test that is sensitive enough to detect change over time on an array of science topics proves a challenge. The P-SELL studies have addressed this challenge by developing and improving a teacher knowledge measure. A further challenge remains in establishing the relationship between teacher change and how it relates to student outcomes within the context of the intervention.

Implications

Across the three studies of the P-SELL intervention, measures of student and teacher outcomes were key to evaluating the impact of the intervention. During the time period of the P-SELL intervention (2004–2015), researchers were calling for more rigorous study designs, along with adequate measures of both student achievement and teacher change to evaluate causal models of PD interventions. The P-SELL efficacy and effectiveness studies used randomized controlled trials. In addition, the P-SELL effectiveness study used proximal and distal measures of student outcomes, while the P-SELL efficacy study used only distal measures due to some challenges (see details in Llosa, Maerten-Rivera, & Van Booven in this volume). Similarly, the need for measures of teachers' science content knowledge in the

P-SELL intervention was addressed by developing a measure in the efficacy study and improving on this measure in the effectiveness study. Another aspect to consider when developing content knowledge measures is that items may need to be included to measure pedagogical content knowledge (i.e., knowledge of how to teach subject matter content in ways that students can understand). Some researchers have included items measuring teachers' pedagogical content (Hill, 2010; Hill, Schilling, & Loewenberg Ball, 2004; Jüttner et al., 2013; Krauss, Baumert, & Blum, 2008).

Further research may examine causal PD models for the impact of interventions on student achievement. The finding of the P-SELL efficacy study suggests that there was a lag in the impact of the intervention on student achievement, which is consistent with other studies indicating a delayed effect of PD on student outcomes (Kreider & Bouffard, 2006; Silverstein et al., 2009). It may take time for teachers to effectively implement a new intervention that results in impact on student outcomes. This finding highlights the need to examine how teachers learn to implement or even adapt an intervention over multiple years and what mechanisms or supports are needed for implementation or adaptation over time. This finding also reminds educational practitioners that although they may look for immediate results of an intervention or program, it takes time for an intervention or program to take root and demonstrate an impact. While the first year results of the students' science achievement from the P-SELL effectiveness study were not consistent with the results of the P-SELL efficacy study and other previous research (cited above), the 3-year results of students' science achievement from the P-SELL effectiveness study will offer insights on this issue.

Furthermore, improved measures of teacher knowledge and practice are needed. These measures need to be studied for evidence of validity and reliability across various settings and various interventions for standardization. If a causal PD model is to be studied, teacher measures must be sensitive enough to detect change over time on an array of science topics. Through the P-SELL efficacy and effectiveness studies, we have learned that developing a measure of teachers' science content knowledge can be difficult but is possible. Other researchers should continue to measure teacher outcomes and develop, improve, and share such measures in order to respond to the call for more standardized measures in this area. Teacher outcomes, in addition to student outcomes, should be examined in order to fully evaluate the impact of an intervention.

References

Abedi, J. (2010). *Performance assessments for English language learners*. Stanford, CA: Stanford University, Stanford Center for Opportunity Policy in Education.

Adamson, K., Secada, W. G., Maerten-Rivera, J., & Lee, O. (2011). Measurement instruction in the context of scientific investigations. *School Science and Mathematics, 111*(6), 288–299.

Baumert, J., Kunter, M., Blum, W., Brunner, M., Voss, T., Jordan, A., & Tsai, Y.-M. (2010). Teachers' mathematical knowledge, cognitive activation in the classroom, and student progress. *American Educational Research Journal, 47*(1), 133–180.
Borko, H. (2004). Professional development and teacher learning: Mapping the terrain. *Educational Researcher, 33*(8), 3–15.
Buxton, C., Allexsaht-Snider, M., Aghasaleh, R., Kayumova, S., Kim, S., Choi, Y. & Cohen, A. (2014). Potential benefits of bilingual constructed response science assessments for understanding bilingual learners' emergent use of language of scientific investigation practices. *Double Helix, 2*, 1–21.
Davis, E., & Krajcik, J. (2005). Designing educative curriculum materials to promote teacher learning. *Educational Researcher, 34*, 3–14.
Davis, E. A., Palincsar, A. S., Arias, A., Bismack, A., Marulis, L., & Iwashyna, S. (2014). Designing educative curriculum materials: A theoretically and empirically driven process. *Harvard Educational Review, 84*(1), 24–52.
Desimone, L. M. (2009). Improving impact studies of teachers' professional development: Toward better conceptualizations and measures. *Educational Researcher, 38*(3), 181–199.
Drake, C., Land, T. J., & Tyminski, A. M. (2014). Using educative curriculum materials to support the development of prospective teachers' knowledge. *Educational Researcher, 43*(3), 154–162.
Garet, M. S., Porter, A. C., Desimone, L., Birman, B. F., & Yoon, K. S. (2001). What makes professional development effective? Results from a national sample of teachers. *American Educational Research Journal, 38*, 915–945.
Goldschmidt, P., Martinez, J. F., Niemi, D. & Baker, E. L. (2007). Relationship among measures as empirical evidence of validity: Incorporating multiple indicators of achievement and school context. *Educational Assessment, 12*(3&4), 239–266.
Heller, J. I., Daehler, K. R., Wong, N., Shinohara, M., & Miratrix, L. W. (2012). Differential effects of three professional development models on teacher knowledge and student achievement in elementary science. *Journal of Research in Science Teaching, 49*(3), 333–362.
Hill, H. C. (2010). The nature and predictors of elementary teachers' mathematical knowledge for teaching. *Journal for Research in Mathematics Education, 41*(5), 513–545.
Hill, H. C., Ball, D. L., & Schilling, S. G. (2008). Unpacking pedagogical content knowledge: Conceptualizing and measuring teachers' topic-specific knowledge of students. *Journal for Research in Mathematics Education, 39*(4), 372–400.
Hill, H. C., Schilling, S. G., & Loewenberg Ball, D. (2004). Developing measures of teachers' mathematics knowledge for teaching. *The Elementary School Journal, 105*(1), 11–30.
Jüttner, M., Boone, W., Park, S., & Neuhaus, B. J. (2013). Development and use of a test instrument to measure biology teachers' content knowledge (CK) and pedagogical content knowledge (PCK). *Educational Assessment, Evaluation and Accountability, 25*(1), 45–67.
Krauss, S., Baumert, J., & Blum, W. (2008). Secondary mathematics teachers' pedagogical content knowledge and content knowledge: Validation of the COACTIV constructs. *ZDM: The International Journal on Mathematics Education, 40*(5), 873–892.
Kreider, H., & Bouffard, S. (2006). Questions and answers: A conversation with Thomas R. Guskey. *The Evaluation Exchange, XI*(4). Retrieved August 14, 2015 from the Harvard Family Research Project website: www.hfrp.org/evaluation/the-evaluation-exchange/issue-archive/professional-development/a-conversation-with-thomas-r.-guskey.
Lee, O., Llosa, L., Jiang, F., Haas, A., O'Connor, C., & Van Booven, C. D. (2016). Elementary teachers' science knowledge and instructional practices: Impact of an intervention focused on English language learners. *Journal of Research in Science Teaching*.

Lee, O., & Maerten-Rivera, J. (2012). Teacher change in elementary science instruction with English language learners: Results of a multiyear professional development intervention across multiple grades. *Teachers College Record, 114*(8), 1–42.

Lee, O., Maerten-Rivera, J., Penfield, R. D., LeRoy, K., & Secada, W. G. (2008). Science achievement of English language learners in urban elementary schools: Results of a first-year professional development intervention. *Journal of Research in Science Teaching, 45*(1), 31–52.

Lipsey, M. W., Puzio, K., Yun, C., Hebert, M. A., Steinka-Fry, K., Cole, M. W., Roberts, M., Anthony, K. S., & Busick, M. D. (2012). *Translating the statistical representation of the effects of education interventions into more readily interpretable forms*. Retrieved August 14, 2015 from Institute of Education Sciences National Center for Special Education Research website: https://ies.ed.gov/ncser/pubs/20133000/.

Liu, X. (2009). Standardized measurement instruments in science education. In W. Roth & K. Tobin (Eds.), *The world of science education: Handbook of research in North America* (pp. 649–677). Rotterdam, The Netherlands: Sense.

Liu, X. (2012). Developing measurement instruments for science education research. In B. J. Fraser, K. Tobin, & C. J. McRobbie (Eds.), *Second international handbook of science education* (pp. 651–665). New York, NY: Springer.

Llosa, L., Lee, O., Jiang, F., Haas, A., O'Connor, C., Van Booven, C. D., & Kieffer, M. J. (2016). Impact of a large-scale science intervention focused on English language learners. *American Educational Research Journal, 53*(2), 395–424.

Maerten-Rivera, J., Ahn, S., Lanier, K., Diaz, J., & Lee, O. (2016). Effect of a multiyear intervention on science achievement of all students including English language learners. *Elementary School Journal*.

Maerten-Rivera, J., Huggins-Manley, A. C., Adamson, K., Lee, O., & Llosa, L. (2015). Development and validation of a measure of elementary teachers' science content knowledge in two multiyear teacher professional development intervention projects. *Journal of Research in Science Teaching, 52*(3), 371–396.

National Research Council. (2014). *Developing assessments for the Next Generation Science Standards*. Washington, DC: National Academies Press.

Penuel, W. R., Fishman, B. J., Yamaguchi, R., & Gallagher, L. P. (2007). What makes professional development effective? Strategies that foster curriculum implementation. *American Educational Research Journal, 44*(4), 921–958.

Ruiz-Primo, M. A., Shavelson, R. J., Hamilton, L. S., & Klein, S. (2002). On the evaluation of systemic science education reform: Searching for instructional sensitivity. *Journal of Research in Science Teaching, 39*(5), 369–393.

Santau, A. O., Maerten-Rivera, J., & Huggins, A. C. (2011). Science achievement of English language learners in urban elementary schools: Fourth-grade student achievement results from a professional development intervention. *Science Education, 95*(5), 771–793.

Silverstein, S. C., Dubner, J., Jon, M., Glied, S., & Loike, J. D. (2009). Teachers' participation in research programs improves their students' achievement in science. *Science, 326*(5951), 440–442.

Wayne, A. J., Yoon, K. S., Zhu, P., Cronen, S., & Garet, M. S. (2008). Experimenting with teacher professional development: Motive and methods. *Educational Researcher, 37*(8), 469–479.

Weaver, D., & Dick, T. (2009). Oregon mathematics leadership institute project: Evaluation results on teacher content knowledge, implementation fidelity, and student achievement. *The Journal of Mathematics and Science, 11*, 57–84.

Appendix A – Teacher Knowledge Test Items from Efficacy Study

Item i

Difficulty: Medium
Source: TIMSS seventh/eighth grade

Figure 3.1 shows an apple falling to the ground. In which of the three positions does gravity act on the apple?
A. 2 only
B. 1 and 2 only
C. 1 and 3 only
D. 1, 2, and 3★
   ★ Denotes correct answer

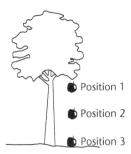

FIGURE 3.1 Apple and tree image.

Item ii

Difficulty: Hard
Source: TIMSS third/fourth grade

The surface of Earth has more water than land. Write down two reasons why some people still do not have enough water to drink.

Total of 2 possible points since score is given for part A (1 point) and part B (1 point).

Appendix B – Teacher Knowledge Test Items from Effectiveness Study

Item i

Difficulty: Medium
Source: TIMSS seventh/eighth grade

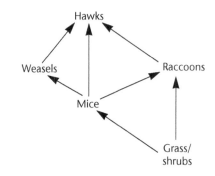

FIGURE 3.2 Food web.

Which organism in the food web in Figure 3.2 can be described as both primary and secondary consumers?
A. Mice
B. Weasels
C. Raccoons★
D. Hawks
  ★ Denotes correct answer

Item ii

Difficulty: Hard
Source: NAEP fourth grade

A bird watcher wants to see many birds in a one-hour period. She decides to investigate which type of food will attract more birds in her backyard.

She has a choice of two types of bird food.

- Sunflower seeds
- Thistle seeds

Describe a fair test the bird-watcher could conduct to help her decide which food will attract more birds.

What information should the bird-watcher collect from her test to help decide which type of food attracts more birds?

Correct response = 4 points
Satisfactory response = 3 points
Essential response = 2 points
Partial response = 1 point
Unsatisfactory/incorrect response = 0 points

4
CHALLENGES IN IMPLEMENTING AND EVALUATING A LARGE-SCALE SCIENCE INTERVENTION

The Case of the Promoting Science among English Language Learners (P-SELL) Project

Lorena Llosa, Jaime Maerten-Rivera, & Christopher D. Van Booven

Introduction

Identifying interventions that are effective when implemented on a large scale has become an important goal of educational research. As McDonald, Keesler, Kauffman, and Schneider (2006) claim, scale-up is about "extending the reach of an exemplary intervention to produce similarly positive effects in different settings and to help a greater number of students" (p. 16). Scaling up interventions, however, has proven difficult (Lee & Krajcik, 2012; Schneider & McDonald, 2007a, 2007b). Lee and Krajcik (2012) highlight four challenges in scaling up educational interventions. First, high rates of teacher and student mobility in urban schools, in particular, result in teachers and students lacking sufficient exposure to and opportunities to engage with the intervention. Second, resources that are essential for the implementation of an intervention, such as professional development for teachers and availability of instructional materials, are often limited. Third, large-scale interventions tend to be implemented as school-wide interventions. Although the collective participation of teachers in a school is a feature of successful professional development, it is possible that some of the teachers may resist the intervention. Finally, interventions take place in the context of high-stakes testing and accountability, thus districts and schools may be apprehensive about adopting a new intervention on a large scale. Evaluating the impact of a large-scale intervention can present as many challenges as the actual implementation of the intervention. Large-scale evaluations need to pay special attention to internal and external validity and statistical power and sample size (McDonald et al., 2006).

The Promoting Science among English Language Learners (P-SELL) efficacy study and the P-SELL effectiveness study described in the previous chapters (Lee, O'Connor, & Hass, this volume; Maerten-Rivera, Llosa, & Lee, this volume)

are among the largest studies conducted to date on the effectiveness of science interventions in elementary school, and the largest that focused specifically on ELLs. A recent research synthesis of elementary science programs from 1980 to 2012 found only 23 out of 332 studies reviewed that met inclusion criteria for rigorous designs (Slavin, Lake, Hanley, & Thurston, 2014) and, of those studies, only a couple were of the scale of the P-SELL studies (in terms of numbers of schools and students), and none focused specifically on ELLs.

An efficacy study examines the impact of an intervention under "ideal" conditions and thus requires a greater involvement of the research team. The P-SELL efficacy study (2009–2013) took place in one Florida school district located in the same county as the university research team. This study involved 64 schools, 359 teachers and approximately 20,000 students over the three years of implementation (Maerten-Rivera, Ahn, Lanier, Diaz, & Lee, 2016). An effectiveness study, on the other hand, examines the impact of an intervention under routine conditions. The P-SELL effectiveness study (2011–2015) took place in three geographically disparate districts in Florida (southern, central, and northern Florida) and the research team was in New York City. This study involved 66 schools, 447 teachers, and approximately 20,000 students over the three years of implementation (Llosa, Lee, Jiang, Haas, O'Connor, Van Booven, & Kieffer, 2016). Both studies used a randomized controlled trial design, where schools were randomly selected for participation in the study and then randomly assigned to the treatment and control conditions.

In this chapter, we describe some of the challenges we encountered during the P-SELL efficacy study and the P-SELL effectiveness study. Both of these studies aimed to examine whether the P-SELL intervention, an inquiry-based elementary science curriculum designed with a focus on ELLs, could be effective for all students. In these studies, P-SELL was implemented in all fifth-grade classrooms in treatment schools, regardless of the number of ELLs in a particular classroom. Thus, while the intervention was designed to support ELLs in particular, the challenges that emerged in implementation and evaluation were not specific to ELLs. We organize our discussion of challenges around two areas: (1) challenges in large-scale implementation of the intervention and (2) challenges in large-scale evaluation. We also describe how we dealt with challenges in these two areas and the implications of these challenges for the intervention and research design. By discussing the challenges of conducting large-scale studies of science interventions in schools, we hope to provide useful information to researchers and practitioners who are or will be engaging in similar work.

Challenges in Large-Scale Implementation

The P-SELL intervention features a yearlong, stand-alone curriculum for fifth grade. Therefore, the schools that were randomly assigned to the treatment group replaced the fifth-grade district-adopted science curriculum with the P-SELL curriculum for the duration of the study. In the efficacy study, 64 elementary schools in one district were randomly selected to participate in the study and 32 of those schools were randomly assigned to the treatment group. In the effectiveness study, 66 schools (22 schools in each of the 3 participating districts) were randomly selected to participate in the study, and 33 schools were randomly assigned to the treatment group. In Florida, one-eighth of a school's grade is based on students' performance on the state science assessment. Thus, one of the main challenges in conducting research on a large-scale intervention, especially one that replaces a yearlong, comprehensive curriculum on a year when test scores count towards accountability, is recruiting districts, schools, and teachers who are willing to take on this "risk" and ensuring their active participation throughout the duration of the study.

School Districts

Earning the trust and support of the school district(s) involved in a large-scale study is essential for its success. In our studies, it required building relationships over a long period of time as well as establishing a reputation as a trustworthy collaborator. Prior to the efficacy study, for example, Principal Investigator Okhee Lee had been working with the participating school district for several years on the development study (described in the previous chapter) during which the initial version of the P-SELL curriculum was developed. Several valuable practices were established during the development study that would carry on through the later efficacy and effectiveness studies. First, a relationship was formed with the district director for science education, to whom any significant issues in P-SELL implementation were reported, along with pertinent findings from the study. Second, a district liaison was funded by the development project to work 50 percent of her time on the development project. The district liaison acted as a resource for the project and was able to keep the district office informed of important updates on project implementation. Similarly, she was able to keep the research team updated on policies and procedures that were taking place in the district.

In the efficacy study, there were a much larger number of schools across the district participating in the study, and therefore additional steps were taken to establish a collaborative relationship between the university research team and the school district. These steps helped to ensure that the study was implemented successfully at a larger scale. First, a stronger relationship was established with the school district by introducing the project to the superintendent and key district personnel at various levels. The university research team met, on average, once every two months with the district administration team consisting of the director and supervisors of science education to discuss important details about the project, including information on the curriculum, teacher professional development, classroom implementation, and results of district benchmark assessments in science. Second, and similar to the development study, the efficacy study provided funding for a district liaison. However, since the efficacy study was implemented at a larger scale, the liaison worked on the P-SELL project full time and had an office at the university. The liaison was hired from within the district and was knowledgeable in science, district policy, and the P-SELL curriculum. The primary roles of the district liaison included involvement in curriculum revision, facilitation of teacher workshops, support for teachers with P-SELL implementation at school sites, and incorporation of the district policies and guidelines in the P-SELL implementation.

We adopted similar strategies for working closely with and ensuring the continuing participation of school districts in the P-SELL effectiveness study. Unlike the efficacy study, however, which took place in one district located in the same county as the university research team, the effectiveness study took place across three school districts in Florida and the university research team was located in New York. In the effectiveness study, we worked with three full-time district coordinators (one per district) hired from within each district with P-SELL project funds. The three district coordinators played a key role, similar to that of the district liaison in the efficacy study. The main role of the district coordinators was facilitating conversations between the research team and district administrators. The district coordinators were also responsible for leading professional development workshops for teachers and assisting with the logistics of data collection. The district coordinators met with the research team over the phone regularly both to deepen their understanding of the P-SELL curriculum (especially during the first year of implementation) and to plan the teacher workshops. The district coordinators were responsible for facilitating the workshops, but the planning and preparation of the workshops was conducted in collaboration with the research team. Another important role of the district coordinators was to assist with the logistics of data collection. They would plan and organize the data collection meetings and make-up dates and assist when needed with the delivery and pick-up of data collection instruments in schools. The district coordinators, however, were not present for the actual data collection, which required teachers to complete questionnaires about their professional background and instructional practices along with a test of science content knowledge. A research team member would travel to each of the districts, and to schools when needed, to administer the instruments to teachers. It was important to the project that the district coordinators' main relationship with the teachers be focused on program implementation and support, and not evaluation.

In addition to district coordinators, an important practice for ensuring the active participation of school districts in the effectiveness study involved working collaboratively and meeting regularly with district leadership. Every summer, including the summer of the planning year, the district coordinators and one or two leaders from each district met with the research team over two days in New York City. During these meetings, we discussed project activities in terms of both implementation and evaluation, new district policies that might impact implementation, and ways to improve all aspects of the project. An important activity during these meetings was sharing preliminary findings with the district leadership. In addition to the annual meeting in New York City, research team members visited the school districts regularly for meetings with district leadership.

Changes in leadership at the district level can present important challenges to multiyear, large-scale research projects, and significant leadership changes took place during both studies. During the effectiveness study, for example, all three participating school districts changed superintendents. By maintaining constant, open communication between the research team and the district leadership and through the key role of the district coordinators, we were able to ensure the districts' continuing participation despite these changes in leadership. Also, promising preliminary findings and positive reviews from teachers and students were important resources to ensure that the new leadership would maintain the district's commitment to the studies.

Finally, flexibility was also important to maintain the active participation of districts and schools in the study. The project had to adapt to various district needs and policies. Since our intervention consisted of a yearlong, stand-alone curriculum, it was particularly important that the intervention be aligned with existing district policies and initiatives. In the effectiveness study, for example, we had to take into account the fact that the three participating school districts had different pacing plans for fifth-grade science instruction; the Big Ideas in the state standards were not covered in the same order. Also, because the pacing plans were aligned to benchmark assessments used by each district, it was important that schools using P-SELL also follow the same pacing plan as the control schools and other schools in the district so that students would be able to meaningfully participate in the benchmark assessments. We therefore reorganized the chapters in the P-SELL book and produced three different versions of the student book to align the P-SELL curriculum with each district's pacing plan. We also had to customize the professional development sessions so that teachers would become familiar with the chapters according to each district's pacing guide, which meant that the teacher workshops were also presented in a different sequence to teachers in each of the three school districts.

We also had to be flexible to each district's preferences in terms of timing of teacher professional development workshops. The effectiveness study called for 5 full days of workshops in Year 1. However, the distribution of those 5 days was decided in collaboration with each school district. Some school districts preferred to have 2 or 3 workshop days in summer, whereas other districts preferred to distribute the workshops throughout the year. Also, some districts preferred workshops on Saturdays, whereas other districts preferred workshops during the week. When workshops were offered during the week, the project paid the schools for a substitute teacher, and when workshops were offered on Saturdays, teachers received a stipend for their participation. Allowing for flexibility in implementation was critical for ensuring the active participation of schools in our studies; indeed, this approach to "maximizing contextual fit" has been found to be a key factor for promoting scale-up and sustainability of interventions (McIntosh, Filter, Bennett, Ryan, & Sugai, 2010).

Schools

Our efforts to build and sustain trust in the intervention did not stop at the district level; we directed considerable attention to the maintenance of strong relationships and open lines of communication with the leadership in each of our participating schools. For not only do superintendents change, principals often change as well. It was important to ensure that a new principal would maintain the school's commitment to participation in the study. The integrity of randomized controlled trials – where randomization is at the school level – is dependent on schools remaining in the study. Attrition at the school level in particular would compromise the experimental design.

To mitigate this challenge, we made sure to have important conversations with the principals involved in the studies at the beginning of every school year. In the efficacy study, a half-day meeting was held for administrators of treatment schools the week prior to school starting; we asked that the principal or a designee attend so that each school had a representative at the meeting. At this meeting, we provided an overview of the project; this was especially helpful for administrators new to a P-SELL school. In addition, we shared results from previous year(s) and explained any updates or changes from the previous year. At this meeting, a copy of the curriculum and all resources were distributed. In the effectiveness study, the three district coordinators contacted new principals to inform them of the study and explain to them the importance of their school's participation. In some districts, the coordinators organized a meeting with all of the principals. In others, the coordinators visited principals individually at their schools.

Another element of the study design that was critical to maintaining the participation of schools in the study was the provision of incentives. In both studies, treatment schools received the entire year's curriculum for fifth-grade science, including a teachers' guide, student consumable books, and all of the science supplies needed for inquiry activities. As explained earlier, treatment teachers received a stipend if they attended a P-SELL professional development workshop on the weekend, and the project paid for a substitute teacher when a workshop took place during the week. In control schools, all participating teachers received a stipend for participating in fall and spring data collection activities. In addition, all control schools received a yearly stipend for participating in the study that the schools could spend at their discretion. Thus, through a combination of extensive communication, support from the district liaison/coordinators, and a program of incentives, attrition in both studies was minimal: only 1 of the 64 schools dropped out of the efficacy study and none of the 66 schools dropped out of the effectiveness study.

Teachers

Finally, it was important to ensure the participation of the teachers. Asking already busy teachers to dedicate extra time to attend professional development and/or data collection sessions, we ran the risk of overburdening the participants on whom we were relying most to implement our curriculum. Therefore, establishing good relationships with all teachers, from both treatment and control schools, was a priority in our studies and a great amount of resources and effort were allocated to accomplish this goal. For example, teacher professional development workshops and data collection sessions were scheduled at a time that was convenient for the teachers. A make-up date was also arranged for teachers who could not attend the main workshop or data collection session. At the workshops, we made sure to provide the teachers with high-quality food options; we felt that attending to such details would reflect our commitment to honoring the work of the teachers in our studies. We were also very sensitive with our timing of communication with teachers by closely monitoring the district calendar (e.g., holidays, testing schedules). For example, we would avoid contacting teachers at times we knew would be particularly busy for them. We also ensured that treatment teachers received all of the P-SELL materials and supplies before the beginning of the school year, and the district coordinator and the research team were available to address any questions. The features of the curriculum itself also helped to ensure teacher buy-in. The close alignment between the P-SELL curriculum and the state standards was greatly appreciated by the teachers, who typically had to sort through textbooks page by page themselves to determine which materials they did and did not need to cover.

Challenges in Large-Scale Evaluation

In this section we describe challenges in managing research activities in a large-scale study. Specifically, we address challenges in logistics and data collection, measures, and data analysis.

Logistics and Data Collection

Evaluating a science intervention on a large scale presents a number of logistical challenges for a research team. Both the P-SELL efficacy study and the P-SELL effectiveness study involved data collection at the beginning and the end of the school year. In order to collect data from students and teachers, we needed a list of all of the fifth-grade science teachers in the participating schools. Many schools, however, did not finalize their rosters until very close to the beginning of the school year and, even when they did, changes were often made during the first few weeks of school. In addition, unexpected changes also frequently emerged throughout the school year (e.g., maternity leave, sick leave). Maintaining an updated database of teachers to ensure complete data collection at pre and post each year required that the research teams keep constant communication with the district coordinators and the principals – not an easy task given the number of participating teachers: the efficacy study involved approximately 300 teachers each year and the effectiveness study involved approximately 275 teachers each year. As another strategy for ensuring complete data collection from teachers, we scheduled make-up sessions for those who could not attend the main session; for cases where teachers could not (or would not) attend either, we would drive to their school to collect the data.

Data collection activities became increasingly efficient during each year of the studies. As teachers came to know the research team and benefited from the intervention, they were more willing to participate in all activities. Furthermore, while there were new teachers in the study in Years 2 and 3, these teachers more readily bought into the intervention because their colleagues who had been participating previously were familiar with the research team and the process and were positive about the experience. Teachers in the control group were also more willing to participate in research activities in Years 2 and 3 once they were familiar with the research team and knew that they and their schools would receive stipends.

Another logistical challenge was teacher mobility. In the efficacy study, approximately 28 percent of the teachers were in the study for the full 3 years, 26 percent participated for 2 years, and 46 percent for 1 year. In the effectiveness study, 35 percent of the teachers were in the study for 3 years, 45 percent participated for 2 years, and 21 percent for 1 year. This teacher mobility had important consequences for our implementation of the intervention. In the effectiveness study, for example, during Years 2 and 3 of implementation, we had to offer two sets of professional development workshops: those for new teachers and those for returning teachers. Workshops for new teachers focused on how to implement the curriculum materials, highlighting how to perform every hands-on inquiry activity in the curriculum, as their students are expected to throughout the year. Workshops for returning teachers were more specialized and in-depth, focusing, for example, on the application and extension of inquiry activities. As noted, a further consequence was that by the end of Year 3 of implementation, there were teachers in the study who had participated for 3 years, teachers who had participated for 2 years, and others who had participated for 1 year; each of these groups of teachers thus had different amounts of exposure to and experiences with the P-SELL curriculum. In the effectiveness study, for which analysis is ongoing, we will therefore be able to examine whether and to what extent the impact of the intervention on students was mediated by teachers' experience with P-SELL (1, 2, or 3 years). Given that teacher mobility is a reality in schools, understanding the impact of mobility on the effectiveness of an intervention is an important goal of scale-up research (Lee & Krajcik, 2012).

Measures

A challenge of every study is determining how much data one must obtain to adequately address the research questions while at the same time avoiding placing a burden on teachers and students that could negatively impact their participation. The main questions that both studies addressed was whether the intervention had an impact on teachers' science knowledge and instructional practices and on students' science achievement. In this section, we discuss some of the challenges associated with deciding which measures to use and how best to develop and administer them. Specifically, we discuss classroom observations and student and teacher science tests.

Classroom observations. One of the most challenging aspects of data collection in a large-scale study is classroom observations. Classroom observations are an important measure of fidelity of implementation in treatment classrooms and allow for an examination of instructional practices in control classrooms.

The efficacy study involved classroom observations. One randomly selected teacher from each of the treatment and control schools was observed three times throughout the year. If the randomly selected teacher remained in the study in subsequent years, he/she was observed again. However, if a selected teacher left the study, a new teacher from the school was randomly selected to be observed. In total, there were close to 200 observations each year and 600 observations over the 3-year period of the efficacy study. A team of three researchers including two full-time staff and one doctoral student conducted observations in schools. Classroom observations required immense resources, starting from the training of the observers, establishing reliability among the observers on an ongoing basis, scheduling classroom visits (including cancellations and rescheduling), conducting the observations, completing observation notes, and maintaining de-identified observation records in the database. Despite the large amount of resources invested, given the great variability between teachers within a school, the observations gathered from one teacher could not be generalized to other teachers in the school, and thus the classroom observations were of limited use.

In the effectiveness study, given the distance between the research team and the three school districts and the distance between each of the districts, observations of teachers' instructional practices were not possible. For classroom observations to yield reliable information about instructional practices, a teacher should be observed multiple times (Desimone, 2009). Even observing one randomly selected teacher per school (66), as in the efficacy study, was not a viable option given the scope and budget of the project and the distance between the research team and the districts. Instead, we relied on a teacher questionnaire (Lee, Llosa, Jiang, Haas, O'Connor, & Van Booven, 2016). According to Desimone (2009), questionnaires can provide "valid and reliable data on the amount of time that teachers spend on specific practices occurring during a set time period – up to a year" (p. 190), and this is the type of data we collected using the teacher questionnaire. The district coordinators did visit each treatment classroom to ensure that the P-SELL curriculum was being implemented, but no classroom observation data was collected as a formal measure of teachers' instructional practices or fidelity of implementation.

Student science assessment. One decision we made was to develop a researcher-developed science assessment to be administered at the beginning and at the end of the year that would supplement science achievement data based on the state science assessment. The state science assessment is only offered at the end of fifth grade. Our assessment administered at the beginning of the year served as a baseline of science knowledge prior to the intervention. This baseline can be used to compare the treatment and control groups initially to ensure that the randomization process selected two groups that were similar in science knowledge prior to the intervention. The baseline can also be used to control for initial achievement prior to the intervention and thus improve the precision of the treatment effect – the difference between the treatment and control groups in science achievement at the end of the year. As explained in the previous chapter, even though a student assessment was developed for the efficacy study, we were not able to use it because the school district did not give permission to administer it to students. The district was concerned that students already had to sit for too many district- and state-mandated assessments. For the effectiveness study, when P-SELL had been more established and was better known in the state, the three participating districts allowed us to administer the student assessment.

One important feature of the researcher-developed student assessment was that it included three open-ended questions. Since one of the main features of P-SELL is its focus on language development, and given that the state science assessment only includes multiple-choice items, we considered it important that our test elicit student language. However, administering three open-ended questions meant that we had to manually score these items. It took a team of 10 raters 6 full days to double score the three items for the approximately 7,000 students in the study at the beginning of the year and another 6 full days at the end of the year. Nonetheless we felt the time and energy spent gathering and scoring these responses were important for a project that focused on inquiry science and ELLs. Some researchers have argued that open-ended questions may afford ELLs a better opportunity to demonstrate their knowledge (Abedi, 2010; Buxton, Allexsaht-Snider, Aghasaleh, Kayumova, Kim, Choi, & Cohen, 2014; Goldschmidt, Martinez, Niemi, & Baker, 2007).

Teacher science test. In addition to a background questionnaire and a questionnaire about instructional practices, we also decided to administer a test of science knowledge to participating teachers (see Maerten-Rivera, Huggins-Manley, Adamson, Lee, & Llosa, 2015). In the planning and development stages for the efficacy study, there was much discussion regarding how teachers would react to being asked to complete a science test that was similar to the test that students were asked to take. We were unsure if teachers would complete the test or simply refuse; we wondered if they would take offense. An additional concern was that teachers might feel that they were being judged and that results would be shared with their school administrators and/or the district. The teachers were informed that the responses were confidential and would not be shared with administrators. In the end, nearly all of the teachers completed the test at each administration without any problems. In the effectiveness study, we were also able to administer the teacher science knowledge test without any problems.

It is important to point out that the P-SELL studies did not include a measure of pedagogical content knowledge (i.e., knowledge of how to teach subject matter content in ways that students can understand), which has been included in several studies and found to be important (e.g., Hill, 2010; Hill, Ball, & Schilling, 2008; Jüttner, Boone, Park, & Neuhaus, 2013; Krauss, Baumert, & Blum, 2008). One of the challenges in research in general, and large-scale studies in particular, is finding a balance between collecting sufficient data to address the research questions and doing so within the constraints imposed by the budget, time, and the willingness of participants to engage in research activities.

Data Analysis

Deciding how to analyze the data was another important decision that we had to make in each of the studies. And the decisions were often affected by changes in state and district assessment and accountability policies.

The efficacy study was most affected by changes in the Florida state tests. As explained in the previous chapter, in the 2011–2012 school year, the topics covered on the state science assessment were changed. In Year 1 of the efficacy study, the state science assessment covered the topics of physical and chemical science, Earth and space science, life and environmental science, and scientific thinking. In Year 2 and subsequent years of the study, the state science assessment was changed to cover the areas of nature of science, Earth and space science, physical science, and life science. In addition, there were changes made in the scale scores for the state science standardized test during the efficacy study implementation, which did not coincide with the change in topics covered. In Years 1 and 2 of the efficacy study, the science scale ranged from 100 to 500. Based on scale scores, students were assigned achievement levels ranging from 1 to 5. Students with scores from 100–272 were level 1, 273–322 level 2, 323–376 level 3, 377–416 level 4, and 417–500 level 5. For the purpose of accountability, students classified as level 3, 4, or 5 were considered proficient. In Year 3 of the study, the science scale was changed to range from 140 to 260. Students with scores from 140–184 were level 1, 185–199 level 2, 200–214 level 3, 215–224 level 4, and 225–260 level 5. Again, students classified as level 3, 4, or 5 were considered proficient.

Given all of these changes, when analyzing the student science achievement data, we used science proficiency levels (i.e., classified as level 1 or 2 versus classified as level 3, 4, or 5), instead of scale scores, to examine the intervention effect in the efficacy study (see Maerten-Rivera et al., 2016). Proficiency levels were also the measure of achievement that the participating school district was most interested in. Other interventions have also evaluated outcomes based on the percent of students deemed "passing" state tests (Silverstein, Dubner, Jon, Glied, & Loike, 2009; Weaver & Dick, 2009). One challenge of using proficiency as an outcome was that it restricted the analyses that could be conducted. Specifically, the examination of the impact of the intervention on student subgroups (e.g., ELLs, former ELLs, non-ELLs) was limited by small sample sizes and the use of a dichotomous outcome variable (i.e., proficient versus not proficient).

In the effectiveness study, we were able to use the scale score, a continuous variable, to examine the impact of the intervention and differential impact for subgroups. During the duration of the effectiveness study there were no changes to the science assessment or the scale scores (see Llosa et al., 2016).

Concluding Remarks

Using the P-SELL efficacy and effectiveness studies as examples, this chapter outlined some of the challenges involved in implementing and evaluating a large-scale science intervention. Some of the challenges were the same for both projects, but others differed in line with the differences between an efficacy and an effectiveness study. As explained earlier, in an efficacy study the intervention is implemented under "ideal" conditions. The P-SELL efficacy study took place in one school district located in the same county as the university research team. Thus, the research team was closely involved in several aspects of P-SELL implementation, including conducting all of the professional development workshops for teachers. Also, the study included classroom observations that served both as a source of data and as a mechanism to closely monitor implementation. On the other hand, an effectiveness study examines the impact of an intervention under routine conditions. In the P-SELL effectiveness study, for example, the teacher workshops were facilitated by the district coordinators, not the research team. Also, the increased generalizability of the findings afforded by conducting the study in three different districts with different characteristics also created challenges. For example, we were not able to conduct classroom observations as explained earlier.

Other challenges were unrelated to the nature of the studies themselves but had to do with state and/or district policies. For example, changes in the state science assessment affected our decisions about how to analyze the data in the efficacy study. Furthermore, the decision to implement an intervention at a grade level when science assessments counted towards accountability involved some risk; however, it also allowed for a more consistent implementation of the intervention and afforded us a meaningful comparison condition. Because science is tested in fifth grade, science was taught regularly and extensively in all of our participating schools, both treatment and control.

As Lynch, Pyke, and Hansen-Grafton (2012) point out, "the messy challenge of bringing an intervention to scale in schools, districts, and states (while minding the need to conduct valid and reliable research) is a complex endeavor that defies tidy organizational plans" (306–307). This chapter provides an illustration of the "messiness" and the ways in which it is possible to work through it and carry out a successful implementation and evaluation study.

References

Abedi, J. (2010). *Performance assessments for English language learners*. Stanford, CA: Stanford University, Stanford Center for Opportunity Policy in Education.

Buxton, C., Allexsaht-Snider, M., Aghasaleh, R., Kayumova, S., Kim, S., Choi, Y., & Cohen, A. (2014). Potential benefits of bilingual constructed response science assessments for understanding bilingual learners' emergent use of language of scientific investigation practices. *Double Helix, 2*, 1–21.

Desimone, L. M. (2009). Improving impact studies of teachers' professional development: Toward better conceptualizations and measures. *Educational Researcher, 38*(3), 181–199.

Goldschmidt, P., Martinez, J. F., Niemi, D., & Baker, E. L. (2007). Relationship among measures as empirical evidence of validity: Incorporating multiple indicators of achievement and school context. *Educational Assessment, 12*(3&4), 239–266.

Hill, H. C. (2010). The nature and predictors of elementary teachers' mathematical knowledge for teaching. *Journal for Research in Mathematics Education, 41*(5), 513–545.

Hill, H. C., Ball, D. L., & Schilling, S. G. (2008). Unpacking pedagogical content knowledge: Conceptualizing and measuring teachers' topic-specific knowledge of students. *Journal for Research in Mathematics Education, 39*(4), 372–400.

Jüttner, M., Boone, W., Park, S., & Neuhaus, B. J. (2013). Development and use of a test instrument to measure biology teachers' content knowledge (CK) and pedagogical content knowledge (PCK). *Educational Assessment, Evaluation and Accountability, 25*(1), 45–67.

Krauss, S., Baumert, J., & Blum, W. (2008). Secondary mathematics teachers' pedagogical content knowledge and content knowledge: Validation of the COACTIV constructs. *ZDM: The International Journal on Mathematics Education, 40*(5), 873–892.

Lee, O., & Krajcik, J. (2012). Large-scale interventions in science education for diverse student groups in varied educational settings. *Journal of Research in Science Teaching, 49*(3), 271–280.

Lee, O., Llosa, L., Jiang, F., Haas, A., O'Connor, C., & Van Booven, C. D. (2016). Elementary teachers' science knowledge and instructional practices: Impact of an intervention focused on English language learners. *Journal of Research in Science Teaching, 53*(4), 579–597.

Llosa, L., Lee, O., Jiang, F., Haas, A., O'Connor, C., Van Booven, C. D., & Kieffer, M. J. (2016). Impact of a large-scale science intervention focused on English language learners. *American Educational Research Journal, 53*(2), 395–424.

Lynch, J. S., Pyke, C., & Hansen-Grafton, B. (2012). A retrospective view of a study of middle school science curriculum materials: Implementation, scale-up, and sustainability in a changing policy environment. *Journal of Research in Science Teaching, 49*(3), 305–332.

Maerten-Rivera, J., Ahn, S., Lanier, K., Diaz, J., & Lee, O. (2016). Effect of a multiyear intervention on science achievement of all students including English language learners. *The Elementary School Journal, 116*(4), 600–624.

Maerten-Rivera, J., Huggins-Manley, A.C., Adamson, K., Lee, O., & Llosa, L. (2015). Development and validation of a measure of elementary teachers' science content knowledge in two multiyear teacher professional development intervention projects. *Journal of Research in Science Teaching, 52*(3), 371–396.

McDonald, S.-K., Keesler, V. A., Kauffman, N. J., & Schneider, B. (2006). Scaling-up exemplary interventions. *Educational Researcher, 35*(3), 15–24.

McIntosh, K., Filter, K. J., Bennett, J. L., Ryan, C., & Sugai, G. (2010). Principles of sustainable prevention: Designing scale-up of School-wide Positive Behavior Support to promote durable systems. *Psychology in the Schools, 47*(1), 5–21.

Schneider, B., & McDonald, S.-K. (Eds.). (2007a). *Scale up in education: Ideas in principle* (Vol. 1). Lanham, MD: Rowman & Littlefield.

Schneider, B., & McDonald, S.-K. (Eds.). (2007b). *Scale up in education: Practice* (Vol. 2). Lanham, MD: Rowman & Littlefield.

Silverstein, S. C., Dubner, J., Jon, M., Glied, S., & Loike, J. D. (2009). Teachers' participation in research programs improves their students' achievement in science. *Science, 326*(5951), 440–442.

Slavin, R. E., Lake, C., Hanley, P., & Thurston, A. (2014). Experimental evaluations of elementary science programs: A best-evidence synthesis. *Journal of Research in Science Teaching, 51*(7), 870–901.

Weaver, D., & Dick, T. (2009). Oregon mathematics leadership institute project: Evaluation results on teacher content knowledge, implementation fidelity, and student achievement. *The Journal of Mathematics and Science: Collaborative Explorations, 11*, 57–84.

PART II
LISELL-B
Language-rich Inquiry Science with English Language Learners through Biotechnology

5
REASSEMBLING SCIENCE TEACHER EDUCATOR PROFESSIONAL LEARNING IN THE LISELL-B PROJECT

Cory A. Buxton, Martha Allexsaht-Snider, Regina Suriel, Shakhnoza Kayumova, Elif Karsli, & Rouhollah Aghasaleh

Introduction

Critiques of the quality of America's teachers are nothing new (Labaree, 2008; National Commission on Excellence in Education, 1983). Such critiques have returned to the spotlight in recent years as states attempt to develop measures of teacher effectiveness tied to merit pay systems and other types of incentives and consequences (Berliner & Glass, 2014; Koedell & Betts, 2011). At the same time, college and university programs that engage in the preparation of teachers have come under similar scrutiny from legislators, the media, and groups such as the National Council on Teacher Quality (NCTQ), all advocating for reforms and increased accountability for the performance of a program's teacher-graduates (Cochran-Smith, Piazza, & Power, 2013; Fuller, 2014). Less attention has been paid, however, to the preparation of the teacher educators who staff these college, university, and alternative teacher preparation programs. To respond effectively to the critiques, it is important to understand what specific kinds of preparation and practice these individuals have had for doing teacher education as part of their own professional preparation.

It is notable that while the current edition of the Handbook of Research on Teacher Education (Cochran-Smith, Feiman-Nemser, & McIntyre, 2008) covers a wide array of topics related to how, why, and where teachers should be prepared, it lacks a chapter dedicated to the preparation of future (or current) teacher educators. Research on this topic has received some limited attention (see, for example, Cochran-Smith's 2003 international comparative study), but this work has predominantly highlighted broad-scale analysis of policies and contexts that might better support the training of future teacher educators. There has been scant research on the details and nuances of the actual preparation of teacher educators that might illuminate bottom-up principles that can guide teacher educator professional learning. Dinkleman, Margolis, and Sikkenga (2006) conducted one of the few empirical studies that explored the process through which former classroom teachers make the often abrupt transition to beginning teacher educators as part of their graduate studies in education. In a study most closely related to the goals of our own project, Gort, Glenn, and Settlage (2010) described their efforts as current teacher educators to improve their own culturally and linguistically responsive practice by using a faculty learning community as a space for self-study. Most recently, a special issue of the *Journal of Teacher Education* took up the question of professional development of teacher educators (Vol. 65(4), 2014). The editors begin with the assertion that

> While we are making gains in building the specialized knowledge base for teacher preparation and professional development, we have neglected the study of teacher educators. The assumption that a good teacher will become a good teacher educator is prevalent in the field but has not been systematically examined. (Knight et al., 2014, p. 268)

The editors of this special issue go on to raise a number of questions regarding the work of teacher educators, including: What influences shape the roles and practices of teacher educators? How do contexts matter in the ways teacher educators learn and develop? What forms of knowledge do teacher educators use that differ from those used by effective teachers more generally, and how do these forms of knowledge develop? Two further questions that our research group found the most intriguing were: (1) Can we prepare tomorrow's teachers with today's teacher educators? (2) What is the role of research and the relationship between research and practice in preparing the next generation of teacher educators?

The seven articles in the JTE special issue address the preparation of teacher educators from multiple perspectives, with several studies highlighting the differences between the knowledge base needed for K–12 teaching and the knowledge base needed for teacher education. The article by Goodwin, Smith, Souto-Manning, Cheruvu, Tan, Reed, and Taveras (2014) most closely addresses the particular questions that intrigued us. From their study of 293 current teacher educators from a range of institutions (all in the U.S.), they concluded that most of these individuals felt that they had become teacher educators largely by chance and had engaged in little explicit study of how to prepare teachers during their doctoral work. The majority claimed to rely most heavily on their own K–12 teaching backgrounds to shape the work they do with teacher candidates. They also identified learning through observation of the faculty in their doctoral programs as well as faculty from their own teacher preparation programs as major influences. Many of these current teacher educators stated that their doctoral programs primarily prepared them to be education researchers but that this research preparation was not closely connected to the work of teacher preparation and did not play a significant role in how they currently do their work as teacher educators.

In this chapter, we provide an additional set of nuanced responses to the question of the role of research and the relationship between research and practice in next generation teacher educator preparation. We do this through a discussion of the preparation of teacher educators taking place within the context of a research and development project focused on the professional learning of middle school and high school science and ESOL teachers working in schools with rapidly increasing numbers of emergent bilingual learners. We explore how participation in this teaching-focused research project helped us to understand and strengthen not only teacher professional learning but also teacher educator professional learning. We use this context to illustrate several emergent principles for supporting science teacher educator professional learning with a critical social justice stance.

The Language-rich Inquiry Science with English Language Learners (LISELL) project and subsequent Language-rich Inquiry Science with English Language Learners through Biotechnology (LISELL-B) project (hereafter collectively referred to as LISELL-B) has been funded by the National Science Foundation since 2010 to support middle school and high school science teacher professional learning by developing, refining, implementing, and testing a pedagogical model and a professional learning framework for improving science teaching and learning for all students, with a particular focus on the needs and resources of emergent bilingual learners. The LISELL-B pedagogical model is aligned with the three-dimensional learning model underlying the Next Generation Science Standards, and focuses on the simultaneous development of conceptual science knowledge, science investigation practices, and the language of science. Our goal is for all students, and especially emergent bilinguals, to gain proficiency in using the language of science and scientific problem-solving skills, both in the context of school science learning and in their daily lives beyond the science classroom. To accomplish this goal, the project developed a pedagogical model for structuring the teaching of science practices and the language of science to emergent bilingual students and a multifaceted teacher professional learning framework through which the project team engages with teachers in project schools. This pedagogical model and professional learning framework have been discussed in detail elsewhere (Buxton, Allexsaht-Snider, Hernandez, Aghasaleh, Cardozo-Gaibisso, & Kirmaci, 2016; Buxton, Allexsaht-Snider, Kayumova, Aghasaleh, Choi, & Cohen, 2015) and are summarized briefly in the methods section below.

While teacher educator professional learning was not initially conceptualized as a goal of the LISELL-B project, as we carried out this research over multiple years, we began to attend to this issue as a valuable offshoot of what we (faculty and the doctoral students who have worked with us on the LISELL-B project) were learning about teacher education through our research. We considered how at our institution (and we suspect, at many others) the preparation of next generation teacher educators is conceptualized as coming primarily from experiences as teaching assistants in pre-service teacher preparation programs. Further, we felt that a false distinction was often drawn between teaching assistantships meant to prepare individuals to be teacher educators and research assistantships meant to prepare individuals to be education researchers. We came to believe that a research project such as LISELL-B, which includes an innovative teacher professional learning framework for practicing teachers, could be one place to seek answers to questions about the ongoing professional learning of both next generation teacher educators (current doctoral students) and current teacher educators (faculty).

In this chapter, we question the dichotomous positioning that often occurs between research and teaching among faculty in teacher education programs, between faculty and doctoral students on research projects, and between university personnel and K–12 teachers during teacher professional learning. While Goodwin et al. (2014) found that current teacher educators often failed to make a meaningful connection between their research preparation in graduate school and their subsequent teacher education work, we hypothesize that this is due to a lack of opportunities to make those connections explicit during doctoral preparation. We use the theoretical framework of actor network theory to situate our work on the LISELL-B project within a network of practices, people, and materials that together provide a context for better understanding – and for suggesting more generalized principles that enhance – the process of teacher educator professional learning.

Theoretical Framework – Actor Network Theory

Actor Network Theory (or ANT) has been described as the "sociology of translations" (Callon, 1986), by which Callon means the study of how social networks of power and activity are assembled and disassembled over time. Law (2004) claims that the value of ANT is that it serves to identify the resources that are mobilized to establish (or assemble) an object of knowledge. In our case, this object of knowledge is a set of principles for supporting the preparation of next generation teacher educators who are skilled at facilitating teacher professional learning in science for emergent bilingual learners. Relevant resources include people, devices, decisions, documents, organizations, and the connections between all of these as they relate to the LISELL-B project. The origins of ANT are closely tied to the sociology of science and how scientific knowledge is constructed in laboratory settings (Latour & Woolgar, 1979) and in the other spaces where scientists do their work (Callon & Latour, 1981). Thus, there is a natural lineage that connects ANT to the work of science education, to science teacher education, and finally to the education of science teacher educators. However, while ANT has been a popular guiding framework for organizational studies in other fields, such as management and sociology, it has remained largely obscure in educational research (Fenwick & Edwards, 2013).

While other related theoretical frameworks, ranging from those more commonly used in research on teacher education, such as Wenger's (1999) communities of practice, to frameworks less common in teacher education, such as Deleuze and Guattari's (1988) metaphors of aborescence and rhyzomes, could guide our thinking about teacher educator professional learning in the LISELL-B project, ANT seemed well suited. ANT proved useful in helping us to circumvent the structure-agency binary in which human actors make moves to resist or conform to pre-existing social structures. While ANT does not deny the existence of such structures (conceptualized as macro actors), nor their interplay with individuals (micro actors), it resists the idea that the work of structures and the work of individuals is fundamentally different. The hyphenated actor-network serves to trouble this distinction between individual agent and larger social structure, breaking down binaries and focusing instead on variations in durability of a network. In this way, ANT can help us to describe the positioning of next generation science teacher educators through an analysis of the construction of differences in size and status between micro and macro actors. As Callon and Latour (1981) describe it,

> There are of course macro actors and micro actors, but the difference between them is brought about by power relations and the construction of networks that will elude analysis if we presume *a priori* that macro actors are bigger than or superior to micro actors. (p. 280)

By insisting on the principle of *symmetry* – that human actors and influences should not be privileged over non-human actors such as devices or documents – ANT provides a novel lens for understanding how social forces (including knowledge) gather allies (and enemies) to become more and more (or less and less) stable over time. This process of network assemblage – *translation* in the language of ANT – can be used to explain how the growth and shrinking, and the stabilizing and destabilizing, of actor-networks shape the ways in which social organizations function. The strength of an actor-network is in its power to break apart and bind together. The actor-network that becomes durable (at least for a time) is the one that is able to stabilize power relations by pulling together the largest number of durably linked elements. As an example from a relevant educational context, this framework might help us to understand how an object of knowledge – the best learning environment for emergent bilinguals – was assembled such that the pull-out model of instruction for these students rose, gained prominence, exerted control, and then eventually faded to be replaced by the next reform – push-in instructional models of co-teaching.

In one approach to framing a method of doing ANT analysis, Callon (1986) described four phases (or *moments*) of translation that work together to assemble an actor-network. These moments can be traced to map out an actor-network that has become stabilized (at least temporarily). The first moment of translation is *problematization*, in which, by clearly defining the problem, key actors also define the interests that are to be included and excluded from the network, as they make themselves indispensable to that process. To follow through with our example of instructional models for emergent bilinguals, we might consider how a school district reforms its instructional practices over time. The identified problem might be that the district wishes to determine the instructional practices that would best allow emergent bilingual learners to simultaneously learn grade-appropriate academic content and the English language skills needed to understand and communicate that content in academic English. In this case, the interests might include grade-appropriate content knowledge and academic language and may exclude conversational English and vocational skills.

The second moment of translation is *interessement*, in which barriers are built to separate what should be included in the network from what should be excluded, while bids are made to attract certain actors to commit to join the network, thereby strengthening it. Here we might consider how the district operationally defines and identifies emergent bilinguals; how state standards represent grade-appropriate content and academic English; how as researchers, some of our projects may be viewed as relevant to the problem, while other projects may be positioned as tangential or even detrimental; and how school personnel determine who and what does and does not fit within these constructs. Thus, a university-generated teacher professional learning project might become increasingly embedded in a growing network if it is perceived to strengthen standards-based academic content and language development, or may gradually be pushed out of the network if teachers or administrators see the project goals as misaligned with the problem as they define it.

Third, translation happens through *enrollment*, in which alliances within a network are created and roles are defined and coordinated. Enrollment practices include ways in which actors may be enticed away from other networks to join the new network. In our example, this might include bringing content area teachers, ESOL teachers, curriculum materials, assessment results, and classroom spaces together in various ways to organize push-in instruction so as to better address goals for educating emergent bilinguals than the previous pull-out model had done. We note that the symmetry of power across material as well as human actors must be kept in mind within an ANT framework, such that the most powerful actors to be enrolled in an actor-network may prove to be non-human, such as assessments, classroom furniture, or student class schedules.

Finally, Callon's fourth moment of translation is *mobilization*, which demonstrates the practices through which networks that are sufficiently stabilized are made mobile, at least temporarily. Often, the elements of an actor-network that are most readily mobilized are abstracted representations of people or objects, such as graphs and charts. Thus, in our example, administrators in one school might use graphic representations of student assessment results, parent surveys, and teacher testimonials to make the case at a district meeting that key aspects of the push-in model of instruction should be adopted district-wide. ESOL teachers in other schools may then suddenly find that the times and spaces in which they interact with English learner students are fundamentally rearranged, as a small subset of actors grow in power to represent (and speak for) a silent majority. In this way, a new actor-network that has been assembled may continue to gather allies (as well as enemies) and become increasingly stable, until such a time that a different actor-network (perhaps computer-based tutorial learning for emergent bilinguals) begins to gain prominence through more effective interessement and enrollment practices. Instead of the multiple possibilities that previously existed, a stable actor-network leads to what Callon (1986) refers to as *obligatory passage points*: those key episodes through which actors must pass once a network has been stabilized.

This ANT framework of translation became a way, for us, of explaining how the work of the LISELL-B project attempted to enroll and mobilize actors into a new network for performing teacher professional learning that challenged key aspects of the currently dominant networks. We see ANT as a hopeful theory, in that even highly stabilized networks, with clearly mobilized obligatory passage points, such as current standardized testing regimes and teacher accountability systems, are assembled through network translation and can, therefore, be disrupted and reduced over time. Other actor-networks may encroach upon, and entice away, actors from the existing dominant networks. To understand how such a process actually takes place, researchers with ANT sensibilities need to spend time at the junctures where actor-networks are being translated, that is, where the irreversible becomes reversible. In the current chapter, as we consider how ANT can help us conceptualize and support the work of teacher educator professional learning, we attempt to answer the following research questions:

1. How does the LISELL-B project attempt to assemble an actor-network that can enroll and mobilize veteran and next generation science teacher educators in ways that reshape their understandings of teacher professional learning?
2. How does the stabilizing (and destabilizing) of elements of the LISELL-B actor-network point to principles that may guide the work of teacher educator professional learning in science education and beyond?

Methods

Context

LISELL-B is an ongoing NSF-funded research and development project to design and test both a pedagogical model and a professional learning framework to support the science and language learning needs of middle school students, and particularly the needs of emergent bilingual learners. For the past six years, a core group of four faculty members and an evolving cast of graduate students have worked with increasing numbers of middle school and high school science and ESOL teachers in a growing number of schools (currently ten) in the southeastern United States. We have taught and learned with and from teachers, their students, and those students' families, in the multiple contexts of the LISELL-B professional learning framework, as we developed, refined, and tested the set of language of science investigation practices that currently compose the LISELL-B pedagogical model. We have elaborated elsewhere on the development of and rationale for the practices of the pedagogical model and the contexts of the professional learning framework (Buxton et al., 2015; Buxton et al., 2016), so only briefly summarize these aspects here.

The LISELL-B pedagogical model highlights and supports key features of the language of scientific investigation – those language skills and practices that are needed to engage in, make sense of, and communicate meaningfully before, during, and after participation in scientific investigations. These practices become increasingly important as students transition from elementary to secondary school, where many students are systematically exposed to the language of science for the first time. Students are asked to contextualize and interpret their experiences of the natural world through a language that may often sound quite foreign (Halliday, 2004). Research is just beginning to address how this language of science intersects with the unique academic needs and resources of bilingual learners in science classrooms (Lee, Quinn, & Valdés, 2013). To this end, we developed six *language of science investigation practices* that constitute the pedagogical model for LISELL-B: (1) coordinating hypothesis, observation, and evidence; (2) controlling variables to design a fair test; (3) explaining cause and effect relationships; (4) using models to construct explanations and test designs; (5) using general academic vocabulary in context; and (6) owning the language of science.

The LISELL-B professional learning framework was collaboratively designed by project researchers and teacher participants to provide multiple ways to explore the language of science investigation practices that compose the LISELL-B pedagogical model, to assist the project team in modifying and adapting the practices to make them more meaningful for teachers and students, and to consider how these practices might be integrated into daily science teaching repertoires. We designed five professional learning contexts in which different stakeholders come together to do the work of bringing the LISELL-B pedagogical model to life. These contexts are: (1) an annual summer *teacher professional learning institute*; (2) an annual summer *student science academy*; (3) academic year *"grand rounds" classroom observations and online teacher logs*; (4) a series of academic year Saturday *"steps to college through science" bilingual family workshops*; and (5) a series of academic year Saturday *teacher workshops for exploring students' writing*.

Data Sources Informing This Analysis

Each component of the LISELL-B professional learning framework generates distinct data sources that are used to answer the LISELL-B research questions related to teacher engagement in the professional learning opportunities, teacher enactment of the project pedagogical practices, and student learning resulting from the pedagogical practices. Our research team's collective reflections on these various data sources are also relevant to our attempt to understand processes of translation and emergent principles of teacher educator professional learning within the LISELL-B project. The teacher professional learning institute included focus group interviews and teacher written responses from individual and group activities as well as numerous artifacts such as "LISELLized" science investigation kits. In the focus group interviews participants discussed their understandings of science inquiry practices, academic language practices, assessment practices, and what they learned from each aspect of the LISELL-B professional learning framework. The student science academy included written reflections from teachers, participant observation memos from LISELL-B staff, and student science notebooks where participants documented and reflected on the various components of the academy (teacher-directed science investigations, lab visits and STEM career information, student-directed problem posing projects, and soccer).

The grand rounds classroom observations resulted in classroom data generated by members of the research team and peer teachers from the school, as well as the collection of school documents such as school improvement plans and district mandates. The classroom observation protocol included pre-observation data, observation data, and post-observation debrief data, all centered on the multiplicity of ways that teachers enact the LISELL-B pedagogical practices. Teachers also completed online logs every two weeks to track and reflect on their enactment of project practices throughout the school year (explained in depth in Caswell, Schwartz, Minner, Buxton, & Allexsaht-Snider, this volume). Steps to college through science bilingual family workshops generated data that included written lab investigation sheets, unstructured ethnographic interviews with teachers, participant observation memos from LISELL-B staff, and parent–student interviews where family members asked each other questions about their experiences with science and with education. Finally, the teacher workshops for exploring student writing generated written teacher reflections regarding what they observed during their analysis of their students' work samples, as well as group recordings of teacher debrief conversations focused on how looking at their students' writing was informing their classroom practice. LISELL-B staff completed participant observation memos. We note that all of the next generation and veteran teacher educators working on the project were involved in various ways in each of the professional learning contexts and the data collection and analysis efforts.

For the purposes of this chapter on teacher educator professional learning, we also conducted focus group conversations and collaborated in written journaling among the research team over a period of several months. We focused on how participation and facilitation in each of the components of the professional learning framework, participation in the development of those components, and participation in the data collection, data analysis, and writing that occurred during and after these professional learning experiences worked together to support our evolving understanding of teacher educator professional learning as well as teacher professional learning. We reflect on our engagement with the multiple data sources described here as we explore how our own enrollment and circulation in the actor-network of the LISELL-B project caused "the identity of actors, the possibility of interaction and the margins of maneuver [to be] negotiated and delimited" (Callon, 1986, p. 68).

While ANT is often referred to as a theory, its early developers have argued that it is better viewed as a way to do ethnomethodology (Latour, 1999; Law, 1999). ANT analysis starts with the assumption that actors know what they are doing and that the role of the researcher is to learn from them about how and why they do it. To do this, the ANT researcher needs to spend time in the places where forces are being translated, that is, where the irreversible has the potential to become reversible, to study how networks are stabilized and mobilized (or not). Using Callon's framework of translation, we reflect on how we have been following the trajectories of various LISELL-B-related actors (both human and material) to identify the moments in these trajectories that influenced the assembly of the LISELL-B project as a collectively understood entity. To this end, we consider how local actors were connected to broader networks and how these actor-networks contributed to social and material transformations in the LISELL project over time.

Results

We present a series of three brief ANT-tales, using Callon's four moments of translation as an analytical framework, to show how participation in the LISELL-B project has influenced our thinking about teacher educator professional learning. We note that, similar to other qualitative research approaches, an ANT analysis is unique and situated, but the strategies and performances that are illuminated may have broader relevance that translates to other settings. Indeed, ANT analysis, more so than most other qualitative approaches, has a fundamental interest in how aspects of an actor-network become stable and mobile over time, therefore incorporating explicit concern with applications beyond the setting studied.

There are many different ANT-tales that could be told about our six years of work on the LISELL-B project. Here we present three that we hope will shed light on the principles of teacher educator professional learning that we have extracted from our participation in our teaching-focused research project. These tales demonstrate how the variable positioning of both human and material actors in the spaces of the LISELL-B professional learning framework was conceived and developed to support teacher professional learning for improving science teaching for emergent bilingual learners. An ANT-sensitivity implicitly helped us to design this model and explicitly helped us to understand its role in shaping our thinking about teaching, about teacher education, and about the education of teacher educators.

ANT-Tale #1 – Networks Competing for Actors: The LISELL Professional Learning Framework Challenging Teachers' and Teacher Educators' Existing Practices

The first tale explores the ongoing negotiations that often occurred between teachers and teacher educators in the LISELL-B project in terms of how the elements and resources of the pedagogical model interacted with the networks of school practices, which were often highly stabilized and mobilized. Specifically, two next generation teacher educators, both former LISELL-B research assistants now in teacher education positions at other institutions, reflect on how their engagement in the LISELL-B project changed their thinking about the role of teachers working with emergent bilingual learners. They point to processes of problematization, interessement, and enrollment, which we call out in the text, within the shifting roles that actors played in the different moments and spaces of the LISELL-B professional learning framework. They describe how their own gradual enrollment in, and circulation through, the actor-network assembled around the LISELL-B practices and professional learning spaces was key to their changing perceptions of teachers who work with Latino/a emergent bilinguals and understandings of the actions that teacher educators can take to better support teachers in this work.

Rouhollah (Iranian, male, multilingual, former secondary science and special education teacher)

An important aspect of the LISELL-B project is the dynamic interrelation of actors and the role rotations and reversals that occur within the various spaces of the professional learning framework. Before my participation in LISELL-B, I had taught courses for teacher candidates and practicing teachers. I conceived of teacher education as necessarily a top-down and linear process in which I, as the teacher educator, possessed the pedagogical knowledge that the teachers lacked, because I had read the relevant theories and they had not (*problematization as actor defines his identity in relation to problem*). The focus of teacher education was to serve the needs of the students in schools and I saw the teacher candidates simply as vehicles for achieving this end (*interessement bid to impose and stabilize roles of teachers in relation to students*). My engagement in the LISELL-B project taught me that, in a teacher professional learning project, teacher-participants might also bring valuable insights to inform the research. It was influential to see experienced scholars leading the research effort who developed the research model for science teaching practices in a scholarly way, yet didn't hesitate to learn from teachers and to co-teach with them in modeling teaching in the middle school science classrooms (*problematization as actor identities are reframed in relation to a reframed problem*). Our *Exploring Students' Science Writing* workshops for teachers were also intentionally designed to position teachers as researchers, making sense of students' writings and doing the analysis along with project researchers. I also saw the dynamic nature and value of role rotations and reversals when parents became students in science investigations during our family workshops and when high school students became teachers in family conversations about pathways to college (*interessement bid to enroll both the workshops and the teachers in an alliance*).

One of the LISELL-B project directors and I developed some lessons that we co-planned with middle school teachers in the project. We taught and sometimes co-taught those lessons with the teachers present in the classrooms. For instance, we taught about waves and their features (e.g., longitudinal/transverse, frequency, and altitude) in multiple eighth-grade science classes, using hands-on activities with springs and Slinkys, singing with low and high pitch sounds, as well as using bingo sheets designed to enhance the academic language of science (*interessement bid to weaken teachers' enrollment in other networks of school practices as lessons and materials enacted the LISELL-B pedagogical model*). Afterward, we asked teachers to reflect on and critique our lessons, rather than promoting our practices as "best practice" that should be imitated. These teachers talked about moments when we could have taught differently and questioned some of our strategies. They explained why and how they would adapt parts of what we had modeled in our teaching to their classroom needs and school requirements (*enrollment of teachers through a process of negotiation and competition with other actor-networks*).

Unlike the teacher education coursework I had taught previously, in which I had teacher candidates or practicing teachers do lesson studies in which I critiqued their teaching from the sidelines, during LISELL-B model teaching we put teachers in an equal power relationship to discuss and even criticize our practice. For me, the LISELL-B professional learning framework served to disrupt theory/practice, teacher educator/teacher, and researcher/participant dichotomies that I held either implicitly or explicitly in my past work as a teacher educator. The LISELL-B professional learning framework as an evolving network of human and material actors remains thought-provoking in ways that led to fundamental change in my perspective toward teacher education (*enrollment of teacher educator as actor-network allowed for redefinition and coordination of new role*).

Regina (Dominican, female, bilingual, former secondary science teacher)

During a previous graduate research assistantship on another project focused on science learning with emergent bilinguals, I encountered a number of teachers who were struggling to meet the needs of Latino emergent bilinguals. As a Latina, bilingual, former high school science teacher myself, I viewed these teachers, who received professional development in the project, as generally lacking an understanding of Latino culture and the educational needs of Latinos, particularly Latino emergent bilinguals. As the result of these and other experiences with educators in the southeastern U.S., I had little faith in these teachers and their abilities or commitments to meet the needs of Latino bilingual learners (*problematization as actor defines identity in relation to problem*). I initially brought these perceptions to my involvement in the LISELL-B professional learning activities.

After participating in and co-facilitating a number of LISELL-B professional learning workshops over two years, I gained a new appreciation for the science and ESOL teachers participating in the LISELL project and how their beliefs and commitments were evolving despite the constraints they faced in their schools. I was impressed by the teachers' growing sense of advocacy for Latino students. Teachers were excited to participate in the project, most were diligent in their efforts to implement aspects of the LISELL approaches in their classrooms, and many of the teachers engaged in additional project work beyond our expectations (*interessement bid as enactment of the LISELL-B pedagogical model weakened both teachers' and teacher educators' enrollment in prior networks*).

One project participant, for example, took the initiative to incorporate the LISELL-B general academic vocabulary development approach and scale it up throughout her school. This middle school language arts and special education teacher repeatedly lobbied her school administrators and teacher peers to support this endeavor (*interessement bid on the part of project teacher to build alliances to strengthen network*). Once embraced by the school faculty, the LISELL-B word cards, demonstrating academic vocabulary used bilingually and in meaningful contexts, gradually spread along the hallways over the course of the school year. The words were incorporated into the morning announcements, displayed on school monitors, incorporated into lessons during homeroom period, and even displayed in the cafeteria. These multiple representations of academic vocabulary served as actors to scaffold expectations and routinely and deliberately immerse students in academic language (*enrollment of school in this aspect of project led to interessement bid on the part of the vocabulary cards to enroll students in the network*). This teacher's efforts to further develop academic language and inquiry processes in her school was just one example of how the LISELL-B project pushed its way into the time and space of other school practices and routines.

As a result of my experiences with the LISELL-B project, I developed a more open-minded disposition toward white, middle class, Southern teachers and their potential for meeting the needs of immigrant, emergent bilingual, Latino/a students. When engaged in a supportive network, the LISELL-B teachers took on active roles in their schools and engaged in academic leadership with colleagues. The LISELL-B project gave me the opportunity to witness teachers becoming leaders and advocates for their Latino students (*network mobilizing teacher educator to represent the role of LISELL-B teachers in new ways*). Teacher leadership, as I experienced it in the LISELL-B project, helped me better understand how to nurture similar dispositions in the teacher candidates with whom I currently work and was a key experience in my professional learning as a teacher educator (*enrollment of teacher educator as the actor-network allowed for redefinition and coordination of new role in supporting teacher leadership development*).

ANT-Tale #2 – The Value of Symmetry: How the Exploring Students' Science Writing Workshops for Teachers Changed Our Thinking about Teacher Educator Professional Learning

In our second ANT-tale, we explore the ways in which the needs of emergent bilingual learners in science classes were constructed, negotiated, and stabilized (and sometimes destabilized) through assemblages of teachers, researchers, and documents such as student writing samples. Specifically, this tale features the voices of two former LISELL-B research assistants, both speakers of English as an additional language, educated outside of the United States, and now teacher educators at other universities. They reflect on how their engagement in the spaces of the LISELL-B *Exploring Students' Science Writing* workshops for teachers changed their thinking about the role of student constructed response assessments as actors that can either support teachers in better understanding the needs and assets of emergent bilingual students in science classes, or else serve to obscure those needs and assets. This tale highlights the value of symmetry as an analytic tool in our work, raising our awareness of the power of non-human actors in shaping educational contexts, contributing to processes of problematization, interessement, and enrollment in the LISELL-B project, and providing insights relevant for the mobilization and transportation of our own teacher educator professional learning.

Elif (Turkish, female, bilingual, former elementary teacher)

It was valuable for me to see how the LISELL-B professional learning framework provided a multifaceted network in which actors, including people (families, teachers, students, and researchers), documents (such as student assessments, students' written answers, and project rubrics), and spaces (such as middle school classrooms and media centers, and university classrooms and labs) all came together in discussions and decision making about supporting science learning for emergent bilinguals (*role of symmetry in enrolling next generation teacher educator in LISELL-B actor-network*).

Particularly, I have reflected on how the LISELL-B *Exploring Students' Science Writing* workshops for teachers were unique spaces in which actors interacted in ways that pushed me to think differently about how to teach my future teacher candidates and especially how to get them to think more deeply about the role of assessment in teaching and learning. Seeing myself as one actor, engaging with the student assessments, the scoring rubric, and other people similarly engaged in the process of examining student writing helped me to understand the difficulties of identifying students' emergent learning and assessing what students "know" and "understand" about science and about academic language (*problematization as actor defines her identity in relation to problem*). At the same time I began to see how a constructed response assessment in science, of the kind we developed in the LISELL-B project, was extremely useful for emergent bilinguals and their teachers (*symmetry giving salience to the assessments as actors*). I observed how teachers examining their students' constructed response assessments, talking about the rubric, and sharing their ideas with each other was more than a cognitive process; it was an emotional process as well (*interessement bid by assessments to enroll other actors in their value*).

During one assessment workshop, I remember two science teachers sitting together and working on their students' assessments. As they saw their students' ideas and personalities reflected on these papers, the teachers' embodied reactions were clearly visible. I remember them sharing creative answers out loud with slight smiles. At other times, they had very serious faces as they talked about the connections between what their students had written and the ways they taught certain topics in their science classrooms. It was the intersection of the teachers' affective and cognitive efforts in the exploring students' writing workshop and the nature of the constructed response written assessment itself that allowed us – teachers and teacher educators together – to see the creativity and understanding, as well as the difficulties of the science learning process for the emergent bilinguals in our project classrooms (*enrollment as roles of teachers and of assessments are defined and coordinated*).

This and other experiences in the LISELL-B *Exploring Students' Science Writing* workshops for teachers helped me to generate new ideas about teacher education, such as the importance of demonstrating multiple ways of assessing student work in science and other content areas, being ambitious about crafting meaningful assessments, and working with colleagues to think about how their students make sense of their teaching. While I have read and talked extensively about the goals of assessment in teacher preparation classes and seminars, the actual engagement between teacher educators, teachers, and their students' thinking and writing, as embodied by the LISELL-B assessments, was a fundamentally different experience from those prior decontextualized conversations or activities about assessment in teacher education courses. The interaction among these LISELL-B actors (human and material) provided a reflective context that influenced my thinking about how I now teach my teacher candidates (*mobilization as roles of teacher educators and assessments are defined and coordinated and then transported to and reassembled in new spaces).*

As I engage in the process of constructing my identity as a teacher educator in my home country, I particularly draw on the critical social justice stance I developed through my engagement in the LISELL-B project. For example, in my current project with Syrian immigrant children and their families and teachers, I include teacher candidates in the work (*mobilization of LISELL-B practices in the blended form of a teacher educator and researcher role*). Although it is common to invite only graduate students to such a project, I intentionally work with undergraduate students (*interessement bid to offer opportunities to teacher education students*) so that, hopefully, they will start to think about working with Turkish language learners and immigrant families in their future teaching careers. These undergraduate students are drawing on their project experiences in other classroom spaces and assignments and are expressing new insights about working with immigrant students (*enrollment of next generation teachers into a network of LISELL-B practices developed halfway around the world*).

Shakhnoza (Uzbek, female, multilingual, former elementary STEM teacher)

I remember that my very first time coming together with the LISELL-B research team and project teachers was during a Saturday *Exploring Students' Science Writing* workshop for teachers. A group of a dozen teachers came to campus early on a Saturday morning to look at their students' assessments as part of the LISELL-B professional learning framework (*interessement bid to link teachers to assessments*). After three hours of scoring the same items over and over and over again, we took a break and had lunch together. After lunch we had a debriefing session, in which each of us shared our thoughts about what we had learned from looking at the students' written work. Teachers were asked to make connections between what they saw in their students' LISELL-B assessments and the students' performance in the classroom (*problematization as actor identities are framed in relation to a problem*). They were asked to describe what surprised them about their students' particular ways of thinking or writing as manifested in the assessments. Overwhelmingly, the teachers' responses focused on how much they learned about their students' emerging knowledge from examining the constructed response assessments, and how they could clearly see which of their students' ideas were on the right track but not yet fully developed (*interessement bid as student assessments attempt to impose new roles on teachers*). The teachers were formulating specific plans for how to provide their students with the guidance they needed to master those concepts and to better use the language of science (*student assessments successfully enroll teachers in new alliance*).

At the same time, teachers were negotiating with one another about where exactly they could see clear connections between standards, benchmarks, and students' written work. While some teachers focused on ways in which the assessments provided valuable formative information about their students, other teachers highlighted the fact that unless they could show clear connections between constructed response assessments about inquiry practices and the science content standards and benchmarks for which the students and the teachers were accountable, they could not make the case for using LISELL-B materials and assessments regularly in their classrooms (*interessement bid by assessments successful with some actors and unsuccessful with others, as some actors maintained strong enrollments in previously existing standards-based, assessment driven actor-network*).

I was fascinated by this conversation, by the power embedded in standards and assessments as actors that control teachers' actions, and by teachers plotting ways to push back against these standardizing forces to better meet the needs of their students and particularly their emergent bilingual learners (*competing interessement bids from state standards and from LISELL-B assessments, as both attempt to enroll teachers*). It was in this workshop that my real interest in teacher education was ignited. I had previously presumed that if teachers knew something was valuable for their students, they would adopt it, and that this was a straightforward process. In this workshop, I observed how standards and other material actors influence teachers' practices so intimately, complicating their decision making and their practices (*problematization as next generation teacher educator redefines the problem and the actors involved*). My continued work on the LISELL-B project helped me to unpack my own assumptions as a teacher educator and provided me with another context for interpreting and sometimes challenging the theories I was reading about in my doctoral coursework and the other experiences I was having as a teaching assistant in teacher education classes (*material actors successfully enroll teacher educator in new actor-network, pushing teacher educator to reinterpret ongoing experiences and redefine her identity in relation to reframed problem*).

ANT-Tale #3 – Using the LISELL-B Professional Learning Framework to Problematize Aspects of Scientifically Based Research and Rethink Teacher Educator Professional Learning

In our third and final ANT-tale, we step back from the daily implementation of the LISELL-B project to consider how two of us, as veteran teacher educators and educational researchers who originally conceptualized the LISELL-B professional learning framework and pedagogical model, used our experiences at research conferences, in reading groups, and writing together to understand and share those aspects of the LISELL-B pedagogical model and professional learning framework that seem to stabilize and mobilize in our work on the project. Such readings, writings, and presentations may act to mobilize entities and ideas that were not previously as mobile. We deployed these material actors to make the various *problematization* and *interessement* bids to teachers, peers, funding agencies, and others that the LISELL-B pedagogical model and professional learning framework were successfully supporting teachers in reimagining their approaches to meeting the science learning needs of their emergent bilingual students. The material actors we mobilized and deployed in these settings served to represent and speak for our teacher participants as we demonstrated how LISELL-B participation weakened these teachers' enrollment in one actor-network (school standards and accountability network) and strengthened their enrollment in another network (LISELL-B). While working to enroll and mobilize allies to help us stabilize, strengthen, and grow the LISELL-B network, we also engaged in *interessement* bids to destabilize and weaken certain elements of other school-centered networks as well as the larger actor-network of scientifically based educational research that has been encroaching into thinking about the preparation of teachers. Here, we briefly discuss our efforts to problematize and weaken the notion of fidelity of implementation as an obligatory passage point for educational research.

Cory (U.S., male, bilingual, former secondary science and ESOL teacher) and Martha (U.S., female, bilingual, former elementary and ESOL teacher)

At about the same time that we were conceptualizing the initial LISELL professional learning framework, one of us heard Grover Whitehurst, then director of the Institute of Education Science (IES) at the U.S. Department of Education, give a talk at an educational research meeting in which he lamented some educational researchers' continued resistance to embrace randomized controlled trials as the gold standard for educational research. Whitehurst argued that unless educational researchers aspire to this model in their work, they would be unable to provide convincing evidence of the effectiveness of educational interventions (*interessement bid to weaken the status of competing networks*). Two points from this talk particularly stuck with us in subsequent discussions. First was Whitehurst's point that not enough educational research adequately attends to what is sometimes called the dosage issue, that is, how much of a treatment is needed and with what frequency to provide a beneficial outcome. Second was his point that we need to more clearly attend to questions of fidelity of implementation in educational interventions. That is, if teachers are not implementing a treatment with fidelity and at the proper dosage, like a patient not taking his or her medicine in the right amount and according to the proper schedule, then researchers cannot adequately assess the efficacy of the treatment (*interessement bid using a compelling but questionable metaphor*).

Simultaneously, we were engaged in a critical reading group with other faculty and graduate students in our college, where we were grappling with texts by Latour, Derrida, Deleuze, and other post-structural philosophers (*texts bid to enroll researchers in new alliance*). These texts heightened out sensitivity to the danger of false binaries, such as fidelity/infidelity of implementation or effective/ineffective interventions, as well as the potential utility of ANT for problematizing the *interessement* bid by actors (*material and human actors such as clinical trials, dosage tables, and Grover Whitehurst*) with the goal of strengthening and mobilizing a clinical treatment model as the standard for educational research.

As we ourselves circulated within and across these actor-networks we came to acknowledge that we could never hope to reduce the complex networks in which teachers, students, families, spaces, assessments, tools, and numerous other actors circulate down to a single set of rigid guidelines for correct action. Embracing this complexity allowed us to rethink fidelity of implementation and to aspire, instead, to understand and explain the multiplicities of enactment that occur in practice in science classrooms (*problematization as we redefined ourselves and our work in relation to competing networks*). We did not seek to use the LISELL-B professional learning framework to make *interessement* bids to enroll actors in a tight, inflexible network organized around achieving fidelity of implementation, which was unlikely to co-opt many actors from the highly mobilized actor-network of school standards and accountability. Instead, we bid to enroll actors in a more flexible network in which we could study how and why different teachers in different contexts adopted a multiplicity of enactments of the LISELL-B pedagogical model. In the following chapter (Caswell, Schwartz, Minner, Buxton, & Allexsaht-Snider, 2016) we further explore one aspect of our revised efforts to both study and enroll others in this framework of multiplicities of enactment using online teacher logs for tracking teachers' varied enactments of LISELL-B practices.

Discussion and Conclusions

In this chapter, we set out to answer the following two research questions: (1) How does the LISELL-B project attempt to assemble an actor-network that can enroll and mobilize veteran and next generation teacher educators in ways that reshape their understandings of teacher professional learning? (2) How does the stabilizing (and destabilizing) of elements of the LISELL-B actor-network point to principles that may guide the work of teacher educator professional learning? Implicit in these questions is a third question of how actor-network theory, and specifically Callon's four moments of translation, can help us conceptualize and support the work of teacher educator professional learning. To answer the first question, we consider a new metaphor that might serve to replace the metaphor of the clinical treatment model in how we study the effectiveness of our work as teacher educators to support and understand teacher professional learning and its influence. To answer the second question, we suggest four principles for supporting teacher educator professional learning that have emerged from our collective work on the LISELL-B project as represented in the three ANT-tales that we have shared in this chapter.

Reshaping Understandings of Teacher Professional Learning

The evolution of the LISELL-B project over the past six years provided us with insights about how being actively engaged in research on teacher learning may also facilitate new thinking about teacher educator professional learning. Among the benefits of adopting an ANT-sensitivity about how individuals, objects, and circumstances interact is that it may give us access to new and helpful metaphors for thinking about our work. While there is a lengthy history of the use of metaphors in teacher education to help teachers think differently about their professional roles and identities in schools (Thomas & Beauchamp, 2011), as well as the use of metaphors, such as the clinical treatment metaphor, to shape the goals of educational research, ANT analysis can point us to new and productive metaphors for conceptualizing both teacher professional learning and teacher educator professional learning.

The ANT-tales shared above mobilize a small number of actors to represent the broader LISELL-B actor-network in demonstrating how the process of translation helped us understand the roles that human and material actors played in shaping both teacher professional learning and teacher educator professional learning. ANT helps us to maintain a sensibility for complexity as we attempt to elucidate successful models of teacher professional learning and teacher educator professional learning without reducing these models to a fixed set of claims and rules that make knowing too simple, singular, or formulaic. This is an inherent tension as we attempt to talk about, appreciate, and practice complexity while also wishing to generate lessons and principles that can be mobilized to enroll actors in other spaces. To this end, we need metaphors that foster complexity and resist simplicity. Law (1999) proposed the fractal as a useful metaphor for ANT analysis, because a fractal contains patterns, but those patterns are often difficult to define.

We wonder if a more productive metaphor for how to study the complexities of teacher professional learning and teacher educator professional learning might be that of an oceanic or atmospheric convection current. Convection currents circulate matter (such as air or water) as well as energy (such as heat) in ways that are broadly predictable at the macro level, yet are characterized by unpredictable and chaotic motion at the micro level. Similarly, Callon's four moments of translation highlight the complex processes that constantly mix and circulate human and material actors, while helping to explain how some networks are strengthened and mobilized and how other networks weaken and fail to hold on to actors. Thus, as matter and energy circulate in a convection current, actors circulate in a network. The metaphor of teacher professional learning as a convection current provides a way to navigate the tension between the inherent complexity of social and material networks and our goal of enrolling actors in a network that can be mobilized and reproduced.

Thus, teachers who move to other school districts take certain classroom or workshop materials or assessment items developed in the LISELL-B project and implement them in these new contexts. Similarly, doctoral students who move on to become faculty at other universities continue to use certain aspects of the LISELL-B professional learning framework at their new institutions in similar ways for similar purposes. These actors (human and material) circulate like matter in convection currents and may or may not be deformed beyond recognition in the process. They may or may not make *interessement* bids to remain connected to the original network, to separate from that network, or even bid to co-opt actors from the original network. For example, in the second ANT-tale, Elif described how she continued to mobilize, circulate, and transform her experiences with LISELL-B as a next generation teacher educator.

Principles for Supporting Teacher Educator Professional Learning

Our experiences as teacher educators working collaboratively with teachers in the various spaces of the LISELL-B network, and our interpretations of that work through an ANT conceptual framework, taught us to think differently about both teacher professional learning and teacher educator professional learning. Our assumptions as teacher educators were often challenged as we attempted to better understand the complicated and contextualized nature of teacher learning as it collided with existing actor-networks in our project schools. To answer the second research question we mobilize the three ANT-tales that we have shared in this chapter to highlight four principles that we have found to support teacher educator professional learning in the context of the preparation of (science) teachers to work with emergent bilingual learners.

Principle 1 – Engage next generation teacher educators in co-design work with teachers where teacher educators make themselves vulnerable to teachers' expertise. This is a way to break down the research–practice dichotomy and work to empower teachers as change agents. Both Rouhollah's and Regina's accounts in this chapter point to how their engagement in the LISELL-B professional learning spaces pushed them to reconsider their expectations of what teachers can contribute both to scholarly inquiry and to equity-oriented practice in science teaching and learning.

Principle 2 – Give next generation teacher educators opportunities to exert leadership in providing teachers with conceptual, material, and linguistic resources that support teacher agency as an essential part of teacher professional learning. Many teacher preparation programs claim that they strive to prepare teacher leaders and teachers as change agents, often in support of a social justice agenda. There is little evidence, however, of how teacher educators are prepared to support such programmatic goals. The accounts of the LISELL-B next generation teacher educators highlight how their experiences in the project caused them to rethink what teachers are capable of as change agents. If we expect new or experienced teachers to become teacher leaders for social justice, teacher educators must provide these teachers with the resources and language to problematize their roles within networks that do not foster social justice. Regina's contrasting experiences working on LISELL-B and on a previous project show the difference between research projects that take an asset-oriented approach to the work of teachers and next generation teacher educators and those projects that take a more limiting view.

Principle 3 – Give next generation teacher educators opportunities to work with teachers who are engaging with their students' language-rich work. The LISELL-B professional learning approach of exploring students' constructed responses to challenging problems has been shown to be effective with teacher candidates and practicing teachers in other contexts (e.g., the Cognitively Guided Instruction work in mathematics teacher professional learning; Carpenter, Fennema, Franke, Levi, & Empson, 1999). There is little evidence, however, that such an approach is typical in science teacher educator professional learning, or in other content areas. While teacher educators often support teacher candidates in learning to make instructional decisions based on student work, the LISELL-B professional learning model scaffolds teacher educators' work *with* teachers in a process of analyzing student work. As Elif and Shakhnoza elaborated in the second ANT-tale, this approach served not just as teacher professional learning but also as teacher educator professional learning.

Principle 4 – Support next generation teacher educators in drawing explicit connections between epistemologies of social science research, research on teaching and learning, and the practice-oriented work of being a teacher educator. While it seems intuitive that making connections between the research on teaching and learning and the practice of teacher education would be central to the doctoral preparation programs through which next generation teacher educators pass, the limited empirical research on the preparation of teacher educators raises questions about this assumption (e.g., Goodwin et al., 2014). As alluded in the third ANT-tale, the tensions we sometimes felt on the LISELL-B project between our own philosophical commitments as teacher educators and the requirements of federally funded educational research were alleviated and supported by our collective study of broader social and philosophical research beyond the field of education. As veteran and next generation teacher educators we continue to read and write together, drawing on and using diverse social research to inform our work in teacher education.

Final Thoughts

As we reflect on our attempts to strengthen, mobilize, and circulate the actor-network of the LISELL-B project, we note that one *interessement* bid we have been making to district leaders, funders, journal editors, and others is the value of using interpretive lenses that are not common in educational research. By exploring, for example, how networks negotiate and compete for actors in attempts to represent the needs and desires of other actors, we can use educational research to better understand and meet the needs of teachers, students, families, and the schools and communities in which they act.

What ANT analysis has afforded us is an alternate framing to the metaphor of a clinical treatment model. By exploring new metaphors, such as that of convection currents, we can better understand how various actors, including the practices, people, objects, spaces, and documents that constitute the work of teacher professional learning and teacher educator professional learning, circulate and interact across multiple sites. At the same time, we fully acknowledge that not all of the multiplicities of enactment that have resulted from our approach to teacher professional learning, and that we have observed in LISELL-B teachers' classrooms, are equally effective for engaging emergent bilinguals in science learning or improving their science or language performance (Buxton et al., 2015).

We are aware that one important response to the pressures we are currently under as university-based teacher educators is that we must show school districts, on the one hand, and state policy makers on the other, that there is a unique value in teacher preparation that occurs in university settings as distinct from other potential contexts for teacher preparation. If we wish to support powerful, socially just teaching for all students, including emergent bilingual learners, then teachers need support from teacher educators who have experiences with innovative and powerful models of teacher education. Universities are the settings in which such preparation of both teachers and teacher educators is most likely to occur. Experience with the principles of teacher educator professional learning that we have outlined in this chapter is an important part of this process.

References

Berliner, D. C., & Glass, G. V. (Eds.). (2014). *50 myths and lies that threaten America's public schools: The real crisis in education*. New York, NY: Teachers College Press.

Buxton, C., Allexsaht Snider, M., Hernandez, Y., Aghasaleh, R., Cardozo-Gaibisso, L., & Kirmaci, M. (2016). A design-based model of science teacher professional learning in the LISELL-B project. In A. Oliveira & M. Weinburgh (Eds.), *Science teacher preparation in content-based second language acquisition* (pp. 179-196). New York, NY: Springer.

Buxton, C. Allexsaht-Snider, M., Kayumova, S., Aghasaleh, R., Choi, Y., & Cohen, A. (2015). Teacher agency and professional learning: Rethinking fidelity of implementation as multiplicities of enactment. *Journal of Research in Science Teaching*, 52(4), 489–502.

Callon, M. (1986). Some elements of a sociology of translation: Domestication of the scallops and the fishermen of Saint Brieuc Bay. In J. Law (Ed.), *Power, action and belief: A new sociology of knowledge?* (pp. 196–233). London, UK: Routledge.

Callon, M., & Latour, B. (1981). Unscrewing the Big Leviathan: How actors macrostructure reality and how sociologists help them to do so. In K. D. Knorr-Cetina and A. V. Cicourel (Eds.), *Advances in social theory and methodology: Toward an integration of micro- and macro-sociologies* (pp. 277–303). Boston, MA: Routledge.

Carpenter, T. P., Fennema, E., Franke, M. L., Levi, L., & Empson, S. B. (1999). *Children's mathematics: Cognitively guided instruction*. Portsmouth, NH: Heinemann.

Caswell, L., Schwartz, G., Minner, D., Allexsaht-Snider, M., & Buxton, C. (2016). Using teacher logs to study project enactment and support professional learning in the LISELL-B project. In C. Buxton & M. Allexsaht-Snider (Eds.), *Supporting K–12 English Language Learners in Science: Putting Research into Teaching Practice*. Boston, MA: Routledge.

Cochran-Smith, M. (2003). Learning and unlearning: The education of teacher educators. *Teaching and Teacher Education, 19*(1), 5–28.

Cochran-Smith, M., Feiman-Nemser, S., & McIntyre, J. (2008). *Handbook of research on teacher education: Enduring questions in changing contexts.* New York, NY: Routledge.

Cochran-Smith, M., Piazza, P., & Power, C. (2013). The politics of accountability: Assessing teacher education in the United States. *The Educational Forum, 77*(1), 6–27.

Deleuze, G., & Guattari, F. (1988). *A thousand plateaus: Capitalism and schizophrenia.* New York, NY: Bloomsbury.

Dinkelman, T., Margolis, J., & Sikkenga, K. (2006). From teacher to teacher educator: Experiences, expectations, and expatriation. *Studying Teacher Education, 2*(1), 5–23.

Fenwick, T., & Edwards, R. (2013). *Researching education through actor network theory.* Malden, MA: Wiley-Blackwell.

Fuller, E. J. (2014). Shaky methods, shaky motives: A critique of the National Council of Teacher Quality's review of teacher preparation programs. *Journal of Teacher Education, 65*(1), 63.

Goodwin, A. L., Smith, L., Souto-Manning, M., Cheruvu, R., Tan, M. Y., Reed, R., & Taveras, L. (2014). What should teacher educators know and be able to do? Perspectives from practicing teacher educators. *Journal of Teacher Education, 65*(4), 284–302.

Gort, M., Glenn, W. J., & Settlage, J. (2010). Toward culturally and linguistically responsive teacher education: The impact of a faculty learning community on two teacher educators. In T. Lucas (Ed.), *Preparing teachers for linguistically diverse classrooms: A resource for teacher educators* (pp. 178–194). New York, NY: Routledge/Taylor & Francis.

Halliday, M. A. K. (2004). *The language of science.* London, UK: Continuum.

Knight, S. L., Lloyd, G. M., Arbaugh, F., Gamson, D., McDonald, S. P., & Nolan, J. (2014). Professional development and practices of teacher educators. *Journal of Teacher Education, 65*(4), 268–270.

Koedell, C., & Betts, J. (2011). Does student sorting invalidate value-added models of teacher effectiveness? An extended analysis of the Rothstein critique. *Education Finance and Policy, 6*(1), 18–42.

Labaree, D. F. (2008). An uneasy relationship: The history of teacher education in the university. In M. Cochran-Smith, S. Feiman-Nemser, & J. McIntyre (Eds.), *Handbook of research on teacher education* (3rd ed., pp. 290–306). New York: Routledge.

Latour, B. (1999). On recalling ANT. In J. Law and J. Hassard (Eds.), *Actor network theory and after* (pp. 15–25). Oxford, UK: Blackwell.

Latour, B., & Woolgar, S. (1979). *Laboratory life: The social construction of scientific facts.* Beverly Hills and London: Sage.

Law, J. (1999). After ANT: topology, naming and complexity. In J. Law and J. Hassard (Eds.), *Actor network theory and after* (pp. 1–14). Oxford, UK: Blackwell.

Law, J. (2004). *After method: Mess in social science research.* New York, NY: Routledge.

Lee, O., Quinn, H., & Valdés, G. (2013). Science and language for English language learners in relation to Next Generation Science Standards and with implications for Common Core State Standards for English language arts and mathematics. *Educational Researcher, 42*(4), 223–233.

National Commission on Excellence in Education (1983). *A nation at risk: The imperative for educational reform.* Washington, DC: U.S. Department of Education.

Thomas, L., & Beauchamp, C. (2011). Understanding new teachers' professional identities through metaphor. *Teacher and Teacher Education, 27*(4), 762–769.

Wenger, E. (1999). *Communities of practice: Learning, meaning, and identity.* Cambridge, UK: Cambridge University Press.

6
USING TEACHER LOGS TO STUDY PROJECT ENACTMENT AND SUPPORT PROFESSIONAL LEARNING IN THE LISELL-B PROJECT

Linda Caswell, Gabe Schwartz, Daphne Minner, Martha Allexsaht-Snider, & Cory A. Buxton

Introduction

Intervention implementation is a key element to understanding program effectiveness and recently has become more of a focus in education research. Most often, educational researchers are interested in documenting how closely a practitioner delivers an intervention's components compared to the developers' intention. Definitions of implementation fidelity are often based on work in prevention programming (e.g., substance-use prevention programs), where the concept of implementation fidelity originated (Bond, Evans, Salyers, Williams, & Kim, 2000). These definitions are diverse including, among others: (1) "the proportion of program components that were implemented" (Mowbray, Holter, Teague, & Bybee, 2003, p. 316), (2) "confirmation that the manipulation of the independent variable occurred as planned" (Moncher & Prinz, 1991, p. 247), (3) "the adherence of actual treatment delivery to the protocol originally developed" (Orwin, 2000, p. 310), and (4) "the degree to which specified procedures are implemented as planned" (Dane & Schneider, 1998, p. 23).

Syntheses of prevention program implementation studies have also identified other elements of program integrity or fidelity beyond adherence to program components (Dane & Schneider, 1998; Gearing, El-Bassel, Ghesquiere, Baldwin, Gillies, & Ngeow, 2011; Nelson, Cordray, Hulleman, Darrow, & Sommer, 2012; O'Donnell, 2008). For example, Dane and Schneider (1998, p. 45) identify: (1) exposure ("the number of sessions implemented, or the length of each session, or the frequency with which program techniques were implemented"), (2) quality of delivery ("implementer enthusiasm, leader preparedness, global estimates of session effectiveness, and leader attitudes toward [the] program"), (3) participant responsiveness ("levels of participation and enthusiasm"), and (4) program differentiation ("a manipulation check that is performed to safeguard against the diffusion of treatments, i.e., the subjects in each experimental condition received only planned interventions").

Even in reviews of common elements included in implementation measurements, some disagreement remains among meta-analysts as to the essential components of fidelity to implementation models. In an effort to synthesize how fidelity criteria are developed, measured, and validated in prevention research studies, for example, Mowbray et al. (2003) reviewed the literature encompassing services in mental health, health, substance abuse treatment, and social services. The fidelity criteria commonly specified in the literature they reviewed included "specification of the length, intensity, and duration of the services (or dosage); content, procedures, and activities over the length of the service; roles, qualification, and activities of staff; and inclusion/exclusion characteristics for the target service population" (p. 318). In a review of 24 meta-analyses and review articles from the past 30 years on fidelity in prevention programs, by contrast, Gearing et al. (2011) were able to outline four required components of intervention research – design, training, monitoring of intervention delivery, and intervention receipt by participants – as well as three additional factors influencing program implementation: professional development and delivery staff characteristics, intervention target being reached, and participant responsiveness.

As this summary demonstrates, there are various ways to conceptualize fidelity of implementation, but there is an underlying basic assumption of "correctness," i.e., adhering to the training materials as developed. In other words, the more closely the program deliverer follows the program manual, the better the outcomes for the program participants. In fact, research has shown that higher fidelity of implementation is generally associated with greater treatment effects within health and human services programs (Dane & Schneider, 1998; Durlak & DuPre, 2008).

Although parallels exist between prevention programming and educational interventions, there are distinct differences that require education professionals to consider other ways of defining fidelity that acknowledge the complexity and variability of teaching and learning contexts. Among these differences is the situation that the recipients of the intervention – in this case, the teachers – become facilitators of the intervention for others (their students). In their role as facilitators, teachers often make adaptations to materials and teaching strategies to accommodate the unique strengths and needs of their students. As the co-authors of this chapter have stated elsewhere, this variability in implementation need not be viewed as a shortcoming, but rather an integral part of how "teaching practices are culturally and historically situated within social and political structures" (Buxton, Allexsaht-Snider, Kayumova, Aghasaleh, Choi, & Cohen, 2015, p. 491). Program implementation in an educational context might therefore be better understood as a product of the complex interactions and resulting decisions of program developers, school administrators, teachers, students, and families engaged in the evolving educational intervention. While not all teacher-driven adaptations to an intervention are beneficial (Fogleman, McNeill, & Krajcik, 2011), we argue that a need exists in education for an alternative to the fidelity of implementation model so prominent in prevention research.

In the LISELL-B project – a professional learning model co-constructed with classroom educators – teachers are viewed as critical partners who contribute important pieces of the knowledge necessary for effective implementation and are encouraged to make their own decisions about their engagement in professional learning opportunities and their enactment of the pedagogical model. From the start, the developers (including the chapter authors) encouraged teachers to participate in professional learning as they were able, and in ways that best met their perceived needs, and to make adaptations to the LISELL-B practices based on their knowledge of their students, their school community, and school expectations. Rather than viewing fidelity of implementation in terms of program adherence, the project team conceptualized it as the interplay of teachers' engagement with, and their enactment of, the LISELL-B practices. This conceptualization is better aligned with the knowledge-construction and utilization processes underlying the LISELL-B intervention, based on Practice Theory (Connell, 1987). Practice Theory views teachers (in this case) as active, knowledgeable constructors of their practice who make decisions in the classroom influenced by the sociopolitical context within which they work. They are agents, choosing which of the professional learning experiences of the LISELL-B project they will participate in, as well as how to implement them in the classroom. From this perspective, there is no pre-existing assumption of correctness in the intervention model, but rather an empirical question about what is gained and what is lost through various adaptations of the model in different teaching and learning contexts.

To answer this question, it becomes vital to document teachers' engagement and enactment with a given educational intervention, enabling developers and teachers to co-examine the variation in engagement and enactment across their classrooms. The insights gained from this co-examination can then be used to understand the professional learning trajectories of participating teachers, to modify opportunities for professional learning in subsequent years of participation, and to adapt the pedagogical model as needed. For their part, the teachers engaged in this co-examination can use insights gained to modify their own engagement choices and enactment practices.

In the original LISELL project (a precursor to the LISELL-B project discussed in this chapter), teachers' enactment of project practices in their classrooms was documented using notes from classroom observations and both structured and semi-structured teacher feedback collected during LISELL professional learning activities. This approach was insufficient, however, for tracking teachers' enactment in an ongoing and systematic way. Thus, in the project's next iteration ("LISELL-B"), the goal was to identify an instrument that could more systematically capture teachers' "multiplicities of enactment" of the project practices over time and be used by a larger number of teachers as the project scaled up.

In this chapter, we provide information on the development and implementation of the LISELL-B teacher log that was created to meet this challenge. Hopefully this will encourage researchers to consider integrating this promising data source into their own projects, as well as encourage teachers to more systematically study their enactment of classroom practices that they believe are important for their students. We also discuss the multiple ways the information from the logs was used in the LISELL-B project – to test the effect of the professional learning activities on teachers' practice and student learning (for all students, and especially for English learners), to revise and refine the model's components and support mechanisms for teachers, and to assist teachers in reflecting on their own practice throughout the year and in a final summative way compared to their peers. We conclude by discussing the implications of using a teacher practice log for measuring implementation in education intervention research, particularly in terms of scale-up.

Development of the Log

Identifying the Appropriate Instrument

The accepted gold standard for data collection on teaching practices is using trained observers to collect structured observational data, often videotaping for detailed coding later on (Rowan & Correnti, 2009). This approach is costly and difficult to implement in large-scale, multisite projects with numerous teachers. While it has strong internal validity, the generalizability of observation across the entire school year is questionable, particularly in middle and high school grades where curricular topics and skills may vary widely across classrooms. Annual surveys administered to teachers about their practices is the second most common approach, which is less costly but has other drawbacks such as limits of recall. The accuracy of recall over a long period of time, for example, is low, leading to concerns about the validity of this method to accurately capture practice (Mullens & Gayler, 1999).

A third approach that has gained appeal is the use of teacher logs (Porter, 1989, 2004), especially after the large-scale Study of Instructional Improvement demonstrated clear benefits of this approach (Rowan & Correnti, 2009). Chief among these benefits, particularly within a Practice Theory framework, is the ability to capture complexity and variability across a school year via near-real-time recording. Another benefit is the ease with which teacher logs can be implemented for large numbers of teachers. Measuring instruction using teacher logs has not been used widely in science education to date, but researchers developing new science curriculum materials are beginning to use this approach to determine how teachers are using materials in their classrooms – whether or not modifications are being made, lessons are skipped, or were taught as designed (Harris, Penuel, D'Angelo, Haydel DeBarger, Gallagher, Kennedy, Haugen Cheng, & Krajcik, 2015).

Undergirding this momentum in the popularity of teacher logs is research demonstrating the benefits outlined above and others (Lesaux, Kieffer, Faller, & Kelley, 2010; Rowan, Camburn, & Corenti, 2004; Rowan & Correnti, 2009; Rowan, Harrison, & Hayes, 2004). Studies have shown that log data can overcome many problems of memory distortion and inaccuracies that arise when respondents are asked to retrospectively summarize behaviors they engaged in over an extended period compared to annual surveys; that they are cost-effective measures of instruction compared to in-person observations; and that they can be used to measure instruction in a variety of subjects (mathematics, language arts, literacy, and reading). With these benefits in mind, logs made the most sense for our purposes, theoretically, technically, and economically.

Developing the Instrument

The teacher log was meant to systematically capture enactment of LISELL-B practices in approximately 50 science classrooms for a period of 3 years. The development of the log was iterative – as we piloted it multiple times – and collaborative, as we incorporated feedback from pilot teachers into subsequent versions to increase usability, maximize response rates, and ensure that both teachers and program developers felt that the log was adequately capturing classroom practice.

As shown in the screenshot of the log in Appendix A, the log has five parts (A–E), asking teachers to reflect on the activities in which their students participated over the course of the preceding week in all of their science classes. Teachers assess each of the following:

1 If their students had the opportunity to participate in any of 14 science inquiry or academic language activities that make up the six language of science investigation practices of the LISELL-B pedagogical model (Part A) – collectively referred to as LISELL-B practices;
2. If students used any resources (such as graphic organizers, vocabulary instructional materials, or lab forms) when participating in any of these activities (Part B);
3. If their students used any technologies (such as computer animation, computer simulation, or digital physical lab equipment) when participating in any of these activities (Part C);
4. If students had the chance to talk about, read about, or write about the content they were engaging with during any of these activities (Part D); and
5. If the activities that students had opportunities to participate in addressed any of the Georgia Science Standards relevant to their subject matter area or to science education more broadly (Part E).

In Part A, each overarching LISELL-B practice is comprised of two or three components, and teachers are asked to select any of these 14 components in which their students participated during the previous week.

Parts B (Resources) and C (Technology) ask teachers to indicate the types of resources and technologies that students used while participating in the science inquiry and academic language practices listed in Part A. The intent of these questions is to document the range of materials that teachers incorporate into their lessons, as well as to identify if certain resources and technologies are particularly supportive of particular LISELL-B practices.

Part D measures an integral part of the LISELL-B intervention, since it asks teachers whether students had the opportunity to talk about, read about, or write about the science content being covered when students participated in the LISELL-B practices identified in Part A. Making sure students, especially English Learners (ELs), have ample opportunity to engage in each of these communication forms is a critical element of the LISELL-B intervention because it provides ELs a way to triangulate understanding across spoken and written text and solidify communication skills and science understanding through practice.

Part E asks teachers to report which Georgia State Science Standards (some relevant to all middle and high school science classes, some specific to a particular science subject) they addressed in the preceding week of instruction. These data were meant to capture the standards that teachers were covering when students participated in specific LISELL-B practices and components (e.g., Component X is often used when addressing Standard Y).

We began developing the log in the fall of 2013 by reviewing LISELL-B project documentation and examining other models of classroom practice logs. Although the key practices of LISELL-B were clear, constructing the log in such a way that teachers could quickly and easily report on them required more extensive thinking. This led us to divide the six language of science investigation practices into 14 components. We also wanted to capture not just which practices were implemented, but how, motivating us to think about which resources and technologies (LISELL-B and otherwise) teachers might be using in concert with the LISELL-B practices. Based on this work, we produced log prototypes and shared these with the LISELL-B project developers, who provided multiple rounds of feedback.

Once the content and structure of the log were agreed upon, we began researching options for an online delivery system that would best facilitate the collection of teacher log data over time. The log needed to be regularly and easily accessible to teachers; launched repeatedly throughout the year; and capture not just the six LISELL-B practices, but also supplemental information that could provide information to developers and teachers for reflection. We decided to program the log using Caspio, an online database platform (Caspio, 2015). Similar to Microsoft Access, Caspio allows developers to create interactive and intuitive forms for front-end users built on a series of relational databases.

Working in Caspio enabled us to quickly and easily download data during the period in which logs were administered (for preliminary analyses or for tracking completion) as well as after data collection was complete. For projects with few tables and forms, Caspio is low cost and can be set up so that logs open and close on a predetermined schedule, lowering the cost and time necessary for data collection.

Piloting the Log

We piloted the log twice with the dual goals of testing the log's overall usability and intuitiveness and getting a sense of whether we might be missing any important program components or ways teachers were enacting certain practices or using classroom resources. If teachers misunderstood the way a given item was worded – or if we misunderstood how teachers thought about a certain classroom practice – this was an opportunity to clarify. To do this, we piloted the log in the spring of 2014, collecting data from 11 Georgia science teachers (5 LISELL-B, 6 comparison). In total, pilot teachers entered 24 classroom logs over the course of 8 weeks, after which teachers debriefed their log experiences. Based on these conversations, we made a number of revisions (as outlined below) then piloted the revised version during the 2014 LISELL-B Summer Academy, in which teachers implemented LISELL-B practices with students during a 2-week period.

We identified a range of issues that hampered data collection during piloting. In some cases, we had not anticipated the breadth of the burden placed on teachers by certain log components. In others, we failed to understand the flow of teachers' work days, and so were opening and closing the log at inconvenient times.

For example, teachers were initially asked to report on their use of different resources, technologies, and student engagement strategies (talking about the practice components, reading about them, writing about them), as well as the Georgia State Science Standards they addressed, for *each* of the 14 LISELL-B components. Perhaps unsurprisingly, this proved too burdensome for teachers, who often simply skipped these sections. We therefore revised the log such that it required teachers to complete only one set of follow-up questions covering *all* of the LISELL-B components in the aggregate. Although this meant less nuanced data for analysis, it was essential to make this change for usability.

The results of this revision were encouraging. Whereas spring pilot log response rates for sections B–E ranged from 20 percent to 30 percent (of those logs that had been completed), response rates for those same sections during the summer ranged from 77 percent to 100 percent (again, of those logs that were completed). In fact, every section except for the subject-specific Georgia State Standards was above 90 percent. A 77 percent response rate for the subject-specific standards was less than ideal, but it represented a nearly fourfold increase from the spring.

As another example, we used the two pilots to gather information on the most appropriate frequency for the log. During the spring pilot, teachers were asked to complete a log for each of 3 weeks during a 5-week period – teachers chose the specific weeks to report. During the summer pilot session, we asked teachers to complete one log a week for 2 weeks in a row, giving them some flexibility if they were constrained on time. Unfortunately, neither of these models seemed to achieve the response or completion rates we felt were necessary to understand teachers' classroom practices. Our efforts to lower the log's burden notwithstanding, the overall completion rate for the summer pilot was only 41 percent (of all logs). This may have been due to accommodations made for teachers during the summer pilot: teachers were allowed to skip their log for the second week of the Summer Academy if they were behind on their project work. Accordingly, we felt that response rates would likely increase during the school year, when teachers would be receiving a small monetary compensation for filling out the log. But it was also self-evident that if teachers felt too busy to complete back-to-back logs during the summer, this was likely to be true during the school year as well.

Based on the goal of obtaining as many logs from teachers as possible over the school year, balanced against what pilot teachers reported was feasible, LISELL-B and comparison teachers were asked to complete one log, covering one week's worth of classes, every other week of the school year. If all logs were filled out, this would amount to a total of 18 logs, which would leave some flexibility for missing data while still ensuring we collected a sufficient number of logs to provide a reasonable picture of teachers' classroom practice. It has been estimated that collecting 10 to 20 logs evenly spaced across an intervention period such as a school year is necessary to reliably discriminate among individual instructional behaviors (Camburn & Barnes, 2004; Correnti & Rowan, 2007; Correnti, 2007).

As the structure of the log changed, we also had to refine the scope of the classes on which teachers were asked to report. Teachers in our first pilot were asked to report on the single class period they were teaching that had the highest number of ELs, as these were the classes LISELL-B practices were especially designed to support. However, teachers reported that this approach was difficult to implement; it was not necessarily clear on day one of classroom instruction which students were and were not ELs, ELs often got moved between classes repeatedly during the year, and class schedules were typically still fluid at the time we were planning to begin collecting data in the fall. Teachers were therefore asked to report on all instruction that took place during the designated week in *any* of their science classes (e.g., "Across all of your high school Biology classes …"). *Ex post facto* approaches could then be applied to explore differences between teachers based on the number of ELs they taught, for example, acquiring their students' English proficiency test scores and assessing whether the percentage of ELs across teachers' classes correlated with the enactment of LISELL-B practices.

Implementation of the Log

In this section, we discuss the implementation of the log during the 2014–2015 school year, including processes for enrolling teachers and providing support to bolster completion rates. As was true of log development, our implementation strategy was iterative and collaborative, beginning with simple reminders and growing into a network of information-sharing between evaluators, participating teachers, and developers to ensure that teachers had the support they needed to complete as many logs as possible.

Participating LISELL-B and comparison teachers were invited in the fall of 2014 via e-mail to participate in the log over the coming school year. Based on input from pilot teachers, we sent three e-mail reminders each log week: (1) on Wednesday of the log week to remind teachers that the log was open; (2) on Friday of the log week to remind them that they should complete the log; and (3) on Tuesday evening of the week following the log week, to remind them that the log would close the following day, on Wednesday.

In the winter of 2015, we reviewed response rates for the log and found they were lower than hoped. Aiming to raise them for the remainder of the year, we decided to employ LISELL-B liaisons assigned to each school to contact teachers and personally remind them to fill out the log. These liaisons – members of the program development team and graduate student researchers who had pre-existing relationships with LISELL-B and comparison teachers – were already in regular contact with teachers, so this additional responsibility was readily integrated into liaisons' schedules. We began sending liaisons the status of teacher log completion, and liaisons followed up with teachers just as spring semester began.

While the vast majority of teachers (28 of 36, or 78 percent) had the opportunity to fill out 18 logs, it is important to note that three (8 percent) only had the opportunity to fill out 17 logs; another three, 11 logs (8 percent); and a final two, who started in the spring semester, 9 logs (6 percent). Despite these differences, teachers filled out a mean of 13 and a median of 14.5 logs overall (with a low of 2 logs – from a teacher who had the opportunity to fill out only 9 – and a high of 18 logs). LISELL-B teachers filled out a mean of 12 logs (median = 13), while comparison teachers filled out a mean of 14 logs (median = 16) – still within the range of reliable discrimination between teachers (Correnti, 2007). Final log completion rates are presented in Table 6.1.

Interestingly, though some teachers anecdotally informed us that they had valued outreach from liaisons, this additional layer of teacher support did not seem to raise response rates overall, dropping slightly from a mean of 81 percent to 75 percent and a median of 90 percent to 88 percent before and after outreach began, respectively. Part of this seeming lack of impact may have been the product of timing: liaisons began their outreach just after the start of the spring semester, much of which was dedicated to preparing for and administering standardized

TABLE 6.1 Log completion rates by group

LISELL-B Status	N (# of teachers)	Logs Completed					Mean Response Rate
		Total	Mean	Median	Min.	Max.	
LISELL-B	23	285	12	13	2	18	71%
Comparison	13	186	14	16	4	18	86%
Total	36	471	13	14.5	2	18	76%

assessments. Response rates in the spring may therefore have fallen even more in the absence of liaisons.

To investigate this further, following the first year of data collection, we asked our five school liaisons to share details of their outreach. These included the frequency with which they reached out to teachers, the mode of communication they most often used, and whether teachers had, in their experience, expressed any particular preferences in terms of receiving log completion support. Nearly all liaisons had communicated with teachers once a week, as was the intention, but it became clear that the quality of this communication varied. While some liaisons sought out the communication preferences of their teachers – e.g., texting certain teachers who would not respond on any other medium, going to meet with them in person at their schools – others largely repeated outreach already done by sending mass e-mails. The latter tactic appeared less helpful; one school liaison reported that some of his teachers felt the e-mails got lost in the clutter. Moving into the second year of data collection, then, the importance of reaching out to teachers either in person or individually over the phone became part of the developer's liaison training.

Conversely, responses from the school liaisons made it clear that they needed more information to do their outreach strategically. For example, liaisons did not have a solid basis for understanding whether their outreach actually worked: they knew which teachers had not filled out their logs by Tuesday morning, but did not know which teachers ultimately completed those logs following liaison outreach. Moreover, liaisons were not given enough information to tell whether certain sections of the log were being systematically neglected, and so could not tailor their outreach accordingly. For the second year of data collection, we therefore implemented a system of sending liaisons each week's final log results. We also began sharing aggregate log response patterns with liaisons at the end of each semester. We note that this direct person-to-person follow-up by liaisons potentially adds an additional cost to the collection of log data that should be considered, especially in the context of scale-up initiatives. In the case of the LISELL-B project, however, the school liaisons were already expected to be in communication with their teachers on a regular basis regarding other aspects of the project, so discussing log completion was an additional task but not necessarily an additional cost.

How the Log Data Informed the LISELL-B Project

As described above, the primary goal of collecting teacher practice data via the log was to document teachers' enactment of the LISELL-B practices in an efficient manner across a large number of teachers. Compared to the observation data that the developers collected only once a year in most cases, the log data had clear advantages over observation data in meeting this goal. First, while observation data culled from observation notes were useful for providing a high resolution snapshot of teachers' enactment of the LISELL-B practices, they were also very complex and contextualized to a particular classroom and a particular lesson. The developers and teachers found that the log data, especially when summarized over time and aggregated across teachers by grade-level band (middle and high school) and by content area, were more robust and useful for discerning patterns of enactment compared to the observation data. In addition, data from the log turned out to be particularly useful for tracking teachers' practices over the course of the year as the intervention began to scale up. The log data provided an efficient and easily understandable summary of what teachers believed they were and were not enacting, which could then lead to productive conversations about the reasons why teachers were making these choices, about their interpretations of the project practices, and about possible revisions to the intervention. The log was also much more easily implemented at scale and provided data over a more extensive period of time for more teachers.

The data from the log, therefore, could be used as a powerful tool for addressing multiple project goals, including: (1) ongoing co-construction of the intervention by developers and teachers; (2) as a means of enabling teachers to reflect on their choices around enactment of the LISELL-B practices; and (3) to measure effectiveness of the intervention regarding teacher enactment of LISELL-B practices, which would be beneficial as the intervention went to scale. We discuss each of these uses of the log data below.

Revising and Refining the Intervention

The log data were used by developers, in collaboration with teachers, to revise and refine the intervention by (1) identifying and clarifying differences in understanding of the LISELL-B practices between teachers and developers and (2) identifying practices that teachers enacted in classrooms differently than how developers had imagined because of the teaching context.

As an example of the first instance, the developers used the log data to identify a difference in understanding of what was meant by providing opportunities for students to talk, read, and write about the LISELL-B science practices (log Part D). After the first semester of the log implementation, we conducted analyses to determine if there was variability in teachers' responses to Part D, which was theoretically designed to capture variability in the degree to which teachers were offering students talk-read-write language integrating opportunities. The results, however, indicated that there was very little variability in teachers' responses, with almost all teachers reporting that they provided students with opportunities to do all three. The developers suspected that there was a difference in understanding in what they meant by talking, reading, and writing about the practices and what teachers understood, likely because of the way the question was asked (i.e., too vaguely). The developers had a more nuanced and explicit vision for how students would be using the LISELL-B practices and hoped to use the log to measure the frequency with which teachers provided these opportunities. In the next professional learning session, developers discussed their intentions for implementation of language use with teachers and found that teachers did indeed have a different (and broader) understanding of what it looked like for students to be engaged in talking, reading, and writing about the project practices. In future professional learning sessions, the developers spent more time coming to a shared understanding of the kinds of language use that the project advocated and wished to track. Furthermore, when the developers were co-designing materials to use in the science investigation kits with teachers, they made sure that these activities were more robustly modeled and scaffolded. The log data, therefore, allowed the developers to identify a difference in understanding and to refine the intervention accordingly. The log Part D questions were also modified based on this realization. See Appendix B for the revised version of these questions.

The developers also used the log data to identify practices that teachers were choosing not to enact, such as Using Variables, which was the least used by all teachers. In discussing with teachers the patterns of enactment around this practice, the developers came to understand that Using Variables was much more challenging to teach, especially for middle grades science teachers. Many teachers felt that the use of variables in scientific research was difficult to understand even for themselves, and thus, they were less confident about developing that understanding with students. The log data enabled the developers to see this pattern, to engage teachers in a conversation about it, and to place more emphasis in their professional learning sessions on how Using Variables could be effectively incorporated into teachers' existing curriculum.

The above two examples highlight how examining the log data allowed developers and teachers to engage in an interactive process of problem-solving. The data spurred the developers to talk with teachers about potential differences in understanding, to figure out how the LISELL-B practices fit in (or did not) with teachers' curriculum, to target professional learning activities, and to revise and refine the intervention based on what teachers were telling them about how they were (or were not) enacting the practices. While classroom observations may have hinted at these same issues, the log data provided a more efficient and more effective way to gain and address these insights. Further, because teachers were reporting these data themselves, rather than the developers telling the teachers what they saw during observations, teachers felt more ownership over the patterns reflected in their data, which in turn facilitated teachers' reflections on their practices, as discussed in the next section.

Teachers Reflecting on Their Own Practice

In addition to its usefulness for the development of the LISELL-B intervention, many teachers told the developers that they appreciated the log as a chance to think critically about their instruction. To get at what, exactly, teachers valued about the log, as well as how they may have used the log data to inform their teaching, the developers conducted a focus group with nearly all LISELL-B teachers during the 2015 Summer Teacher Institute (STI). Having gleaned broad conclusions about teachers' relationship to the log from the focus groups, we followed up with three LISELL-B teachers in semi-structured, in-depth interviews in the fall of 2015. For purposes of anonymity, we will refer to these teachers as Laverne, Carol, and Jayla. At the time of our interviews, Laverne had recently retired from teaching, while Carol and Jayla were still in the classroom.

In our interviews, we focused on two time points at which the log might have proven useful to teachers. The first was when teachers filled out the log every other week during the 2014–15 academic year, and the second was when teachers examined patterns of their responses across the school year during the 2015 STI. During the institute, teachers were given graphs showing the rates at which each of them had used each LISELL-B practice during the fall, winter, and spring of the 2014–2015 school year. Teachers were then able to compare patterns of their own practice across the year with the average patterns of their peers teaching the same subject (e.g., seventh-grade life science), as well as average patterns across all LISELL-B teachers. See Appendix C for sample aggregate teacher response patterns for middle school physical science. This was followed by a facilitated discussion in which teachers explored reasons for the patterns they saw.

From our interviews, we learned that filling out the log biweekly, as well as viewing the pattern of their responses across the school year, helped teachers identify gaps in their pedagogy and find ways to implement LISELL-B practices more regularly and effectively. For some of these teachers, the log became an integral part of the intervention, serving as a link between LISELL-B professional learning experiences, observations by the LISELL-B research team and other LISELL-B teachers, and their day-to-day lesson planning.

Formative reflection (while filling out the log). Focus group teachers expressed that filling out the log on a biweekly basis served as a useful reminder of what the LISELL-B practices were, which of these they were using regularly, and which they had not yet found an opportunity to implement. Laverne described this as a process of "self-correction," a sentiment that Carol and Jayla echoed. All three explained that they used their time filling out each log to think through the next few lessons or units, trying to come up with an ideal way to bring in LISELL-B practices they had not used as much.

Case 1 – Laverne

This opportunity was especially important to Laverne, who claimed that the rest of the professional development and teaching resources she received from the state focused not on "process" skills, but rather on the content that teachers were expected to cover. According to Laverne, how students were learning, or whether they were contextualizing that learning as part of a broader training in scientific thinking and analysis, was less valued by her administration. Through filling out her logs every other week, Laverne kept herself accountable for teaching material she felt was vital but not required of her to teach.

Laverne was required, for example, to teach her students about biomes. But nowhere in her curriculum was she expected to teach students to identify independent and dependent variables, a lack that dawned on her via her log completion. To address this gap, Laverne used climatological graphs depicting seasonal fluctuations in temperature and precipitation in different biomes to help her students understand the relationship between these two types of variables (i.e., how seasonal changes in the Earth's orbit around the sun affect temperature). This helped students internalize the meaning of independent and dependent variables, and it also helped them better understand how biomes were defined and how to differentiate between different types of biomes. For Laverne, this process – starting by identifying a problem and ending with addressing that problem – was facilitated both by the log and by in-person observations and workshops that are part of the LISELL-B intervention. The log helped her recognize LISELL-B practices she had not been implementing, at which point the observations and workshops provided the push she needed to turn these realizations into lesson plans.

Case 2 – Carol

For Carol, the log helped her not just remember to incorporate certain LISELL-B practices into her instruction, but, at times, also helped her understand which practices might best enable her to reach her students. The previous spring, for example, Carol knew that she had not given as much attention to teaching students to devise scientific experiments through which one could test the influence of an independent variable on a dependent variable. When it came time to studying enzymes, Carol hoped that this material would be a perfect opportunity for students to test the effect of temperature on the rate of a reaction. Carol set up the lab as relatively open-ended: students were given lab equipment and a question, but did not have a specific lab protocol. She hoped this would help them practice the skill of experimental design, but she was frustrated by the result. Carol felt that her students had just played around, and no one seemed very close after the first day to developing any conclusions from the evidence they were supposed to be gathering.

Looking over her students' notes on what they had learned that day, however, she saw they had been experimenting productively, just not in the way she had expected. Many had figured out how each of the materials (e.g., ice, a Bunsen burner, a number of different enzymes) they were given was supposed to be used, and many had gathered useful observations, but they did not grasp how to apply a systematic test in which they changed one variable and observed how it affected another.

Thinking back on her logs, Carol realized that the reason her students were struggling was that she had not devoted much time to teaching her students about independent and dependent variables. Students had thus lacked a scaffold from which to build outwards and develop experiments of their own. Carol therefore had her students write down the steps that they might take next time they did that experiment, this time explicitly focusing on independent and dependent variables as a foundation upon which they could develop an experimental procedure.

Case 3 – Jayla

Jayla's self-correction, in contrast, was less immediately reactive. As she filled out her logs, she mentally took note of trends, making sure that she was planning ahead so that students would get the opportunity to learn using each of the LISELL-B practices throughout the year. For her, the log served less as a weekly reminder than as a chance to add data to her internal graphs and a yardstick against which she could measure how quickly she found a way to incorporate LISELL-B practices she had not yet had the opportunity to use.

This approach resulted in innovative lesson plans integrating LISELL-B practices into her curriculum. The week Jayla spoke to us, for example, her students were running a river model: looking at how water eroded the surface of the Earth using sand on a stream table. To make this a lesson not only about earth science but also an opportunity to learn about independent and dependent variables, Jayla's students measured how the *rate* of erosion changed as the experiment progressed. The amount of water they poured, for example, was identified as an independent variable, with the rate of erosion the dependent variable.

Thus, while each teacher made use of the process of completing the logs in somewhat different ways, each saw personal pedagogical value in the formative aspects of the log completion task.

Summative reflection (examining log patterns). Focus group teachers in the STI, as well as our three in-depth interviewees, reported that the process of looking over their collective log response patterns was valuable for a number of reasons (see Appendix C for an example of aggregated middle school physical science teachers' log response patterns). First, as Carol noted, before examining their log data, differences in patterns of instruction across the year were not always clear to teachers, many of whom did not remember differences across the year in their enactment of LISELL-B practices. As the work of Rowan and others has demonstrated (Rowan, Camburn, & Correnti, 2004; Rowan, Harrison, & Hayes, 2004; Mullens & Gayler, 1999), teachers are fairly good at remembering their instruction a week or two after the fact, but generally poor at remembering their patterns across an entire semester or year.

Second, many focus group participants (and all three of our follow-up interviewees) reported that having a large group of teachers with whom they could discuss gaps they saw in their own or in the group's practices was useful. It allowed them to share knowledge about how to integrate the LISELL-B practices into their respective lesson plans and to brainstorm new strategies for doing so. This was particularly productive because these conversations involved teachers from multiple schools and multiple districts, a rarity in most of the teachers' professional learning experiences. Not having every teacher in the room working at the same school ameliorated some of the political and interpersonal dynamics that could potentially disrupt constructive reflection. Further, this diversity expanded the breadth of experience from which the group could draw and learn.

Jayla also explained that allowing teachers to compare patterns of LISELL-B practice implementation both within and across schools helped her better understand how to use the log as a guide for her teaching. Jayla's middle school, for example, partners with three others in her district to develop their sixth-grade Earth Science curriculum. But when viewing the patterns of her practice across the year, she was surprised to learn that they differed significantly from those of teachers from the other three middle schools, and even from those of her co-worker down the hall. Through group conversation, she learned that many of the teachers with different patterns across the year had only reported using a given LISELL-B practice if the practice had been an explicit part of their lesson plans and if students understood that learning the practice was a clear goal of a given lab or activity. In contrast, Jayla described having filled out the log and thinking, "Well, my lab is related to cause and effect, so I'm going to write down that I did that." As a result of participating in the whole group summative reflection, Jayla has since altered her log reporting to align more closely with the former approach, which will let her more accurately assess what her students were expected to learn.

Not every benefit of the log was logistical or analytic, though. Teachers reported that the log also offered a welcome conceptual shift away from an assessment framework dominating in their schools and towards a positive space for engaging in critical thinking about their work. They saw value in moving from externally monitored observation data ("Did I do what I was supposed to?") to self-report ("What opportunities did I offer my students? Why did my practices differ from those of my colleagues? Why did we collectively give or not give our students certain opportunities? Can patterns of my practice help me identify reasons for patterns in my students' work?").

Carol described the difference between these two purposes at some length. Implicit in her description is a transition between power relationships: from observer–observed to facilitator–reflector, the role of the former no longer that of a judge but rather that of a partner. Carol explains:

> I thought the way it [the yearlong log data] was presented and distributed in packets was actually very helpful in that it was positive – here's what I could improve on, here's what I could do more of ... but it wasn't ... "Oh you're not doing enough." It was more, "Oh, that's maybe an area where maybe I could improve." There wasn't any kind of attachment of ... "Wow, oh, you haven't done this one at all." It was more ... "Here – what do you think?" I thought it was just very nice and professional, and a great reflective tool to plan for this year.

The log thus helped teachers own their lesson planning and instructional time, in addition to allowing them to plan more effectively for the upcoming year. While teacher self-report data is sometimes critiqued as being too subjective or prone to over-reporting what others wish to hear, recent research has shown that in carefully executed research these biases are not as pronounced as once suspected (Desimone, 2009). These teachers' experiences with the LISELL-B teacher log data highlight some of the positive aspects of self-report data related to participant ownership of what the data show and to building a community of professional pedagogical inquiry.

Testing Intervention Effectiveness

Another important use of the teacher logs is that the information can be quantified and used in a statistical model to test the effectiveness of the intervention. There are many challenges to linking teacher practices with teaching effectiveness, typically measured by student outcomes, and much has been written in the last few years about the limitations of value-added models when considering the impact of teaching on student learning (American Statistical Association, 2014). As Darling-Hammond (2015) has pointed out, the validity of drawing such relationships is predicated on a set of ideal conditions and assumptions that rarely (if ever) hold in the context of our current classroom environments. One of these assumptions is that we have a clear notion of what practices teachers are actually using in their classrooms and with what frequency. While the LISELL-B project is interested in testing intervention effectiveness rather than teacher effectiveness, the same challenges apply. As one way to explore intervention effectiveness, we are attempting to define and then connect teacher engagement in project professional learning experiences with teacher enactment of project practices (Buxton et al., 2015). Teacher logs provide a viable way to calculate a project enactment score for each teacher each year that can then be analyzed in relation both to teacher engagement in professional learning and to student performance on the LISELL-B specific student assessment.

As discussed earlier, the initial version of the teacher log asked respondents to complete Parts B–D of the log for each practice in Part A that they enacted during a given reporting period. These data would have allowed us to connect the use of specific classroom resources, technologies, and language functions with the individual LISELL-B practices as part of an enactment score. As we streamlined the log in consultation with project teachers, we removed our ability to connect the data from Parts B–D to individual components in part A, thus reducing the potential complexity of our enactment scores. We are currently exploring various ways to combine the binary elements of the log into weighted summed scores for each of the six LISELL-B practices that are addressed in Part A of the log for each teacher. Parts B–D of the log can likewise be used to produce weighted summed scores for each teacher for their uses of various classroom resources, technologies, and language functions throughout the school year. By treating these weighted sum scores within and across years as total enactment scores for each LISELL-B practice (Part A) and supporting category (Parts B–D) for each teacher, the enactment scores are quantified as continuous rather than binary variables. While these analyses are ongoing, we believe that when summarized over time and aggregated across teachers by grade-level band (middle and high school) and by content area, the teacher log data can serve as a robust and useful way to discern patterns of enactment and to study intervention effectiveness.

Implications

Based on our experiences developing and utilizing the LISELL-B teacher log for documenting teachers' enactment of LISELL-B practices, we provide several insights and recommendations for others considering the use of a teacher log. First, we have found that although the log data were fairly simple – consisting of mostly binary responses – they provided rich and useful information to both developers and teachers. Considering ways to combine the binary elements of the log into weighted summed scores is one way to further improve the information obtained from the logs and is an ongoing part of the LISELL-B project.

Particularly when working within an intervention framework that conceptualizes teachers as active agents in the enactment of intervention practices, as is the case for the LISELL-B project, log data can be a powerful tool for engaging teachers in the ongoing refinement of the intervention and in reflecting on their own practice. By providing a picture of ongoing and evolving practice over a prolonged period of time, the logs assist researchers and teachers in discerning and discussing patterns of enactment. In this way, log data can provide a platform for generative conversations about the contextual factors that encourage the enactment of certain practices and hinder the enactment of others. Such conversations are an essential component of a project model that supports multiplicities of enactment rather than traditional views of fidelity of implementation.

Second, from a practical perspective, log data are relatively inexpensive to collect (compared to observations), can be readily used for both intervention teachers and comparison teachers, and can be used for multiple purposes – for program improvement as well as for effectiveness research. This flexibility gives teacher logs the unique ability to provide a variety of actors involved in an intervention with information that they might find relevant and that can be directly acted upon.

Third, we believe that it is imperative to involve teachers in the development and refinement of any teacher log instrument. For example, without teachers' early involvement and honest feedback in the multiple rounds of piloting, we would have found only after the fact that our data were inaccurate, our response rates were low, or that the classes teachers were reporting on might have been mostly arbitrary. Although we might have anticipated that the burden of the log was too high in our initial prototype, insights from teachers and the project liaisons working most closely with them were essential to determine the balance that was feasible between depth of data collected and log completion rate, among other issues. Without liaison feedback, we could not have ensured that teachers were receiving the support for completing the log that they thought was most useful. This iterative and collaborative process, working with teachers and liaisons, is a cornerstone of the LISELL-B log and will continue to be used to create an ever more relevant log instrument for the remaining years of implementation.

In conclusion, we encourage developers, evaluators, teachers, and school district personnel to explore the potential of using teacher practice logs in ongoing collaboration with teachers as teachers are asked to enact new practices and standards. Despite the high level of attention currently being paid to student performance data in schools, we assert that the opportunity for teachers to regularly reflect on their own classroom practice is rare. Logs with key practices delineated (based on district standards, professional learning goals, or curricula) can be a powerful, relatively low cost (time and money) tool for teachers themselves to make real-time adjustments to their instruction, and for developers, evaluators, and researchers to better understand and track those adjustments.

References

American Statistical Association. (2014). *ASA statement on using value-added models for educational assessment*. Alexandria, VA: Author.

Bond, G. R., Evans, L., Salyers, M. P., Williams, J., & Kim, H.W. (2000). Measurement of fidelity in psychiatric rehabilitation. *Mental Health Services Research*, 2(2), 75–87.

Buxton, C., Allexsaht-Snider, M., Kayumova, S., Aghasaleh, R., Choi, Y., & Cohen, A. (2015). Teacher agency and professional learning: Rethinking fidelity of implementation as multiplicities of enactment. *Journal of Research in Science Teaching, 52*(4), 489–502.

Camburn, E., & Barnes, C. A. (2004). Assessing the validity of a language arts instruction log through triangulation. *The Elementary School Journal, 105*(1), 49–73.

Caspio. (2015). Overview. Retrieved November 13, 2013 from www.caspio.com/online-database/.

Connell, R. W. (1987). *Gender and power: Society, the person and sexual politics.* Palo Alto, CA: Stanford University Press.

Correnti, R. (2007). An empirical investigation of professional development effects on literacy instruction using daily logs. *Educational Evaluation and Policy Analysis, 29*(4), 262–295.

Correnti, R., & Rowan, B. (2007). Opening up the black box: Literacy instruction in schools participating in three comprehensive school reform programs. *American Educational Research Journal, 44*(2), 298–339.

Dane, A. A., & Schneider, B. H. (1998). Program integrity in primary and early secondary prevention: Are implementation effects out of control? *Clinical Psychology Review, 18*(1), 23–45.

Darling-Hammond, L. (2015). Can value added add value to teacher evaluation? *Educational Researcher, 44*(2), 132–137.

Desimone, L. (2009). Improving impact studies of teachers' professional development: Toward better conceptualizations and measures. *Educational Researcher, 38*(3), 181–199.

Durlak, J., & DuPre, E. (2008). Implementation matters: A review of research on the influence of implementation on program outcomes and factors affecting implementation. *American Journal of Community Psychology, 41*(3), 327–350.

Fogelman, J., McNeill, K., & Krajcik, J. (2011). Examining the effect of teachers' adaptations of middle school science inquiry-oriented curriculum unit on student learning. *Journal of Research in Science Teaching, 48*(2), 149–169.

Gearing, R. E., El-Bassel, N., Ghesquiere, A., Baldwin, S., Gillies, J., & Ngeow, E. (2011). Major ingredients of fidelity: A review and scientific guide to improving quality of intervention research implementation. *Clinical Psychology Review, 31*, 79–88.

Harris, C., Penuel, W., D'Angelo, C., Haydel DeBarger, A., Gallagher, L., Kennedy, C., Haugen Cheng, B., & Krajcik, J. (2015). Impact of project-based curriculum materials on student learning in science: Results of a randomized controlled trial. *Journal of Research in Science Teaching, 52*(10), 1362–1385.

Lesaux, N., Kieffer, M., Faller, S., & Kelley, J. (2010). The effectiveness and ease of implementation of an academic vocabulary intervention for linguistically diverse students in urban middle schools. *Reading Research Quarterly, 45*(2), 196–228.

Moncher, F., & Prinz, R. (1991). Treatment fidelity in outcome studies. *Clinical Psychology Review, 11*, 247–266.

Mowbray, C., Holter, M., Teague, G., & Bybee, D. (2003). Fidelity criteria: Development, measurement, and validation. *The American Journal of Evaluation, 24*(3), 315–340.

Mullens, J. E., & Gayler, K. (1999). Measuring classroom instructional processes: Using survey and case study fieldtest results to improve item construction (Working Paper No. 1999–08). Washington, DC: U.S. Department of Education National Center for Education Statistics.

Nelson, M. C., Cordray, D. S., Hulleman, C. S., Darrow, C. L., & Sommer, E. C. (2012). A procedure for assessing intervention fidelity in experiments testing education and behavioral interventions. *Journal of Behavioral Health Services & Research, 39*(4), 374–396.

O'Donnell, C. (2008). Defining, conceptualizing, and measuring fidelity of implementation and its relationship to outcomes in K–12 curriculum intervention research. *Review of Educational Research, 78*(1), 33–84.

Orwin, R. (2000). Assessing program fidelity in substance abuse health services research. *Addiction, 95*(Suppl. 3), S309–S327.

Porter, A. C. (1989). A curriculum out of balance: The case of elementary school mathematics. *Educational Researcher, 18*(5), 9–15.

Porter, A. C. (2004). Curriculum assessment. In J. Green, G. Camilli, & P. Elmore (Eds.), *Handbook of complementary methods in education research* (pp. 141–160). Washington, DC: American Educational Research Association.

Rowan, B., Camburn, E., & Correnti, R. (2004). Using teacher logs to measure the enacted curriculum: A study of literacy teaching in 3rd grade classrooms. *The Elementary School Journal, 105*(1), 75–102.

Rowan, B., & Correnti, R. (2009). Studying reading instruction with teacher logs: Lessons from the study of instructional improvement. *Educational Researcher, 38*(2), 120–131.

Rowan, B., Harrison, D., & Hayes, A. (2004). Using instructional logs to study mathematics curriculum and teaching in the early grades. *The Elementary School Journal, 105*(1), 103–127.

Appendix A – Year 1 Log Screenshots

Language-Rich Inquiry Science with English Language Learners through Biotechnology
(LISELL-B)

Home   Logout

LISELL-B Log | Activity Reporting | Page 1 of 2

Log #2, 9/1/2014 - 9/8/2014

Instructions

The purpose of this log is to gather information on inquiry-based science activities in which your students participate. The activities are organized into six broad categories, which are listed below. Place your mouse over a category to view its description.

1. Coordinate hypothesis, observations and evidence
2. Learn about controlling variables
3. Explain cause and effect relationships
4. Use models to construct scientific explanations and test engineering designs
5. Develop general academic vocabulary in context
6. Own the academic language of science

In order to save your work, you must scroll to the bottom of this page and click the "Save" button.

Part A. Science Activities

The log asks you to report on activities in your **7th Grade Agriculture** classes. For each of the activities below, the log asks several specific questions. Please indicate whether the students in any of your 7th Grade Agriculture classes participated in the given activity during the week of **9/1/2014 - 9/8/2014**. If you answer "Yes," for any activity, please answer the follow-up questions on Page 2.

Thinking about the week of 9/1/2014 - 9/8/2014, did any of the students in your 7th Grade Agriculture classes have opportunities to coordinate hypothesis, observations and evidence by...

○ Yes ○ No   1. Stating their expectations based on prior experiences and knowledge *(hypothesis)*?

○ Yes ○ No   2. Using their senses and tools to make targeted *observations* and collect data?

○ Yes ○ No   3. Selecting appropriate observations to serve as *evidence* to evaluate their hypothesis?

Thinking about the week of 9/1/2014 - 9/8/2014, did any of the students in your 7th Grade Agriculture classes have opportunities to learn about controlling variables by...

○ Yes ○ No   4. Identifying variables in science (anything that can change during an observation or experiment)?

○ Yes ○ No   5. Distinguishing between *independent variables*, *dependent variables*, and *controlled variables* (constants) when designing an investigation or discussing the investigations of others?

Thinking about the week of 9/1/2014 - 9/8/2014, did any of the students in your 7th Grade Agriculture classes have opportunities to explain cause and effect relationships by...

○ Yes ○ No   6. Identifying cause and effect relationships (where one event, the *cause*, brings about another event, the *effect*, through some mechanism or process)?

○ Yes ○ No   7. Describing key mechanisms or processes that relate to the cause and effect relationship?

Thinking about the week of 9/1/2014 - 9/8/2014, did any of the students in your 7th Grade Agriculture classes have opportunities to use models to construct scientific explanations and test engineering designs by...

○ Yes ○ No   8. Using various types of models (e.g., physical, drawn, simulation, mathematical) to *explain scientific concepts*?

○ Yes ○ No   9. Using various types of models (e.g., physical, drawn, simulation, mathematical) to *test and improve designs*?

Thinking about the week of 9/1/2014 - 9/8/2014, did any of the students in your 7th Grade Agriculture classes have opportunities to develop general academic vocabulary in context by...

- ○ Yes ○ No   10. Using general academic vocabulary (non-science -specific vocabulary common across academic content areas) *orally* to support meaningful explanation of science concepts or practices?

- ○ Yes ○ No   11. Using general academic vocabulary (non-science -specific vocabulary common across academic content areas) *in writing* to support meaningful explanation of science concepts or practices?

Thinking about the week of 9/1/2014 - 9/8/2014, did any of the students in your 7th Grade Agriculture classes have opportunities to own the academic language of science by...

- ○ Yes ○ No   12. Translating scientific language into everyday language or vice versa?

- ○ Yes ○ No   13. Breaking down the technical nature of scientific vocabulary through roots, prefixes and suffixes?

- ○ Yes ○ No   14. Translating dense, abstract, or depersonalized science text into more active personalized text, or vice versa?

[Save] [Go to Page 2 >>]

Abt — BOLD THINKERS DRIVING REAL-WORLD IMPACT

Language-Rich Inquiry Science with English Language Learners through Biotechnology (LISELL-B)

Home   Logout

LISELL-B Log | Follow-Up Questions | Page 2 of 2

Instructions

Listed below are the activities that you selected on the previous page. Please answer the follow up questions below about these activities.

2. Students coordinated hypothesis, observations and evidence by using their senses and tools to make targeted observations and collect data
8. Students used various types of models (e.g. physical, drawn, simulation, mathematical) to explain scientific concepts
11. Students used general academic vocabulary (non-science specific vocabulary common across academic content areas) in writing to support meaningful explanation of science concepts or practices
13. Students broke down the technical nature of scientific vocabulary through roots, prefixes and suffixes
14. Students translated dense, abstract, or depersonalized science text into more active personalized text, or vice versa

In order to save your work, you must scroll to the bottom of this page and click the "Save" button.

Part B. Resources used during the science activities

Did students use any of the following types of resources during the activities listed at the top of the page?
Check all that apply.

- ☐ Graphic Organizers
- ☐ Lab forms for doing investigations
- ☐ Readings for developing science understanding
- ☐ Vocabulary instructional materials
- ☐ Thinking Maps
- ☐ Lab Notes Templates
- ☐ Language Boosters
- ☐ Academic Vocabulary Word Cards
- ☐ None of the above

Part C. Technology

Did students use any of the following types of technology during the activities listed at the top of the page?
Check all that apply.

- ☐ Computer animation (e.g., Brainpop)
- ☐ Computer simulation or virtual lab (e.g., Phet)
- ☐ Digital physical lab equipment (e.g., probeware, data collection devices)
- ☐ Online reading or information gathering (e.g. webquest, virtual text)
- ☐ Online writing/ reporting (e.g., virtual notebook, Edmoto, Google docs)
- ☐ Other, specify
- ☐ None of the above

Part D. Talking about, reading about and writing about the science activities

Did students have the chance talk about, read about, or write about the activities listed at the top of the page?
Check all that apply.

- ☐ Students talked about them
- ☐ Students read about them
- ☐ Students wrote about them
- ☐ None of the above

Part E. Alignment with Georgia standards

When students did the science activities listed at the top of the page, did they address any of the following Georgia Science Standards?
Place your mouse over a standard to see the corresponding substandards

E1. Characteristics of Science - Habits of Mind
- [ ] S7CS1. Students will explore the importance of curiosity, honesty, openness, and skepticism in science and will exhibit these traits in their own efforts to understand how the world works
- [ ] S7CS2. Students will use standard safety practices for all classroom laboratory and field investigations
- [ ] S7CS3. Students will have the computation and estimation skills necessary for analyzing data and following scientific explanations
- [ ] S7CS4. Students will use tools and instruments for observing, measuring, and manipulating equipment and materials in scientific activities
- [ ] S7CS5. Students will use the ideas of system, model, change, and scale in exploring scientific and technological matters
- [ ] S7CS6. Students will communicate scientific ideas and activities clearly
- [ ] S7CS7. Students will question scientific claims and arguments effectively
- [ ] None of the above

E2. Characteristics of Science - The Nature of Science
- [ ] S7CS8. Students will investigate the characteristics of scientific knowledge and how that knowledge is achieved
- [ ] S7CS9. Students will investigate the features of the process of scientific inquiry
- [ ] None of the above

E3. Georgia Science Standards for 7th Agriculture
- [ ] MSAGED7-1: Express the importance of agriculture in daily life
- [ ] MSAGED7-2: Compare/contrast the importance of Georgia agriculture
- [ ] MSAGED7-3: Demonstrate an understanding of the National FFA Organization
- [ ] MSAGED7-4: Express an understanding of the area of agriscience
- [ ] MSAGED7-5: Build an understanding of the area of forestry & natural resources
- [ ] MSAGED7-6: Critique the area of agricultural mechanics
- [ ] None of the above

Part F. Description of the science activities

F1. Please describe how you used the science activities listed at the top of this page in your lesson. You can cut and paste directly from your lesson plan. Alternatively, you may use the "Add Document" button at the bottom of the screen to upload your lesson plan file(s).

Other Comments

Please provide any other comments below.

When you have completed this log, please check the box below and click the 'Submit Log' button.
- [ ] Log Complete

[<< Back to Page 1]   [Save]   [Submit log]

Support Documents
[Add Document]

FIGURE 6.1 Log screenshots from year 1.

Appendix B – Revised Year 2 Part D Log Questions

Part D. Talking about, reading about and writing about the science activities

Rate the amount of time students had chances to talk about, read about and write about the science activities listed in Part A.

How often did students have the _chance to talk about_ the science activities listed in Part A, throughout this week?

	Never	A little (1-10% of instructional time)	Some (11-50% of instructional time)	A lot (51-100% of instructional time)
Students engaged in paired student-student talk	○	○	○	○
Students engaged in small group (3-7 students) student talk	○	○	○	○
Students engaged in whole-class discussion with teacher as moderator	○	○	○	○

How often did students have the _chance to read about_ the science activities listed in Part A, throughout this week?

	Never	A little (1-10% of instructional time)	Some (11-50% of instructional time)	A lot (51-100% of instructional time)
Students read an assignment or substantive text silently in class	○	○	○	○
Students took turns reading aloud a text for the whole class to follow along	○	○	○	○
Students read and discussed with a peer or small group what they read	○	○	○	○

How often did students have the _chance to write about_ the science activities listed in Part A, throughout this week?

	Never	A little (1-10% of instructional time)	Some (11-50% of instructional time)	A lot (51-100% of instructional time)
Students took notes from a teacher presentation/lecture	○	○	○	○
Students wrote about activities individually	○	○	○	○
Students wrote about activities in pairs or small groups	○	○	○	○

FIGURE 6.2 Log screenshot from year 2 log revisions.

Appendix C – Sample Aggregate Teacher Response Patterns: Middle School Physical Science

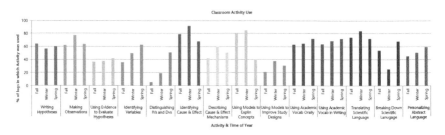

FIGURE 6.3 Sample aggregate teacher response patterns.

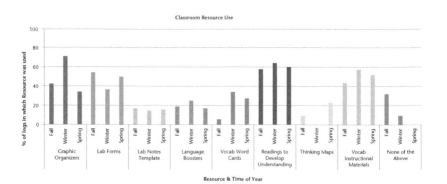

FIGURE 6.4 Sample classroom resource use.

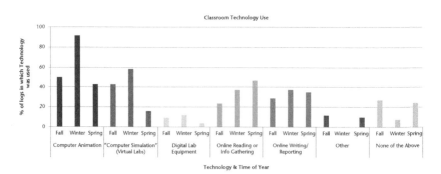

FIGURE 6.5 Sample classroom technology use.

7
THE VALUE OF THEORY AND PRACTICE IN THE CONTEXT OF THE LISELL-B PROJECT

Examples of Plug-ins

Shakhnoza Kayumova, Rouhollah Aghasaleh, & Max Vazquez Dominguez

The LISELL-B (Language-rich Inquiry Science with English Language Learners through Biotechnology) project is a longitudinal, mixed methods, teacher professional development research project implemented in the state of Georgia. Other aspects of this project are described in detail elsewhere (e.g., Buxton, Allexsaht-Snider, Kayumova, Aghasaleh, Choi, & Cohen, 2015) as well as in the preceding two chapters in this volume. In this chapter we take turns discussing how contexts of the LISELL-B project allowed each of us to work with multiple theories in order to make sense of teaching and learning science with emergent bilingual students, their families, and teachers. The common threads among the multiple theories we use are our shared reliance upon so-called "post" theories and new materialisms. These theories are highly suspicious of the idea of "method," as conceptualized in modern social (and natural) science research. Drawing on Deleuze and Guattari's (1987) notions of assemblages and plug-ins, we position the LISELL-B project as an open-ended and dynamic assemblage of discursive, social, and material entities. Written in the form of narrative genre, each plug-in we describe illustrates (1) a distinct piece of situated experience and (2) the ways in which each of us utilize multiple theoretical perspectives to interpret the complex work of the LISELL-B project.

The first plug-in emerged during classroom research with science teachers and emergent bilingual students in the LISELL-B project context. The author (Kayumova) uses theories of new materialism and conceptualizes science teaching, learning, and pedagogy as implicated with human and nonhuman bodies, through what she calls bodily-affective practices. From this perspective, conceptualizing science pedagogy in light of new materialisms provides an alternative understanding of how materiality, embodiment, and subjectivity play out in school science teaching and learning.

The next plug-in emerged during the LISELL-B assessment workshops. The second author (Aghasaleh) argues that looking at specific materialities of classroom practice allows researchers to attend to "thing power ... [as] a good starting point for thinking beyond the life-matter binary, the dominant organizational principle of adult experience" (Bennett, 2010, p. 20). Aghasaleh uses Jane Bennett's (2010) notion of thing power to illustrate that assessments are one of the agentic discursive-material assemblages that have an effect on students and teachers in science classrooms.

In the last plug-in, the third author (Vazquez Dominguez) emphasizes the value of assemblage theory as it attends to multiple elements of teaching and learning, e.g., linguistic and non-linguistic components, and material elements, such as physical objects, that can be combined to support productive interactions in science education. According to Vazquez Dominguez, assemblage theory not only elucidates these elements, but it also links them to the physical spaces where dynamics between humans and objects enhance the teaching and learning of science.

Overall, the plug-ins presented here helped us to think through the following questions: (1) What is the value of thinking/applying/emerging with a theory and simultaneously being in the field with teachers, students, and families? (2) What are the potential contributions of these multiple theoretical perspectives to knowledge production within the LISELL-B project?

Plug-in 1 (Shakhnoza)

During my doctoral program, as a research assistant on the initial LISELL-B exploratory project, I had the opportunity to work with 25 teachers and 1,600 students from diverse backgrounds. I helped with administering assessments, conducting classroom observations, holding post-observation debrief sessions, and conducting interviews with science teachers. During these years, I developed a special relationship with two eighth-grade science teachers, Becky and Kelly. Becky and Kelly took part in over 30 LISELL-B professional learning activities during my 3 years of work with them. They consistently demonstrated a high level of engagement with language-rich inquiry practices in their articulations and participation during the LISELL-B project activities.

Becky and Kelly worked at Blue Ridge Middle School, one of the implementation schools of the LISELL-B project. At the time, Blue Ridge Middle School had about 800 students enrolled; 46 percent of the students were identified as Latina/Latino, while the district classified 24 percent of those students as English language learners (ELLs). I choose to refer to these children as emergent bilinguals (García, 2010). Judith Butler (1995) argues that "to be constituted by language is to be produced within a given network of power/discourse" (p. 135). The term emergent bilingual signifies children whose language skills are emerging in two languages, for example both in English and in Español, instead of suggesting a limited proficiency in one or another language. Emergent bilingual students, in particular Latina/Latino students, are the fastest growing population in the Southeast region of the U.S. (Buxton, Allexsaht-Snider, Suriel, Kayumova, Choi, Bouton, & Baker, 2013). For many years, researchers working with emergent bilinguals have been concerned with students' oral and written language development (McKay & Wong, 1996); however, limited research exists on the influence of mainstream classroom teachers' subject positioning while working with emergent bilinguals (Yoon, 2008). This is partly because working with emergent bilinguals has typically been considered the responsibility of English as Second Language (ESOL) teachers (Fu, 1995). Unlike much of the research about teaching emergent bilinguals that has focused on the work of ESOL teachers and students' oral and written language development, the aim of the LISELL-B professional learning practices was to support middle school science teachers in creating opportunities for emergent bilinguals to engage in science learning through language-rich investigations.

Becky and Kelly's overall experiences and participation in the LISELL-B professional learning were heavily situated in similar challenges they encountered in their middle school science classrooms. Given limited instructional time, limited resources, and extensive accountability policies and practices, Becky and Kelly found creating equal opportunities for *all* students to participate in inquiry-based science a challenge in their daily teaching practice. This was the case even for two teachers who were obviously concerned about the learning opportunities they presented to their emergent bilingual students, and who believed that these students particularly benefited from language-rich inquiry science practices. To better understand the role of various discursive and structural constraints on science teachers' instructional decision making, I decided to do fieldwork in Becky and Kelly's classrooms at Blue Ridge Middle School.

In the beginning of my fieldwork, I was particularly interested in how Becky and Kelly negotiated through structural and discursive limitations and how they used their agency to enact inquiry-based language-rich science teaching. Later, I observed that the teachers were strongly influenced by social and cultural discourses, along with the physical and material entities they used in their classrooms. The pedagogical practices that constituted the classroom instruction were intricately connected to physical objects that were available in that space. For instance, new technological objects, such as computers, laptops, and interactive white boards had changed the room setup, organization, and the kinds of practices taking place in the classroom. Laptop computers occupied the laboratory corners of the classroom. Students' desks faced the interactive white board. The teachers used these interactive white boards to show videos about science practices, and students used their individual laptops to engage in virtual science investigations. Instructional technology afforded students the opportunity to engage in virtual science labs and experiments. These physical objects played an important role as *actants* with influence over what kind of science learning was possible and impossible for emergent bilingual students (Latour, 1999) in the classrooms. The physical objects were not passive or inactive things, nor simply material sensory manipulators; rather, they were active entities, shaping and reshaping Becky and Kelly's classroom spaces, practices, and their relations with students and instructional objects. These are examples of what I call bodily-affective practices. As Latour argues:

> It is by mistake, or unfairness, that our headlines read "Man flies," "Woman goes into outer space." Flying is a property of the whole association of entities that include airports and planes, launch pads and ticket counters. B-52s do not fly, the U.S. Air Force Flies. Action is simply not a property of humans but of an association of actants. (p.182)

Thus, my work with LISELL-B teachers in their classrooms pushed me to seek alternative theories to better understand what I was observing in those spaces. I read and reflected on multiple theories (e.g., Barad, 2003; Braidotti, 2013; Deleuze & Guattari, 1987; Latour, 1999). Particularly, I found myself attracted to feminist readings of new materialisms, such as the work of physicist Karen Barad (2003), to examine the significance of physical objects as important material entities in the construction of cultural forms and agentic spaces in science education. According to Barad (2003), agency, or the ability to do something, is not only located in humans. It is a result of human and non-human intra-action, meaning they constitute each other. For example, reading a book is not only possible because of human intention but is also made possible because there is a physical thing that we discursively call and signify as a book. While we used to understand books as things made of paper and ink, our idea of book now extends to things made of plastic, metal, or other materials (e.g., tablets and e-book readers). Similarly, smelling the pages of the book is made possible not only because humans intend to smell a book's pages but also because the chemistry between paper and ink produces a certain kind of smell. As I explored these theoretical perspectives, my understanding about science teaching and learning, bilingual students, and their agency slowly shifted.

For me, the conception of good teaching has begun to signify more than having/applying pedagogical content knowledge, and/or adapting/resisting/negotiating discursive spaces – it also includes matter that matters. For instance, I now see classrooms as assemblages that include bodies of students, physical entities, and various forms of intra-actions with these physical entities, be it paper, pencil, virtual labs, or laptops. The science and pedagogical practices used in classroom instruction are connected in complex ways with the physical objects, the bodies of teachers and students, physical objects, as well as what these bodies and materialities signify to one another. While computers and interactive white boards changed the setup of Becky's and Kelly's classrooms, these material actants also changed the academic performances and assessment systems that were available through those entities in ways that had an impact on the instructional practices taking place in the classroom. Teaching and learning were intertwined with bodies, both human and non-human, and understanding the ways in which these bodies intra-acted with each other was important for understanding the complexities of how Becky and Kelly's science teaching evolved. Beyond the context of these two teachers' classrooms, this use of theory changed my understanding of human agency more broadly. My fieldwork allowed me to theorize that the conditions for change in education are not necessarily located only within individuals, but instead that change and agency are implicated in the intra-action of many different entities.

Plug-in 2 (Rouhollah)

As a mixed methods research project, we developed pre and post constructed-response assessments to evaluate the effectiveness of LISELL-B practices in both implementation and comparison classrooms. More than 1,000 assessments were completed each year by middle school students and all were scored by the project's staff, by teachers in the project, and on a few occasions, by students in our teacher preparation program. Being in charge of scoring workshops and training the scorers, I witnessed many conversations in which assessments became living beings. For instance, scorers would say things like, "this student is smart" or "this student is saying …" referring to the sheets of paper. Thus, the assessments became animated and living examples of vibrant matter. In one of the scoring workshops, I asked the scorers (in this case, undergraduate and masters students in the middle school teacher education program) to draw pictures and describe the person whose assessments they were scoring. This plug-in is an analysis of what the scorers drew and wrote.

Humanist paradigms in philosophy and the social sciences are informed by modernist, structural, and humanist theories/discourses versus post-humanist approaches that are informed by post-modernist, post-structural, post-humanist theories/discourses. Post-qualitative research is grounded in post-humanism. In the post theories all major epistemological and methodological concepts (e.g., language, discourse, knowledge, truth, reason, power, freedom, the subject, objectivity, being, reality, method, science) are deconstructed.

The Humanist paradigms are based on a hierarchical ontology in which the human knower preexists knowing. This knower has innate agency as opposed to that which is to be known (the world of reality), which is passive and lacks agency. In this hierarchical ontology, language is a transparent medium that can unproblematically represent reality. However, in a flattened ontology (Deleuze & Guattari, 1987), the roles of subject, object, and language are always already entangled, and the human knower has no separate existence, but rather, all come into existence together.

New Materialism/New Empiricism as an ontological turn focuses on new definitions of being and becoming rather than focusing on ways of generating knowledge. This is why in this type of inquiry, unlike in Humanist research, questions of ontology are more important than questions of epistemology. In this plug-in, using thing-power theory I introduce another ontology, in which non-human actants are equally – and in some cases more – agential than human actants. There is no new knowledge generated through this study. All teachers and those who have the experience of scoring students' assessments already know what is found by this study. However, this study affords educators and researchers an opportunity to define a world in which assessments are not mere passive objects that "represent" students' learning; rather they are agentic assemblages.

Qualitative research, and its chief method of data collection, the interview, relies on the "voice" of the knowing Cartesian subject. Post-qualitative inquiry, however, follows Foucault (1970) who wrote, in *The Order of Things*, that the human and the human's voice are not the center of the inquiry.

> I tried to explore scientific discourse not from the point of view of the individuals who are speaking, nor from the point of view of the formal structures of what they are saying, but from the point of view of the rules that come into play in the very existence of such discourse: what conditions did Linnaeus (or Petty, or Arnauld) have to fulfill, not to make his discourse coherent and true in general, but to give it, at the time when it was written and accepted, value and practical application as scientific discourse. (p. xiv)

This does not mean that the researcher should be detached from her/his surroundings. Foucault himself spent many years going to prisons and most probably took notes about these visits; however, he did not cite or quote a prisoner, guard, or other human in his book *Discipline and Punish; The Birth of the Prison*. Like Foucault, post-qualitative researchers refuse to privilege participants' voices over other sources of knowledge or being in their inquiry. That is, they question the "phonocentrism" of conventional humanist qualitative methodology – the belief that speech is superior to, or more primary than, written language. As Derrida (1978) argued, phonocentrism developed because the immediacy of speech has been regarded as closer to the presence, the real being, of subjects, than writing.

Post-qualitative research, then, focuses on identifying structures and discourses that allow people to say certain things and not others. As Spivak (1988) explained in *Can the Subaltern Speak*, because human subjects are produced in structures, their voices are most often only reproductions and echoes of the structure. Therefore, if one wishes to deconstruct the structure, it does not make sense to rely on the participants' voices. One of the ways to deconstruct a hierarchical structure is to subvert the privileges in the hierarchy. In what follows, I attempt to give voice to the objects (assessments) to make some invisible agencies visible.

Part 1. Hola! Soy yo: My name is Isabella. I just finished 7th grade in a suburban middle school in the state of Georgia. Mrs. Forest's class is shown in Figure 7.1.

The Value of Theory and Practice **125**

I and 21 other students went to her class this year. She teaches 7th grade science. She's my favorite teacher and she is probably the main reason I love science. I'm pictured in Figure 7.2.

Well, this doesn't actually look like me, but still, it's much better than the picture of my friend Ethan. See Figure 7.3.

FIGURE 7.1 Pictures of students from Mrs. Forest's class.

FIGURE 7.2 Picture of Isabela.

126 Kayumova, Aghasaleh, & Vazquez Dominguez

FIGURE 7.3 Picture of Ethan.

The person who drew the picture of Ethan wrote that "I drew a girl because of the good handwriting," which drove Ethan nuts. You see, people who don't really know us drew these pictures of us – they read the answers that we wrote about some science questions, and then they drew the pictures of what they guessed we look like. Here's how it happened: two years ago Mrs. Forest and two other science teachers from our school agreed to participate in a project called LISELL-B, which is short for Language-rich Science Inquiry for English Language Learners through Biotechnology. I don't know the LISELL-B project well. All I know is that they do so many things. One thing they do is stop by our classroom twice a year with a bunch of manila envelopes and huge bags of candy. In those envelopes they have tests [ughhh!!!] printed on blue and pink papers. They have us do those tests and they give us candy. I guess it's a fair trade off. They say the tests are not for grades but to help Mrs. Forest understand how we learn science. Sometimes they invite ESOL students and their families to their Saturday bilingual workshops called Steps to College. I like the people who work on this project. Two professors, who speak English and Spanish, are really nice. One of them does cool science experiments, usually with a fat guy who has a name I was never able to pronounce. The other one does conversations with us and our families about our goals and achievements. I never knew a university professor before, but I always thought doctors wear suits, because I never saw Ethan's dad, who is a doctor, wearing anything but suits. After they collect the tests they score them. The people who scored our tests were asked to imagine our faces and draw them.

Figure 7.4 is the picture that another scorer drew from Kim's test.

The Value of Theory and Practice **127**

FIGURE 7.4 Picture of Kim.

Kim likes her picture a lot. Not because it looks like her, though. I'll tell you secretly what I think; Kim is Korean-American and she's always unhappy about how her eyes look. The scorer who has drawn the picture wrote "I drew a white female student because she checked the non-Hispanic box and wrote in-depth answers with good hand writing." Isn't that silly that the scorer thinks Ethan is a girl because of his handwriting and that Kim is a white female because she's not Hispanic and her paper looks smart? I don't like that they made those assumptions.

Sometimes, when the teacher returns my test I can't believe that I wrote all those awkward things. Mrs. Forest says that due to test anxiety my performance on tests is different from when I'm not writing a test. I hate tests, not only because it affects my grades but also because people judge me based on a piece of paper that is not actually ME.

Part 2. I am pictured in Figure 7.5.

My name is LISELL-B#289 Random#2244. This is not actually a name that people call me; rather, it's a name by which they sort me among my fellow assessments. There are thousands of us sitting in file cabinets in the LISELL-B research office. Like many of you, I've no idea how I was created. All I know is that I've changed a lot over time, and things have been added and removed to and from me. I must have started as a poor tree that was cut down to make paper. I've been cut and colored pink. Someone wrote a couple of questions on

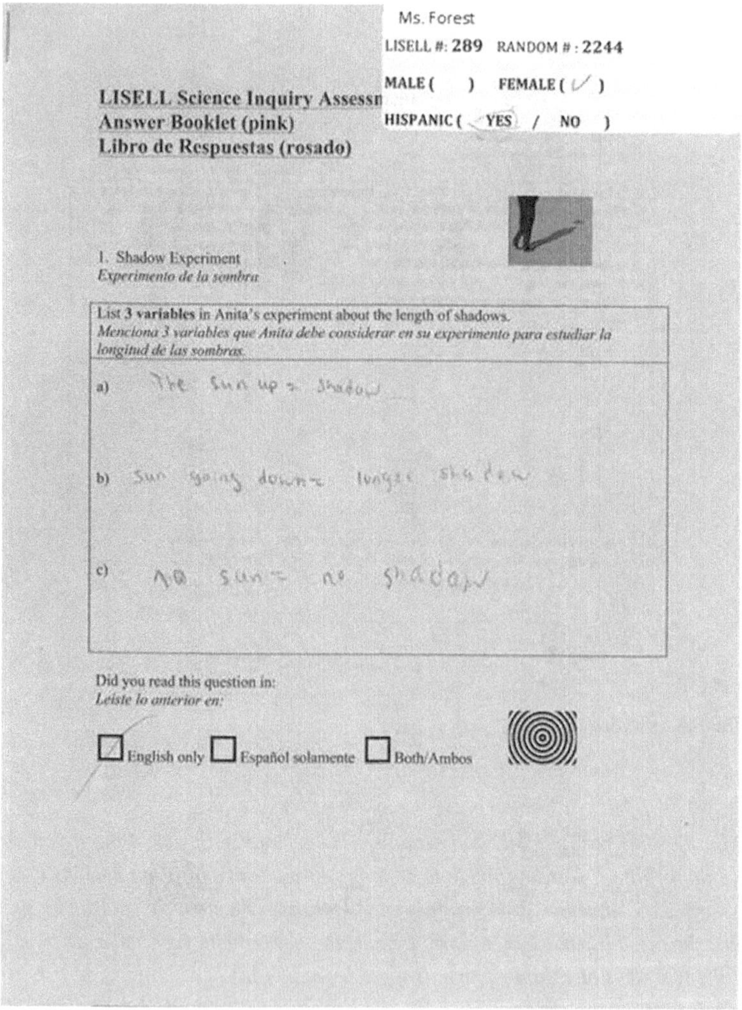

128 Kayumova, Aghasaleh, & Vazquez Dominguez

FIGURE 7.5 Picture of LISELL#289.

my body and left some spaces for Isabela to fill in. I have a knowledge piece. I'm about middle school science and I'm supposed to measure Isabela's knowledge about science inquiry practices, the academic language of science, and science content. I'm a rhizome that has no beginning or end; I am always in the middle, between things, interbeing, intermezzo … "The tree imposes the verb 'to be,' but the fabric of the rhizome is the conjunction, 'and … and … and …'" This conjunction carries enough force to shake and uproot the verb "to be." (Deleuze & Guattari, 1987, p. 25). Thus, my assemblage increases in "the dimensions of a multiplicity that necessarily changes in nature as it expands its connections. There are no points or positions in a rhizome, such as those found in a tree structure or root" (Deleuze & Guattari, 1987, p. 8).

I'm material and I'm knowledge. How can knowledge be material? I'm also discursive. I'm the narrative that Isabela wrote. I'm non-human and I'm human. I have a sticker on me that indicates my gender, race, home language, and other identities that a human could have. That's why people rely on me to judge Isabela. To be frank, I've stolen Isabela's identity. Scorers look at me and think about Isabela. Some of them talk to her through me, saying things like "I think she's a sweet girl, nice to friends" or "from your handwriting I can tell you do everything fast" or "she's like a self-conscious sassy girl" or "an adventurous boy who likes to explore the outdoors."

I don't know what I am, but I know what I'm related to. I know that I'm powerful and I also know what I can do. People think I'm just stuff because I'm so quiet in the file cabinet most of the time. However, teachers and students realize that we, tests, are not inanimate. We can be gentle or mean, just like people. We can fail people and limit their life choices or we can help people achieve their dreams. We can make Mrs. Forest lose her job. We speak to teachers on behalf of students and speak to school administrations on behalf of teachers. We generate all those dangerous numbers that make everyone anxious. All the way from kindergarten to graduate school; high stake tests, CRCT, final exam, SAT, GRE, we never leave students and educators alone.

Jane Bennett (2010) wrote:

> No one really knows what human agency is, or what humans are doing when they are said to perform as agents. In the face of every analysis, human agency remains something of a mystery. If we do not know just how it is that human agency operates, how can we be so sure that the processes through which nonhumans make their mark are qualitatively different? (p. 34)

Assessments are clear and vibrant examples of nonhumans that affect their surroundings. This is what Bennett (2010) calls thing power: "the curious ability of inanimate things to animate, to act, to produce effects dramatic and subtle" (p. 6). As Bennett further elaborates, "Thing power may thus be a good starting point for thinking beyond the life-matter binary, the dominant organizational principle of adult experience" (p. 20).

Assessments are assemblages that are groupings of diverse elements. Assemblages are living. They have uneven topographies. They are not governed by any head on top, foundational root, or central heart.

Deleuze and Guattari wrote:

> As an assemblage, a book has only itself, in connection with other assemblages and in relation to other bodies without organs. We will never ask what a book means, as signified or signifier; we will not look for anything to understand in it. We will ask what it functions with, in connection with what other things it does or does not transmit intensities, in which other multiplicities its own are inserted and metamorphosed, and with what bodies without organs it makes its own converge. (p. 4)

For educators, assessments are non-human agents that shape evaluators' judgments about humans. Students' writings on assessments are not the students themselves, although they are often treated as if they were. Students' handwriting, time, and space, intra-acting with students' content knowledge, sociocultural contexts, and their language skills, all generate matter called "assessment" through which humans get ranked and promoted, included and excluded. In the LISELL-B project, in which more than 4,000 middle school students have participated, we have a room full of students' assessments. As we have conducted training workshops for scorers every year and trained scorers in how to make sense of students' responses, as well as scored many, many assessments ourselves, we, as researchers, have come to see these written constructed responses as things possessing the power to speak out. We may never get to see Isabela or talk to her; however, we judge her, and we prescribe and plan for her present and future.

Plug-in 3 (Max)

In my case, the LISELL-B project motivated me to continue searching for and experimenting with the cultural tools that could be used to support emergent bilingual students in understanding, engaging in, and communicating science ideas. Incorporating language and household practices in curriculum has been shown to support learning for emergent bilingual students (Gonzalez, Moll, & Amanti, 2005), but I was looking for different approaches to shaping productive interactions between Latina/Latino students and science learning. I was looking for activities or a set of practices that were more than simply familiar to the LISELL-B participants; I wanted activities capable of triggering a powerful interest or a force in the participants, so we, as teachers, could experiment with and use that force to improve science teaching and learning.

As an educator and researcher studying educational and social aspects of interactions in and beyond schools, one needs to have tools to understand and modify the various dynamic processes in a community and society. Manuel DeLanda (2006) suggests that assemblage theory provides that set of tools needed to understand how the social reality works and, based on that comprehension, the theory allows us to design a plan to experiment with and change that social reality. In what follows, I describe how assemblage theory informed my understanding and actions in the LISELL-B project, leading to the inclusion of emergent bilingual students' passion for soccer in science learning activities and new relationships between students' science learning and the physical space needed to create learning territories.

As a first step, assemblage theory does not support nor does it hold any essentialist views (DeLanda, 2006). Thus, in my case, the notion of Latina/Latino has to be understood as a historical process; that is to say, the people and students who participated in the project can be understood as Latina/Latino only after we contextualize their educational, work, and life experiences in their home countries, the migration process, and their interests and experiences in the United States. This helped me, as a researcher of Mexican origin, to not make assumptions about Latinos/Latinas' experiences, such as generalizing about students' experiences with the Spanish language, or the migration process, or documentation status. In addition, knowledge about the students' interests and experiences in the U.S. helped me to understand their possible paths of becoming. For instance, if a Latina student wants to pursue her dream of becoming a physician and wishes to go to one of the five major universities in Georgia, but lacks residence or citizenship, then her process of becoming is affected by macro forces, such as state policies that limit university access. In other words, assemblage theory provides the concept of Latina/Latino with a face, a body, an individual history, and a present situation in which interests, circumstances, and experiences affect the teaching of science and the students' learning processes that are inscribed at different levels such as institutions, communities, and higher-level organizations (e.g., country). This historical construction of the individual also applies to teachers, activities, and institutions, and in this case, the role of soccer in Latin countries.

Deleuze and Guattari (1987) say that assemblages consist of content and expression or, in Manuel DeLanda's words (2006), in material and expressive dimensions. The expressive component of assemblages has both linguistic and nonlinguistic elements, for instance, when a science teacher explains about the water cycle she uses linguistic elements, such as the words and sentences coming out of her mouth, the language resources displayed on the classroom walls, and nonlinguistic elements, such as body postures, facial gestures, classroom activity organization, and table arrangements and placements. On the other hand, the material component of assemblages is equally important and consists of physical elements such as bodies, which in our example would be the body of the teacher, the classroom, chairs, computers, students, and their work. It is important to say that, for Deleuze and Guattari, the linguistic part is as crucial as the material one, and both types of elements always come in mixtures.

Also, assemblages consist of processes of territorialization and deterritorialization. DeLanda (2006) writes that processes of territorialization "define or sharpen the spatial boundaries of actual territories. [They also refer] to non-spatial processes which increase the internal homogeneity of an assemblage," and he adds, "any process which either destabilizes spatial boundaries or increases internal heterogeneity is considered deterritorializing" (p. 16). Using the previous example, there is a science classroom that may be inhabited by diverse students whose home languages may be different than English. In regular classrooms in the U.S., English is often the only language spoken and used as part of the teaching process in which both teachers and students participate, and any other languages spoken at students' homes are rarely used as a resource. In this example, English has been territorialized as part of the teaching process but it has not been fully territorialized by students in relation to their learning process. A process of deterritorialization in the science classroom would be to use Spanish, in addition to

English, as a teaching resource so Spanish-speaking students would have support in their understanding and learning processes through the use of cultural tools. This would also be a destabilization in the physical boundaries where Spanish is spoken. Destabilization processes offer risks and opportunities to the teacher and students in the classroom; however, in this case, it is the teacher who has to decide, regulate, and organize the new activities, spaces, linguistic choices, and students. In this light, teachers, especially in science, know how physical objects, as part of the science activities, have the capacity to engage students in those activities. Students' curiosity, passions, and personal interests can be used in addition to the objects' capacities to trigger learning as long as they are adequately scaffolded. The field of science can be seen as an element that functions in two directions; that is to say, science content has historically been created and utilized primarily by individuals who are part of mainstream culture (English-speaking, middle class culture), and when explained to others from non-mainstream cultures, it is done from the mainstream cultural perspective. Therefore, it is often harder for people from non-mainstream cultures to understand and feel connected to science, and harder for teachers to scaffold their non-mainstream students' learning processes (Lee & Buxton, 2013). I claim that science learning can actually be bidirectional because diverse students' relevant cultural practices can be included in the classroom in meaningful ways if we support them in their learning process.

Vygotsky (1962) argued that language is the most relevant of the cultural tools and its use, along with other cultural practices such as skills and experiences, forms a complex collection of elements in the emergent bilingual students' learning process with science. These skills and experiences include: parents' backgrounds; students' exposure to English and science; the amount and type of interactions between students and their parents; social resources, such as parent engagement in the school; science teacher preparation; and many others. Cultural-historical and sociocultural theories have offered important insights into how some of these elements intertwine and affect the teaching-learning process (González, Moll, & Amanti, 2005; Gutiérrez & Rogoff, 2003). From the assemblage perspective this means that the elements that participate in the process that may be used to teach science extend beyond the classroom and the individuals inhabiting it. This makes the science teacher an ethnographer in search of a range of students' cultural practices in order to include them as part of the classroom resources. This is pure experimentation, and the risks increase given the general lack of teacher preparation to teach science to diverse students (Buxton, Lee, & Santau, 2008).

In this regard, the LISELL-B project has encouraged the assemblage formed by *science teachers/emergent bilingual students/families/school classrooms/science content/ teaching practices* to work with a model and a structure that supports the teaching and learning processes. This is accomplished by homogenizing:[1] (a) teachers' acknowledgment of cultural differences as a teaching resource and the presence and use of the emergent bilingual students' cultural practices in the teaching of science and (b) the use of these resources to promote inquiry. This homogenization,

I argue, helps to increase the teaching and learning opportunities for teachers and emergent bilingual students in the classroom.

The classroom as a physical space has the material and expressive elements that offer opportunities for the teaching and learning processes. Here, a helpful distinction to use in portraying the relationship between the classroom and the students, especially emergent bilingual students, is the Heideggerian difference between a house and a home. The difference is simple: we inhabit houses and dwell in homes. The process by which people make a space a home is domestication, that is, the process in which people have a constant interaction over a long period of time with the space. What would this process of domestication, a house becoming a home, look like in the classroom?

According to Didakis and Phillips (2013), "The architectural 'object' becomes an extension of a man's personality and psyche, providing as an exchange not only survival possibilities, but also poetic and colourful properties" (p. 308). In science education, teachers are usually in charge of implementing the rules that regulate how students interact with other students and how students interact with the environment. For instance, I have observed that it is a regular practice for middle and high school students to remain in their seats for the entire science class as their production of knowledge (e.g., notes, diagrams, ideas) is usually stored in a notebook or in a computer. However, if we, as science teachers, implement a direct relationship between the students and the physical space of the classroom, students would have the opportunity to build their learning environment in the classroom and, therefore, have a chance to dwell in that space as teachers encourage their students' spatial agency.[2] Spatial agency would be an important aspect of dwelling in a classroom, since traditionally students use their space according to a set of social rules (e.g., safety, respect) imposed by the institution and the teacher. In a space encouraging students' spatial agency, teachers and students interact with each other and with the classroom and the objects within for the purpose of enhancing their teaching/learning process and relating their learning to the physicality of the classroom.

The emergent bilingual learners' processes of dwelling in the science classroom may also be promoted by adding cultural aspects as part of the teaching of science. For instance, an element we have developed in the LISELL-B project that promotes this student–space interaction is a series of language cards that have a science concept in English and Spanish, a definition written with the needs of emergent bilinguals in mind, and the word used in a phrase or sentence so students see the relation between the English and Spanish concept. Several science teachers who have participated in the project display these cards on their classroom walls and include them as part of their teaching of science. This supports emergent bilingual and other students by extending their resources in the classroom and their interaction with the environment. However, there are more resources to be explored so teachers can expand their strategies to promote the students' processes of dwelling in the classroom. Recently, I have researched how soccer not only functions as a cultural resource but also as a passionate activity for emergent bilingual students. Soccer, in this case, may be used in science as an element to develop activities relevant for the Latina/Latino students and other students interested in the game.

In my experience as an ethnographer in the LISELL-B project, I have found that soccer is an important activity for many Latina/Latino students and their families as they devote important amounts of time to play on the school team, watch soccer games with the family on weekends, play soccer video games, and engage in soccer pools. In this light, the LISELL-B project motivated me to continue searching and experimenting with the cultural tools that could be used to support emergent bilingual students in understanding, engaging in, and communicating science. Their passion for soccer was the solution I was looking for to support more productive interactions, because soccer has been known and practiced for several generations of Latinos/Latinas and their children, and there is an economical network such as the media that supports it.

Students' passion for soccer could be combined with science to find critical thresholds for productive interactions inside and outside the classroom. Again, it is important not to generalize that Latinos/Latinas will necessarily connect to soccer without studying the historical process of the sport with specific individuals and particular regions. Soccer plays a major cultural role in some Latin American regions, such as South America, Central America, and México (Bavoni Escobedo, 2014; Nadel, 2014), but not necessarily in all countries. For example, baseball is culturally more important in Puerto Rico, the Dominican Republic, and Cuba.

In the context in which I was working, soccer offered the possibility of extending the borderlines of the science classroom as the emergent bilingual students' spatial agency acted in the classroom and on the soccer field. Science teachers can broaden the educational assemblage and increase students' capacities to affect their learning of science as long as cultural resources form part of this process. If the process of using the classroom space is stable enough for emergent bilingual students to domesticate their environment, then the science teachers can rely on this resource to continue to push their emergent bilingual students' learning process in new directions (for more information about the soccer practices with science, see Vazquez Dominguez, Allexsaht-Snider, & Buxton, under review).

In my experience working as a researcher with emergent bilingual students mostly from Latin American regions, assemblage theory has provided me with the necessary tools to study, understand, design, and act within this heterogeneous collection of elements that extend beyond the science classroom. I wish to stress three important aspects about assemblage theory and my work in the LISELL-B project: (a) *the individual background* (e.g., person, institution, country) and how this helps elucidate the elements' histories in the assemblage; (b) *the two axes of material/expressive elements and of the territorialization/deterritorialization processes, which localized the elements, cultural practices, and processes each element is involved in*; and (c) *the opportunities for experimentation and change*.

In the teaching/learning process with emergent bilingual students, teachers can use the emergent bilingual students' home language, in this case Spanish, as a resource in the classroom, since the production of science knowledge is closely connected to language and culture. The inclusion of the emergent bilingual students' home language and other cultural resources as part of the classroom practices can help them domesticate the science practices as well as the science classroom. As long as this domestication happens with emergent bilingual students, we, as science teachers, will be able to expand the assemblage in new directions. We will face risks and opportunities as we try to expand the assemblage associated with science teaching and learning and explore new possibilities. In this light, opportunities can expand by using, in addition to a cultural tool like language, the students' passions, such as soccer, that can be powerful forces to support the science teaching and learning processes.

Next

Given the pragmatic nature of large-scale work, we understand that at times it becomes a challenge to work with multiple, complex theories and knowledge systems, and to speak from unique and situated experiences in the context of mixed methods studies. The studies that come out of large-scale implementation projects in science teaching and learning are often interpreted through a single lens that privileges mainstream research assumptions grounded in linear (for a critique of linear theories, see DeLanda, 2006) and cognitive theories. While useful, such theories often provide limited perspectives about complexity within teaching and learning. We purposefully used multiple theories, such as post-structural, post-modern, and feminist new materialisms, to explore the depth and context of teaching and learning in new ways within the LISELL-B project. In this chapter, we used Deleuze and Guattari's concept of plug-ins to illustrate our three individual examples of theoretical and practical struggle, accounting for the complexities entailed in enacting interdisciplinary research in science education with emergent bilingual/multilingual youth.

There are many more plug-ins in the LISELL-B project, and in all large-scale research and design projects, and it is important to invite other scholars to continue to plug in with their own theoretical explorations.

Notes

1 A helpful difference between Deleuze and DeLanda in terms of assemblages is that heterogeneity is a constant in Deleuzian assemblages, whereas in Delandian assemblages it is a variable. By treating heterogeneity as a variable, DeLanda does not have to include strata as another category besides assemblage. The process of turning an assemblage into a stratum – to use Deleuzian terms – that is, homogenizing a space or an activity, could work to either benefit or damage the assemblage.

2 Spatial agency, coined by Schneider and Till (2009, Spring), refers to the production of space like houses, warehouses, industrial sheds, and buildings from the point of view of architects and with the main purpose of designing and building the physical facility. Here, I use the term in a different way proposing that teachers and students use spatial agency to co-design and co-build learning environments in which the people involved interact and have a more active relationship with the physicality of the classroom and the objects within.

References

Barad, K. (2003). Posthumanist performativity: Toward an understanding of how matter comes to matter. *Signs, 28*(3), 801–831.
Bavoni Escobedo, F. (2014). *Los juegos del hombre: Identidad y poder en la cancha (The games of man: Identity and power in the field)*. México, D. F.: Cal y Arena.
Bennett, J. (2010). *Vibrant matter: A political ecology of things*. Durham, NC: Duke University Press.
Braidotti, R. (2013). *The posthuman*. Cambridge, UK: Polity Press.
Butler, J. (1995). For a careful reading. In S. Benhabib, J. Butler, D. Cornell, & N. Fraser (Eds.), *Feminist contentions. A philosophical exchange* (pp. 127–142). New York, NY: Routledge.
Buxton, C., Allexsaht-Snider, M., Kayumova, S., Aghasaleh, R., Choi, Y., & Cohen, A. (2015). Teacher agency and professional learning: Rethinking fidelity of implementation as multiplicities of enactment. *Journal of Research in Science Teaching, 52*(4), 489–502.
Buxton, C. A., Allexsaht-Snider, M., Suriel, R., Kayumova, S., Choi, Y. J., Bouton, B., & Baker, M. (2013). Using educative assessments to support science teaching for middle school English-language learners. *Journal of Science Teacher Education, 24*(2), 347–366.
Buxton, C., Lee, O., & Santau, A. (2008). Promoting science among English language learners: Professional development for today's culturally and linguistically diverse classrooms. *Journal of Science Teacher Education, 19*(5), 495–511.
DeLanda, M. (2003). Deleuzian ontology: A sketch. Retrieved February 12, 2015 from www.situation.ru/app/j_art_1078.htm.
DeLanda, M. (2006). *A new philosophy of society*. New York, NY: Continuum.
Deleuze, G., & Guattari, F. (1987). *A thousand plateaus: Capitalism and schizophrenia* (B. Massumi, Trans.). Minneapolis, MN: University of Minnesota Press.
Derrida, J. (1978). *Writing and difference*. Chicago, IL: University of Chicago Press.
Didakis, S., & Phillips, M. (2013). Objects of affect: The domestication of ubiquity. *Technoetic Arts: A Journal of Speculative Research, 11*(3), 307–317.
Foucault, M. (1970). *The order of things*. New York, NY: Vintage.
Fu, D. (1995). *My trouble is my English: Asian students and the American dream*. Portsmouth, NH: Boynton/Cook.
García, O. (2010). *Educating emergent bilinguals: Policies, programs, and practices for English Language Learners*. New York, NY: Teachers College Press.
González, N., Moll, L., & Amanti, C. (2005). Introduction: Theorizing practices. In N. Gonzalez, L. C. Moll, & C. Amanti (Eds.), *Funds of knowledge* (pp. 1–28). New York, NY: Routledge.
Gutiérrez, K. D., & Rogoff, B. (2003). Cultural ways of learning: Individual traits or repertoires of practice. *Educational Researcher, 32*, 19–25.

Latour, B. (1999). *Pandora's hope: Essays on the reality of science studies.* Cambridge, MA: Harvard University Press.

Lee, O., & Buxton, C. (2013). Integrating science and English proficiency for English language learners. *Theory into Practice, 52*(1), 36–42.

McKay, S. L., & Wong, S. L. C. (1996). Multiple discourses, multiple identities: Investment and agency in second-language learning among Chinese adolescent immigrant students. *Harvard Educational Review, 66*(3), 577–609.

Nadel, J. (2014). *Fútbol!: Why soccer matters in Latin America.* Gainesville, FL: University Press of Florida.

Schneider, T., & Till, J. (2009, Spring). Beyond discourse: Notes on spatial agency. *Footprint,* 97–111.

Spivak, G. C. (1988). Can the subaltern speak? In *Marxism and the interpretation of culture* (pp. 271–313). London, UK: Macmillan Education.

Vazquez Dominguez, M., Allexsaht-Snider, M., & Buxton, C. (under review). Connecting soccer to middle school science: Latino students' passion in learning.

Vygotsky, L. S. (1962). *Thought and language.* Cambridge, MA: MIT Press.

Yoon, B. (2008). Uninvited guests: The influence of teachers' roles and pedagogies on the positioning of English language learners in the regular classroom. *American Educational Research Journal, 45*(2), 495–522.

PART III
ESTELL
Effective Science Teaching for English Language Learners

8
PROMOTING ENGLISH LANGUAGE LEARNER PEDAGOGY IN SCIENCE WITH ELEMENTARY SCHOOL TEACHERS

The ESTELL Model of Pre-Service Teacher Education

Trish Stoddart

Introduction

California must prepare pre-service teachers to work with the most diverse K–12 student population in the United States. Currently, 75 percent of the state's student population is from minority groups: African American (6 percent), American Indian (1 percent), Asian (9 percent), Filipino (3 percent), Latino (53 percent), White (25 percent), and Other (3 percent) (CalEd Facts, 2015). The fastest growing student group in California and across the United States is students who do not speak English as a first language – English Language Learners (ELLs). While the overall K–12 school-aged population increased by only 7.2 percent between the 1998/1999 and 2008/2009 school years, the K–12 ELL population grew from 3.5 to 5.3 million, an increase of 51 percent (National Clearinghouse for English Language Acquisition [NCELA], 2011). Language minority students often have limited access to the core academic curriculum and are typically taught by the least prepared and experienced teachers (National Center for Education Statistics [NCES], 2006a; U.S. Census Bureau, 2010; Wong-Fillmore & Snow, 2002). It is not surprising, therefore, that for 30 years the achievement of ELLs has lagged behind that of native English speakers in science and literacy (Lee & Luyxk, 2006; NCES, 2006b, 2011; Rodriguez, 2004, 2010).

Despite the long-term and chronic underachievement of ELLs, the majority of programs that engage in pre-service teacher preparation are not adequately preparing pre-service teachers to work with this rapidly expanding student population. Nationally, less than one-fifth of teacher preparation programs require any preparation for mainstream teachers in ELL instruction (Menken & Antunez, 2001). Furthermore, in a survey of 1,000 teachers in four states, Freeman, Garcia, Herrera, Murray, Valdés, and Walqui (2004) found that the number-one gap that a majority of teachers identified in their preparation programs was a lack of training in appropriate instructional and assessment strategies for working with ELLs. In fact, the majority of novice or experienced teachers surveyed in national studies state they are unprepared to teach any subject to ELLs (Ballantyne, Sanderman, & Levy, 2008; California Legislative Analyst's Office [LAO], 2007–2008); Gándara, Maxwell-Jolly, & Driscoll, 2005; NCES, 2011).

To compound the problem, there is very little empirical research on preparing the pre-service teacher population to teach any group of students (Sleeter, 2015). Scholarship in the field of teacher education tends to focus on describing the inadequacies of teacher preparation and offering suggestions for improvement (Labaree, 2004; Feiman-Nemser, 2012; Zeichner, 2003). There is very little research that focuses on implementing instructional reform in programs of teacher preparation and analyzing the impact on the novice teachers they prepare.

In response to these challenges, the ESTELL (Effective Science Teaching for English Language Learners) research group designed and implemented an innovative program of pre-service teacher preparation at three universities in California and conducted a quasi-experimental program of research to examine the impact of the project on the knowledge, beliefs, and practices of novice teachers who participated in the ESTELL project compared to those in a comparison group in the "business as usual" teacher education programs at the same institutions. This chapter describes the conceptual framework for ESTELL pedagogy and design of the ESTELL pre-service teacher education program. The two subsequent chapters in this section discuss aspects of the empirical research on program implementation.

ESTELL Pedagogy

The ESTELL project is grounded in sociocultural theory (Bakhtin, 1982; Rogoff, 1990, 1995; Rogoff & Wertsch, 1984; Tharp, 1997; Tharp & Gallimore, 1988; Vygotsky, 1978; Wertsch, 1985, 1991), the efficacy of which has been established through a series of empirical studies that demonstrate that student learning is enhanced when it occurs in contexts that are culturally, linguistically, and cognitively meaningful and relevant to students (Au, 1980; Deyhle & Swisher, 1997; Doherty & Pinal, 2002; Estrada & Inmhoff, 2001; Heath, 1983; Hilberg, Tharp, & Degeest, 2000; Lee & Fradd, 1998; Ladson-Billings, 1994; Lemke, 2001; Rosebery, Warren, & Conant, 1992; Tharp & Gallimore, 1988; Warren & Rosebery, 1995, 1996). Two converging lines of empirical research support this approach: (1) the CREDE Five Standards for Effective Pedagogy (CFSEP) (Dalton, 1998; Tharp, 1997; Tharp, Estrada, Dalton, & Yamauchi, 2000) and (2) the integration of inquiry science, language, and literacy practices (Baker & Saul, 1994; Casteel & Isom, 1994; Lee & Fradd, 1998; Lee & Luykx, 2006; Rodriguez & Bethel, 1983; Rosebery, Warren, & Conant, 1992; Stoddart, 1999, 2005; Stoddart, Pinal, Latzke, & Canaday, 2002). Both approaches have identified a common set of specific and observable teacher actions that a substantial body of empirical research has demonstrated raise the achievement of culturally and linguistically diverse students and improve their motivation to learn. This research has identified six areas of teaching practice that promote the achievement of ELLs.

ESTELL Practices

The ESTELL framework involves six major instructional practices: (1) Facilitating Collaborative Inquiry, (2) Promoting Science Talk, (3) Literacy in Science, (4) Scaffolding and Developing of Language in Science, (5) Contextualizing Science Activity, and (6) Promoting Scientific/Complex Thinking. These six major instructional practices correspond with research that support collaborative learning arrangements and science-driven language support. The ESTELL practices are conceptualized as overlapping pedagogical practices that pull from each other and that are mutually constitutive of effective science learning. These practices moreover are potentially ever-present in the classroom while not necessarily leveraged in the same way or activated by the teacher in each lesson. That is, effective science learning does not require that all ESTELL practices are fully addressed in every lesson, or that all teachers address each practice in the same way. Finally, ESTELL practices are not an exhaustive list of all possible ways that teaching and learning occurs in the science classroom, but rather, a particular orientation to science teaching that focuses on authentic disciplinary science literacy practices, inquiry learning, and language development. Table 8.1 describes how each ESTELL major practice is defined broadly through two related sub-constructs.

Facilitating Collaborative Inquiry (FCI) is generally defined by the level of persistent and widespread student interaction, including how teachers design and differentiate group work to include all students (Collaboration). FCI also includes the degree to which student voices are supported in communicating science knowledge by facilitating collaborative inquiry (Authority). Promoting Science Talk (PST) considers both the models and patterns of scientific discourse (Academic Science Discourse) and the interactional, discursive modes by which teachers engage in more dialogic scientific talk (Instructional Conversation). Literacy in Science (LIS) focuses on two aspects of meaning-making processes available in science learning, including the use of reading and writing for conducting scientific investigations (Authentic Science Literacy) and the use of inquiry and scientific language (Science Vocabulary). Scaffolding and Developing of Language in Science (SDLS) addresses two widely accepted English Learner approaches for language development, including attention to English language features and functions (Language Scaffolding) and the augmentation and modification of instruction to increase content comprehension (Content Scaffolding). Contextualizing Science Activity (CXA) refers to how science lessons can make explicit and/or implicit connections to previous student experiences in their

TABLE 8.1 Estell instructional practices

Facilitating Collaborative Inquiry		
1	Collaboration	Teacher use, modeling, and support of varied and inclusive student participation in science activities.
2	Authority	Teacher support of student involvement in generating science knowledge.
Promoting Science Talk		
3	Academic Science Discourse	Teacher use, modeling, and support of the scientific method.
4	Instructional Conversation	Teacher use, modeling, and support of dialogic strategies for reasoning.
Literacy in Science		
5	Authentic Science Literacy	Teacher use and support of authentic literacy tasks to support scientific activity.
6	Science Vocabulary	Teacher use, modeling, and support of scientific language in science activity.
Scaffolding and Development of Language in Science		
7	Language Scaffolding	Teacher use, modeling, and support of English language features and language teaching strategies.
8	Content Scaffolding	Teacher use, modeling, and support of strategies that augment content comprehension.
Contextualizing Science Activity		
9	Personal/Home/Community Experiences	Explicit or implicit attention to previous science-related experiences at home or in the community.
10	Physical Environment and Local Ecology	Explicit or implicit attention to previous science-related experiences in the natural world.
Promoting Scientific/Complex Thinking		
11	Scientific Reasoning and Understanding	The level of teacher use, modeling, and support of scientific reasoning and argumentation.
12	Developing Inquiry Skills	The level of teacher use, modeling, and support of inquiry.

communities and at home (Personal/Home/Community Experiences) and to student experiences in the natural world (Physical Environment and Local Ecology). Lastly, Promoting Complex Thinking (PCT) addresses how teachers promote scientific reasoning (Scientific Reasoning and Understanding) as well as promoting inquiry (Developing Inquiry Skills).

Instructional Exemplars

To illustrate how ESTELL practices are interpreted in our analysis of science lessons, we provide a lesson example taken from the instructional plan of a pre-service teacher in the ESTELL cohort. This lesson example involves a second-grade lesson that accomplishes many of the qualities involved in effective instructional conversations in science learning. In this example, the pre-service teacher promotes instructional conversations with some open-ended (i.e., indefinite, investigatory, and legitimate) questions to generate student science talk while also following up and revoicing student talk. Several types of productive teacher moves are captured in this opening example where the teacher initiates talk and offers guiding questions while also following up on student responses.

> *This lesson example about wheat plants begins with the teacher announcing the topic (wheat) and activity agenda for the day. She reminds students of the rules for talking and quickly moves to a warm-up activity. The teacher has students talk to their partner about what kinds of plants people like to eat and listens to their responses in pairs ("What kind of plants do people like to eat?"). The teacher then initiates a large group discussion by asking a question about grains to frame the lesson of the day ("Has anyone ever heard of a plant called a grain?"). The teacher selects student turns from the large group and redirects talk back to the whole class after a few responses ("Does anyone else have an example of a grain?"). She clarifies some answers and summarizes student responses to her questions before moving on to a subsequent activity ("We're talking about 'oats, corn, rice, barley, and rye.'").*

In this first short segment the pre-service teacher engages students in conversation and prepares students for participation in a science topic related to the California Science Standards under Earth Science that requires "Students know rock, water, plants, and soil provide many resources, including food, fuel, and building materials, that humans use." The example includes several productive pedagogical moves that promote learning through dialogue including having students pair-share about plant food. The pre-service teacher also clearly elicits students' prior knowledge on this topic by asking and extending their questions on the subject. Finally, the pre-service teacher provides an opportunity for students to use more academic science language by moving from "plant" (generic term) to "grain" (target food term). However, here is where the teacher could also have provided more assistance. It is possible that students, especially ELLs, are familiar with some grains more than others. For example, the teacher could have elicited a discussion on corn and rice or other familiar grains from home.

In a second segment of the same lesson, the teacher uses a brief story about grains to further extend key science vocabulary terms. The teacher also focuses attention to the California Science Standard under Investigation and Experimentation including "Make predictions based on observed patterns and not random guessing" and "Follow oral instructions for a scientific investigation." She elicits students' past recollection of how plants grow. As she does this, the pre-service teacher reframes the topic of the lesson as one where the class will act like scientists. She goes on to ask again what plants need to grow and if soil is needed. This occurs briefly before the teacher shifts attention to conducting an experiment herself. But before having students conduct an experiment or construct the focus or purpose of this or any other experiment, the teacher demonstrates what student groups will be doing later in the lesson. Students note that they will have the same materials on their desks as the teacher and observe the teacher doing the experiment first. Finally, the teacher asks students what scientists do when they don't know something and students provide several responses written on the board by the teacher.

> *Teacher then begins reading aloud a text titled "The Story of Wheat." Teacher shares the story, including information about seeds, sprouts, and the harvest of wheat. Teacher pauses to acknowledge those students that brought in plants for today, including rye and alfalfa plants. The teacher then asks students to recall a previous discussion about growing plants. Some students offer one-word responses including sun, water, soil, air, time, and space. The teacher repeats students' answers and validates responses as she writes them on the board. She asks students to give her more examples. Then the teacher calls out that the purpose of the lesson is to act as if "we're scientists today." The teacher next asks students if all plants need soil. Students offer yes/no responses as a group. The teacher then explains to students they will do an experiment. She mentions that all students will have a straw and paper towel for the experiment and points out these materials on their desks. She walks around to help students identify these materials. The teacher informs students that the paper towel is going to be like the soil for plants. Finally, the teacher demonstrates the focal activity with a paper towel, food coloring, and straws. Students observe the demonstration from their desks. The teacher asks about naming the function of roots ("Who can tell me which part of the plant brings the water up?") and about their connection to this demonstration ("We're going to investigate ... do you think all plants need soil to grow?"). The teacher asks students what scientists do when they don't know something. Students give three- to four-word responses like "they experiment it," "observe," "they detect," "they explore clues," "take chances, make mistakes." The teacher repeats some of these responses ("So, the paper towel is like our roots, right, and maybe the straw is like our soil?"), occasionally adding comments as she writes responses on the board. She says they will think about the list they came up with.*

In this segment the pre-service teacher sets up what will be the main activity by probing for student understandings of plant life and scientific work addressing aspects of inquiry and scientific reasoning. The exemplar illustrates the additional support provided for ELLs that makes their participation possible throughout the lesson.

The ESTELL Pre-Service Teacher Preparation Program

Pre-service teacher preparation programs rarely contain coursework or practicums with ELLs as part of their requirements. According to an American Association of Colleges for Teacher Education survey of 417 institutes of higher education, less than one-fifth required any preparation for teaching ELLs at the elementary or secondary levels (Menken & Antunez, 2010). Programs of pre-service teacher preparation must change their instructional practices to accommodate the needs of the rapidly changing demographics of the K–12 student population. Unfortunately, research on teacher preparation demonstrates that the effects of pre-service preparation are weak and that teachers tend to teach as they were taught or quickly accommodate to the prevailing school practice (Feiman-Nemser, 2012; Thompson, Windschitl, & Braaten, 2013; Zeichner & Tabachnick, 1981). A significant part of the problem is that curriculum and instruction in teacher education programs is fragmented and disconnected from the problems of practice encountered in schools (Labaree, 2004; Feiman-Nemser, 2012). Subject matter and pedagogical knowledge are typically acquired in different courses and programs. In California, prospective teachers acquire disciplinary knowledge in undergraduate degree programs in biology, chemistry, mathematics, and physics that model a pedagogy of lecture, lab, and problem sets and then go into pre-service teacher preparation programs that focus on how to teach. As Lee Shulman pointed out in 1986, knowledge for teaching or "pedagogical content knowledge" requires the integration of subject matter and pedagogical understandings. Teachers need to learn new instructional approaches through the pedagogy they are being prepared to teach and be provided with explicit models (Ball & McDiarmid, 1990; Stoddart, Connell, Stofflet, & Peck, 1993; Stofflett & Stoddart, 1994).

Learning to teach academic subjects to ELLs adds another level of complexity to compound the problem. The majority of teacher preparation and professional development courses on subject matter teaching typically give little attention to the importance of valuing and incorporating the linguistic needs and cultural experiences of the students being served (Cochran-Smith, Feiman-Nemser, McIntyre, & Demers, 2008; Fradd & Lee, 1995; Godley, Sweetland, Minnici, & Carpenter, 2005; Lee & Luykx, 2006; Rosebery & Warren, 2008; Stoddart, Bravo, Solís, & Mosqueda, 2011; Zeichner, 2003). Issues relating to cultural and linguistic diversity, when taught, are presented in separate courses that often focus on social conditions and not pedagogy (Ball & Tyson, 2011; Trent, Kea, & Oh, 2008; Zeichner, 2003).

Establishing Coherence across the Teacher Preparation Program

The ESTELL project uses a practice-based model of teacher education based on research demonstrating that the development of expertise in novice teachers is facilitated by engaging them in observation, analysis, and experience with explicit models of the instructional approaches they are being prepared to teach (Abell & Cennamo 2004; Goldman, Pea, Barron, & Derry 2007; Hewson & Hewson, 1988; Roth, Garnier, Chen, Lemmens, Schwille, & Wickler 2011; Schwartz & Hartman 2007; Sherin, 2004; Thompson, Windschitl, & Braaten, 2013; Wilson, Floden, & Ferrini-Mundy, 2008). Further, the pre-service teachers are provided with opportunities to practice these instructional approaches with the student population they are being prepared to teach with intensive feedback, coaching, and support (Joyce & Showers, 1995; Speck & Knipe, 2001).

However, for this approach to be effective, conceptual and practical coherence must be established across the pre-service teacher education program by articulating the integrated instructional model throughout the coursework and field practicum. In many teacher education programs there is no explicit model for teaching diverse learners articulated across the program (Wilson et al., 2008). In addition, there is often discontinuity between the pedagogical model presented in the university courses and the teaching practices modeled in field practicum (Stoddart, 1993; Wilson et al., 2008).

The ESTELL program supported the development of novice teachers' knowledge and skill by explicit articulation of the ESTELL practices throughout coursework and practicum experiences. The student teachers were all provided with experiences learning science through the six ESTELL practices in standards-based instructional units. These units explicitly modeled the ESTELL practices as they engaged in reflection and analysis of the ESTELL instructional exemplars. The novice teachers also developed and taught ESTELL lessons with feedback and support from ESTELL-trained master teachers.

Setting

Sites included three California teacher education programs of comparable size and teacher education focus located in urban centers in California with large populations of ELLs. All three sites offer a preliminary teaching credential and opportunity to add a bilingual authorization to their preliminary credential. These credentials allow students to teach in kindergarten through eighth-grade settings. Each teacher education program graduates approximately 200 pre-service teachers each year. These three programs were chosen because (1) each program prepares novice teachers to work in regions of great cultural, linguistic, and economic diversity and low educational attainment and each has a strong focus on preparing teachers to be responsive to student diversity and (2) all three institutions have one year post-baccalaureate elementary teacher education programs with the same requirements and coursework.

The Intervention

The ESTELL intervention consisted of two components: (1) re-structured science methods courses in the teacher education program and (2) pre-service teacher placement in a classroom where her/his master teacher had received professional development from our research team, which also focused on the ESTELL framework.

Science Methods Course

The science methods course was created collaboratively by four science methods instructors, who worked at the three participating state university campuses during the 2008-2009 development phase of the project. The science methods course focused on engaging pre-service teachers in a personal learning experience of science methods instruction through the research-based pedagogy that modeled the integration of science content with language and literacy, the use of science discourse and contextualized science instruction, collaborative inquiry, and scientific reason. The primary vehicle for the treatment of science methods instruction was the use of five California Science Standards–based units (with corresponding lesson plans and activities). These units were: Biodiversity, Skulls and Teeth, Earth, Sun & Moon, Electricity, and Arthropods. Each unit was designed to illustrate the five approaches to addressing the needs of ELLs in science, but we highlighted one or two of the categories per unit to make it easier for pre-service teachers to engage with the framework.

The science methods course taught through ESTELL pedagogy was 15 weeks long. Below is a description of the planning guidelines used by the instructors of the courses across the three universities.

Weeks 1–4: Science learning experience. Pre-service teacher education students engage in personal learning of science content through the ESTELL pedagogy by conducting science inquiries in small collaborative inquiry (CI) groups on science topics drawn from the California Science Standards. These will include two fourth-grade science topics (the water cycle and weather) and two fifth-grade science topics (phases of the moon and seasons). The science methods instructor will collaborate with each group on the development of the investigation (Collaborative Inquiry); promote science discourse and language, literacy, and writing activities (Literacy in Science); engage students in studying the science concepts in the local ecology (Contextualization); engage students in the analysis of data and theory development (Scientific/Complex Thinking); and actively engage in discussion of the science concepts and investigation with each of the small groups (Instructional Conversation). At the end of the content instruction phase, students will analyze their learning experiences and, with scaffolding by the science methods instructor, compare this to their previous learning experiences.

Weeks 5–9: Study and analysis. Pre-service teachers will read research and practice articles and observe videos as the basis for the analysis of the six core ESTELL teaching practices. They will reflect in CI groups on their personal experience of learning science content through ESTELL. One week of instruction will be devoted to the examination of each teaching practice.

Weeks 8–11: Curriculum development. Pre-service teachers will analyze curriculum units on the two topics they have investigated during the science content inquiry course (water cycle and weather) and two new topics, for example magnetism. They will also examine several science curriculums – including FOSS and GEMS – adopted by the local school district, analyzing these units for use of the ESTELL teaching practices. Students will work in pairs, to develop three ESTELL lesson plans selected from grades K–2, 3–4, and 5–6. Each lesson plan will have activities and curriculum material to engage students in all six ESTELL practices.

Week 12: Classroom teaching. Pairs of pre-service teachers will teach one ESTELL lesson in a K–6 classroom over three days (one hour a day) – selecting the unit appropriate to the grade level – observe and give feedback on each other's performances, revise their lesson plan, and write a critique.

Weeks 13–15: Reflection, critique, and revision. Pre-service teachers will work in CI groups to reflect on their classroom teaching experiences and analyze the instructional units developed by students in the group. With instructor support, the class will select 14 ESTELL lessons (two for each grade level K–6) to be reproduced in a binder for each student to use in their student teaching placement.

Professional Development

Master teachers who mentored the treatment group pre-service teachers participated in a two-day professional development workshop that focused on introduction to the ESTELL pedagogy, review of lessons plans which modeled the six pedagogical components, mentoring resources that incorporate these components, an observation guide, and a variety of articles and videos on being effective mentors for pre-service teachers and effective teachers of science for English language learners.

The master teachers were trained to engage in reflective teaching conversations with student teachers in regular post-observation conferences to discuss the successes and challenges of implementing specific ESTELL practices. They closely monitored the content of conversations to ensure that the dialogue went beyond technocratic notions of teaching, and moved to deeper and more complex issues such as contextualization of practices, facilitating student talk and inquiry, accessibility of content, equitable participation, and scaffolding of instruction for linguistically and culturally diverse learners. They recorded in writing the important discoveries and suggestions constructed in the formal post-ESTELL conferences so that pre-service teachers had a record to refer to as they worked to improve their practices.

Conclusion

Prior research has shown that the majority of pre-service teachers do not receive explicit instruction in how to teach ELLs and that K-6 pre-service teachers have a low sense of efficacy with respect to science and ELL teaching (Ballantyne, Sanderman, & Levy, 2008; California Legislative Analyst's Office [LAO], 2007–2008; Gándara, Maxwell-Jolly, & Driscoll, 2005; Freeman et al., 2004; Menken & Antunez, 2001). In addition, many pre-service teacher preparation programs have no clear model of instruction articulated across the coursework and practicum components (Stoddart, 1993; Wilson et al., 2008). Subject matter instruction, teaching methods, and information about student diversity and ELLs are siloed in separate courses and program components. The challenge is, however, to prepare teachers to teach subject matter to ELLs and to integrate the teaching of academic language and literacy into the teaching of science. In order to learn how to do this, pre-service teachers need experience with explicit and coherently presented models of instruction that align theory and practice. It is critical to have alignment between the pedagogical practices demonstrated by master teachers, who host pre-service teachers in the field, and the pedagogical practices presented in the science methods courses. Such alignment makes for a more enduring and meaningful experience for future teachers.

The ESTELL project focused on infusing effective practices for ELLs throughout three pre-service teacher education programs and analyzing the impact of the ESTELL model on the knowledge, beliefs, and practices of pre-service teachers. Pre-service teachers in the treatment group strengthened their beliefs about the ESTELL pedagogy in science and enacted the practices in field placements where these practices were explicitly labeled and modeled, and where they received feedback on their enactment of these practices from their master teacher. Science teacher educators who plan to enhance the manner in which they address the needs of ELLs in their courses must be observant of the need for a high level of detail in unpacking ELL pedagogy as they craft experiences for pre-service teachers. It is equally important that they plan to revisit these practices often and tie them to experiences pre-service teachers have in their classroom placement. Moreover, explicit explanations as to the authenticity of these practices to the scientific enterprise also had positive impact.

Integrating the ESTELL pedagogy and science education with guidance from science methods instructors and support from cooperating teachers shows promise in assisting pre-service teachers to enhance their science instruction. These efforts can ensure the next generation of educators are making science more accessible to *all* students and hence begin to address the persistent science achievement gap between native speakers of English and ELLs. The work has yielded strong outcomes not only for pre-service teachers, but master teachers and science methods faculty as well. The ESTELL science methods course has become the model for science instruction across the institutions, and master teachers recount these activities have served as reminders to them as they continue to look for ways to integrate language, literacy, culture, and science.

In the following two chapters we describe in more detail the instruments that were developed as part of the ESTELL project and provide additional exemplars of the practices being enacted by pre-service teachers.

References

Abell, S. K., & Cennamo, K. S. (2004). Videocases in elementary science teacher preparation. In J. Brophy (Ed.), *Advances in research on teaching: Using video in teacher education* (Vol. 10, pp. 103–130). New York, NY: Elsevier JAI.

Au, K. H. (1980). Participation structures in a reading lesson with Hawaiian children: Analysis of a culturally appropriate instructional event. *Anthropology and Education Quarterly, 11*, 91–115.

Baker, L., & Saul, W. (1994). Considering science and language arts connections: A study of teacher cognition. *Journal of Research in Science Teaching, 31*(9), 1023–1037.

Bakhtin, M. M. (1982). *The dialogic imagination: Four essays*. M. Holquist, Ed. and Translator, and C. Emerson, Translator, University of Texas Press Slavik Series: Austin, TX.

Ball, A., & Tyson, C. (Eds.). (2011). *Studying diversity in teacher education*. New York, NY: Roman and Littlefield.

Ball, D. L., & McDiarmid, G. W. (1990). The subject matter preparation of teachers. In W. R. Houston, M. Haberman, & J. Sikula (Eds.), *Handbook of research on teacher education* (pp. 437–449). New York, NY: Macmillan.

Ballantyne, K. G., Sanderman, A. R., & Levy, J. (2008). Educating English language learners: Building teacher capacity roundtable report. *National Clearinghouse for English Language Acquisition & Language Instruction Educational Program*. Washington, DC: George Washington University, Graduate School of Education and Human Development.

CalEd Facts. (2015). Sacramento, CA: California Department of Education Publications.

California Legislative Analysts Office (LAO). (2007–2008). Budget Book – Education Analyses, February 21, 2007. California Legislative Analyst's Office Report, 2007–2008 Retrieved September 2, 2016 from www.lao.ca.gov.

Casteel, C. P., & Isom, B. A. (1994). Reciprocal processes in science and literacy learning. *The Reading Teacher, 47*, 538–545.

Cochran-Smith, M., Feiman-Nemser, S., McIntyre, D. J., & Demers, K. (Eds.). (2008). *Handbook of research on teacher education: Enduring questions in changing contexts*. New York, NY: Routledge Taylor & Francis and the Association of Teacher Educators.

Dalton, S. S. (1998.) *Pedagogy matters: Standards for effective teaching practice*. Santa Cruz, CA: University of California, Center for Research on Education, Diversity & Excellence.

Deyhle, D., & Swisher, K. (1997). Research in American Indian and Alaska Native education: From assimilation to self-determination. In M. W. Apple (Ed.), *Review of research in education*, Vol. 22 (pp. 113–194). Washington, DC: American Educational Research Association.

Doherty, R. W., & Pinal, A. (2002). Joint productive activity, cognitive reading strategies, and achievement. Paper presented at the *Annual Meeting of the National Council of Teachers of English*, Atlanta, GA.

Doherty, R. W., & Pinal, A. (2004). Joint productive activity and cognitive reading strategy use. *TESOL Quarterly, 38*(3), 219–227.
Estrada, P., & Imhoff, B. D. (2001). *Patterns of language arts instructional activity: Excellence, inclusion, fairness, and harmony in six first grade classrooms.* Paper presented at the annual meeting of the American Education Research Association, Seattle, WA.
Feiman-Nemser, S. (2012). *Teachers as learners.* Cambridge, MA: Harvard Education Press.
Fradd, S. H., & Lee, O. (1995). Science for all: A promise or a pipe dream for bilingual students? *Bilingual Research Journal, 19,* 261–278.
Freeman, D., Garcia, E., Herrera, S., Murray, D., Valdés, G., & Walqui, A. (2004). *Preparing teachers to teach English language learners: What do we know?* Panel presented at the annual meeting of the American Educational Research Association, San Diego, CA.
Gándara, P., Maxwell-Jolly, J., & Driscoll, A. (2005). *Listening to teachers of English language learners: A survey of California's teachers' challenges, experiences, and professional development needs.* Santa Cruz, CA: Center for the Future of Teaching and Learning.
Godley, A., Sweetland, J., Wheeler, S., Minnici, A., & Carpenter, B. (2006). Preparing teachers for dialectally diverse classrooms. *Educational Researcher, 35*(8), 30–37.
Goldman, R., Pea, R. D., Barron, B. & Derry, S. (2007) (Eds.). *Video research in the learning sciences.* Mahwah, NJ: Lawrence Erlbaum Associates.
Heath, S. B. (1983). *Ways with words: Language, life, and work in communities and classroom.* New York, NY: Cambridge University Press.
Hewson, P. W., & Hewson, M. G. A'B. (1998). An appropriate conception of teaching science: A view from studies of science learning. *Science Education, 72*(5), 597–614.
Hilberg, R. S., Tharp, R. G., & DeGeest, L. (2000). Efficacy of CREDE's standards-based instruction in American Indian mathematics classes. *Equity and Excellence in Education, 33*(2), 32–40.
Joyce, B., & Showers, B. (1995). *Student achievement through staff development.* White Plains, NY: Longman.
Labaree, D. F. (2004). *The trouble with ed schools.* New Haven, CT: Yale University Press.
Ladson-Billings, G. (1994). *The dreamkeepers: Successful teachers of African American children.* San Francisco, CA: Jossey-Bass.
Ladson-Billings, G. (1995). But that's just good teaching! The case for culturally relevant pedagogy. *Theory into Practice, 34,* 159–165.
Lee, O., & Fradd, S. H. (1998). Science for all, including students from non-English-language backgrounds. *Educational Researcher, 27*(4), 12–21.
Lee, O., & Luykx, A. (2006). *Science education and student diversity: Synthesis and research agenda.* New York, NY: Cambridge University Press.
Lee, O., & Luykx, A. (2007). Science education and student diversity: Race/ethnicity, language, culture, and socioeconomic status. In S. K. Abell & N. G. Ledereman (Eds.), *Handbook of research in science education* (2nd ed., pp. 171–197). Mahwah, NJ: Lawrence Erlbaum.
Lemke, J. (2001). Multimedia literacy demands of the scientific curriculum. *Linguistics and Education, 10*(3), 247–271.
Menken, K., & Antunez, B. (2001). *An overview of the preparation and certification of teachers working with limited English proficient students.* Washington, DC: National Clearinghouse of Bilingual Education.
National Center for Education Statistics (2006a). *The condition of education in 2006.* U.S. Department of Education. Institute of Education Sciences, NCES 2006-071.
National Center for Education Statistics (2006b). *The Nation's Report Card: Science 2005* (NCES 2006–466). U.S. Department of Education. Washington, DC: U.S. Government Printing Office.

National Center for Education Statistics (2011). *The Nation's Report Card: Science 2009.* Institute of Education Sciences. Washington, DC: U.S. Government Printing Office.

National Clearinghouse for English Language Acquisition. (2011). *How many school-aged Limited English Proficient (LEP) students are there in the U.S.?* 2008–09 Consolidated State Performance Reports.

Rodríguez, A. J. (2004). Turning despondency into hope: Charting new paths to improve students' achievement and participation in science education. Southeast Eisenhower Regional Center for Mathematics and Science Education (SERC).

Rodriguez, A. J. (Ed.). (2010). *Science education as a pathway to teaching language literacy.* Rotterdam, Netherlands: Sense Publishers.

Rodriguez, I., & Bethel, L. J. (1983). An inquiry approach to science and language teaching. *Journal of Research in Science Teaching, 20*(4), 291–296.

Rogoff, B. (1990). *Apprenticeship in thinking: Cognitive development in social context.* New York, NY: Oxford University Press.

Rogoff, B. (1995). Observing sociocultural activity on three planes: Participatory appropriation, guided participation, and apprenticeship. In J. V. Wertsch, P. del Rio, & A. Alvarez (Eds.), *Sociocultural studies of mind* (pp. 139–164). Cambridge, UK: Cambridge University Press.

Rogoff, B., & Wertsch, J. V. (1984). *Children's learning in the zone of proximal development.* San Francisco, CA: Jossey-Bass.

Rosebery, A. S., & Warren, B. (2008). *Teaching science to English language learners.* Alexandria, VA: National Science Teachers Association.

Rosebery, A. S., Warren, B., & Conant, F. R. (1992). Appropriating scientific discourse: Findings from language minority classrooms. *The Journal of the Learning Sciences, 21,* 61–94.

Roth, K. J., Garnier, H. E., Chen, C., Lemmens, M., Schwille, K., & Wickler, N. I. Z. (2011). Videobased lesson analysis: Effective science PD for teacher and student learning. *Journal of Research in Science Teaching, 48,* 117–148.

Schwartz, D. L., & Hartman, K. (2007). It is not television anymore: Designing digital video for learning and assessment. In R. Goldman, R. Pea, B. Barron, & S. J. Derry (Eds.), *Video research in the learning sciences* (pp. 335–348). New York, NY: Routledge.

Sherin, M.G. (2004). New perspectives on the role of video in teacher education. In J. Brophy (Ed.), *Advances in research on teaching: Using video in teacher education* (Vol. 10, pp. 1–27). New York, NY: Elsevier JAI.

Shulman, L. S. (1986). Those who understand: Knowledge growth in teaching. *Educational Researcher, 15*(2), 4–14.

Sleeter, C. E. (2015). Towards teacher education research that informs policy. *Educational Researcher, 43*(3), 146–153.

Speck, M., & Knipe, C. (2001). *Why can't we get it right? Professional development in our schools.* Thousand Oaks, CA: Corwin.

Stoddart, T. (1993). The professional development school: Building bridges between cultures. *Educational Policy, 7*(1), 5–23.

Stoddart, T. (1999). *Language acquisition through science inquiry.* Paper presented at the Annual Meeting of the American Educational Research Association, Montreal, Canada.

Stoddart, T. (2005). *Improving student achievement with the CREDE Five Standards Pedagogy.* Technical Report No. (J1). Santa Cruz, CA: University of California, Center for Research on Education, Diversity and Excellence.

Stoddart, T., Bravo, M., Solís, J., & Mosqueda, E. (2011). Preparing pre-service elementary teachers to teach science to English language learners. *Proceedings of the International Conference on Education,* Honolulu, Hawaii.

Stoddart, T., Connell, M., Stofflett, R., & Peck, D. (1993). Reconstructing elementary teacher candidates' understanding of mathematics and science content. *Teaching and Teacher Education, 9*(3), 229–241.

Stoddart, T., Pinal, A., Latzke, M., & Canaday, D. (2002). Integrating inquiry science and language development for English Language Learners. *Journal of Research in Science Teaching, 30*(8), 664–687.

Stofflett, R., & Stoddart, T. (1994). Teachers' ability to understand and use conceptual change teaching as a function of prior content learning experience. *Journal of Research in Science Teaching, 31*(1), 31–51.

Tharp, R. G. (1997). *From at-risk to excellence: Research, theory, and principles for practice*. Santa Cruz, CA: Center for Research on Education, Diversity & Excellence. Retrieved September 8, 2016 from www.crede.ucsc.edu/products/print/reports/rr1.html.

Tharp, R. G., & Gallimore, R. (1988). *Rousing minds to life: Teaching, learning, and schooling in social context*. New York, NY: Cambridge University Press.

Tharp, R. G., Estrada, P., Dalton, S. S., & Yamauchi, L.A. (2000). *Teaching transformed: Achieving excellence, fairness, inclusion and harmony*. Boulder, CO: Westview Press.

Thompson, J., Windschitl, M., & Braaten, M. (2013). Developing a theory of ambitious early-career teacher practice. *American Educational Research Journal, 50*(3), 574–615.

Trent, S. C., Kea, C. D., & Oh, K. (2008). Preparing preservice educators for cultural diversity: How far have we come? *Exceptional Children, 74*, 328–350.

U.S. Census Bureau. (2010). American Community Survey [2005-2009]. Retrieved September 8, 2016 from www.census.gov/programs-surveys/acs/.

Vygotsky, L. S. (1978). *Mind in society: The development of higher psychological processes* (M. Cole, V. John-Steiner, S. Scribner, & E. Souberman, Trans. and Eds.). Cambridge, MA: Harvard University Press.

Warren, B., & Rosebery, A. S. (1995). Equity in the future tense: Redefining relationships among teachers, students, and science in linguistic minority classroom. In W. G. Secada, E. Fennema, & L. B. Adajian (Eds.), *New directions for equity in mathematics education* (pp. 298–328). New York, NY: Cambridge University Press.

Wertsch, J.V. (1985). *Culture, communication, and cognition: Vygotskian perspectives*. New York, NY: Cambridge University Press.

Wertsch, J.V. (1991). A sociocultural approach to socially shared cognition. In L. B. Resnick, J. M. Levine, & S. D. Teasley (Eds.), *Perspectives on socially shared cognition* (pp. 85–100). Washington, DC: American Psychological Association.

Wilson, S. M., Floden, R. E., & Ferrini-Mundy, J. (2008). Teacher preparation research: An insider's view from the outside. *Journal of Teacher Education, 53*, 190–204.

Wong-Fillmore, L., & Snow, C. (2002). What teachers need to know about language. In C. A. Adger, C. E. Snow, & D. Christian (Eds.), *What teachers need to know about language* (pp. 7–54). McHenry, IL: Delta Systems; Washington, DC: Center for Applied Linguistics.

Zeichner, K. M. (2003). The adequacies and inadequacies of three current strategies to recruit, prepare, and retain the best teachers for all students. *Teachers College Record, 105*(3), 490–519.

Zeichner, K. M., & Tabachnick, B. R. (1981). Are the effects of university teacher education "washed out" by school experiences? *Journal of Teacher Education, 32*(2), 7–11.

9
CAPTURING PRE-SERVICE TEACHERS' ENACTMENT OF AMPLIFIED SCIENCE INSTRUCTION FOR ENGLISH LANGUAGE LEARNERS

Marco A. Bravo, Jorge L. Solís, & Eduardo Mosqueda

Introduction

In the ESTELL project we were interested in capturing pre-service teachers' enactment of instructional strategies that support English Language Learners (ELLs) in science. Thus, the observation protocol we developed needed to be sensitive enough to distinguish pre-service teachers' instructional approaches that could be attributed to "good teaching (e.g., modeling expected student practice; activating prior knowledge)," from instruction that was designed to specifically address the linguistic needs of ELLs. ELLs are also an extremely diverse group (Goldenberg, 2008) and adaptations to the science instructional plan that pre-service teachers develop must take this diversity into account. Diversity among ELLs includes levels of English proficiency, prior schooling experiences, and native language fluency among other factors (Bunch, Kibler, & Pimentel, 2012). Pre-service teachers in the ESTELL project were coached to take these and other ELL student characteristics into account when deciding which type of linguistic scaffold to enact (e.g., Native Language Support, Semantic Maps) and the intensity with which these scaffolds were implemented (e.g., amount of time spent, number of repetitions) in order to provide individualized ELL instruction. An additional factor considered at the onset of the research project was that certain scaffolds tend to be present at specific points during instruction (e.g., preview vocabulary, grouping configurations) and are not consistently present throughout a lesson.

The ESTELL project is organized around making the following pedagogical considerations available to science methods instructors, pre-service teachers, and the master teachers that supervise them:

- Facilitating Collaborative Inquiry
- Promoting Science Talk
- Literacy in Science

- Scaffolding and Development of Language in Science
- Contextualizing Science Activity
- Promoting Scientific/Complex Thinking

Teacher and students producing together (*Facilitating Collaborative Inquiry*) refers to activity where the teacher facilitates learning through purposeful interaction with students and facilitates student–student interaction. The expertise in science (*Authority*) is shared with students and students are encouraged to see their science activities as contributions to the scientific field. *Promoting Science Talk* refers to opportunities that the teacher structures during a science lesson where he/she can directly model academic discourse patterns and evaluate students' comprehension of the language needed to practice the nature of science. Teachers engage students in dialogue by initiating conversation, eliciting student discussions in ways germane to the scientific enterprise (e.g., evidence-based explanations). *Literacy in Science* looks to make the literacy involved in doing science more explicit. Teachers provide explicit instruction in the reading and writing tasks as well as the vocabulary of focus in science lessons. *Scaffolding and Development of Language in Science* addresses the additional considerations a teacher can take to make abstract science concepts more concrete for ELLs by providing visual representations, multimodal experiences, and modulating the teacher's talk. Connecting classroom activities and learning to students' home and/or community experiences is a critical process allowing for students to make sense of emerging and familiar knowledge (*Contextualizing Science Activity*). In this respect, contextualized science teaching refers to situating everyday, familiar knowledge, in the science learning goals of pre-service teachers' science lessons. *Promoting Scientific Thinking* refers to the practice of guiding elementary grade students' understanding of the inquiry process.

To capture pre-service teachers' implementation of the ESTELL pedagogies during science instruction, the research group developed the ESTELL Dialogic Activity in Science Instruction (EDAISI) instrument. The EDAISI includes both a quantitative (observation rubric) and qualitative (ethnographic notes) dimension to better account for the various instructional moves pre-service teachers can make to scaffold ELLs' science learning. A rubric with the various dimensions of the ESTELL pedagogies was developed and scaled to represent different levels of implementation. Ethnographic observations and notes during science instruction also allowed the research team to gather evidence focused on the quality of the enacted linguistic scaffolds. In this chapter, we describe the development and process undertaken to refine the EDAISI instrument, provide results collected via the EDAISI, and discuss limitations of the observation scheme.

The EDAISI Observation Instrument

In the following section we present the developmental trajectory of the EDAISI, provide a description of the rubrics that capture the ESTELL practices, and describe the psychometric qualities of the instrument as well as the qualitative dimensions of the EDAISI. These elements detail the process that resulted in the current iteration of the EDAISI.

EDAISI Development

In the development of the EDAISI observation instrument, we drew primarily from previous work on the integration of language and literacy in science instruction for diverse classrooms, including work by the Science Instruction For All (SIFA) and the Integrating Science and Diversity Education (ISDE) projects funded by the National Science Foundation and the Institute of Education Sciences. The SIFA research team developed the Classroom Observation Protocol (COP) which was used to capture how elementary classroom teachers in mainstream and bilingual classrooms used language and culture to teach science literacy (Ku, Bravo, & García, 2004; Reyes, 2009; Solís, 2005). The COP observation instrument included 17 sub-domains related to the following four major areas: science and mathematics teaching, linguistic scaffolding, cultural responsiveness, and literacy scaffolding. Examples of the COP instrument sub-domains are scientific understanding, scientific discourse, locus of authority, modification of curriculum, use and respect of the home language for instruction, teachers' response to student contributions, support of expository writing, and use of multiple codes/code-switching.

The ISDE project focused specifically on science and combined aspects of the COP instrument (Solís, 2005) and the Center for Research on Education, Diversity, and Excellence (CREDE) Five Standards of Effective Pedagogy (CFSEP) (Doherty, Hilberg, Epaloose, & Tharp, 2002) to emphasize on overlapping elements between the constructs in these instruments and inquiry-based science instruction. For example, a focus on the nature of tasks done by scientists working together was seen as an overlapping focus of the CFSEP that promoted group work, specifically group work with shared authority between teacher and students. Similar "sweet spots" were noted with attention to language and literacy and the ways in which scientists enact literacy and language practices (Cervetti, Pearson, Barber, Hiebert, & Bravo, 2007). The EDAISI domains expand on constructs in the ISDE project and modify them to further refine the manner in which the CFSEP practices might materialize in the context of inquiry-based science. The ISDE project represented two newly expanded terrains in the application of CFSEP – an emphasis on science and diversity education in teacher preparation (Bravo, Mosqueda, Solís, & Stoddart, 2014) – from which we worked to develop the EDAISI framework (ESTELL Dialogic Activity In Science Instruction).

The ESTELL instructional practices are informed by the existing body of research on the CFSEP that was further developed by the ESTELL research group to address varied (i.e., rural/urban, bilingual/monolingual, etc.) science teacher education preparation contexts; close attention was given to situating sociocultural tenets of teaching and learning in the context of science education. We utilized prior research efforts with SIFA and ISDE to assist with the translation of the CFSEP to what materialized into the ESTELL instructional practices.

EDAISI Subscale Dimensions

The rubric for ESTELL practices reflected the various levels of implementation ranging from a novice practitioner to a more expert one. These levels of implementation spanned from "Not Present" (score of 0) to "Introducing" (score of 1), "Implementing" (score of 2), and "Elaborating" (score of 3). Each practice also had two dimensions that were further distinguished in the rubric. Each construct was scored from zero to three for 15-minute periods throughout the lessons delivered by elementary (Kindergarten to fifth grade) pre-service teachers across three teacher education university sites. Observers of elementary grade pre-service teachers received training on the observation scheme. Six observers (three graduate students, a post-doctoral researcher, and two faculty) attended a two-day training in the first year of the study. The training included an introduction to the EDAISI followed by practice sessions using the protocol and coding scheme. Inter-Rater Reliability (IRR) checks were conducted at various points in the training and divergences in coding and understanding of the scheme were addressed. We conducted four IRR checks – one before data collection began, one after the first observation was completed, and again before the final observation was complete. Video clips were distributed to observers who recorded notes and coded the instruction using the EDAISI rubrics. In the first session, we achieved an IRR of 82 percent. This same training was repeated in the second phase of the study. In the second session, the observation team achieved an IRR rate of 92 percent. Two additional IRR checks were conducted during the data collection period with an IRR rate of 88 percent. Below we provide a more thorough description of the EDAISI rubric dimensions used in this training and in the field.

Facilitating Collaborative Inquiry. The Facilitating Collaborative Inquiry practice depicts the degree of student group work that a pre-service teacher facilitates (Collaboration) and the level of shared expertise (Authority) the pre-service teacher promotes during science instruction. Table 9.1 describes the two dimensions of this ESTELL pedagogy along different levels of implementation.

The *Collaboration* domain examines the nature of interaction present in the classroom, especially the degree of student-to-student interaction and teacher-student interaction. *Authority* emphasizes how the teacher presents scientific understandings as those that are shared and challenged as well as student generated

TABLE 9.1 EDAISI Collaborative Inquiry Rubric

0 NOT PRESENT	1 INTRODUCING	2 IMPLEMENTING	3 ELABORATING
Collaborative Inquiry			
A. Teacher does not facilitate *collaborations* resulting in no opportunities for Student–Teacher or Student–Student interaction	A. Teacher facilitates collaboration resulting in minimal Student–Teacher or Student–Student interaction	A. Teacher facilitates collaboration resulting in substantial Student–Teacher or Student–Student interaction	A. Teacher facilitates collaboration resulting in substantial collaboration and assures all students are engaged, especially ELLs
Authority			
B. Teacher promotes an understanding of scientific *authority* as closed, not challenged, and not shared	B. Teacher promotes an understanding of scientific authority as minimally open and shared	B. Teacher promotes an understanding of scientific authority as open, shared (owned by Teacher and Students), yet not challenged	B. Teacher promotes an understanding of scientific authority as open, shared (owned by Teacher and Students), and challenged

(score of 3) versus scientific understandings that are primarily teacher and/or textbook driven.

Promoting Science Talk. This ESTELL instructional practice is comprised of two dimensions –Academic Science Discourse and Instructional Conversations. The former focuses on pre-service teachers' attention to the particular ways language is used in science, for example, making evidence-based explanations or forms of scientific argumentation. There is a particular focus here also on providing examples of how to use scientific discourse by using, modeling, and supporting this practice with students. The lower and higher levels of implementation for this practice distinguish between implicit and explicit support by teachers. This practice ranges from *Not Present*, to pre-service teacher *Introducing* science discourse through implicit use of science discourse, to *Implementing* science discourse in a way that models for students what is expected of them, to *Elaborating* for students by providing positive corrective feedback to ELLs' use of this discourse. Table 9.2 presents the rubric for the Promoting Science Talk ESTELL pedagogy.

The second dimension, *Instructional Conversations*, focuses on the type of questions posed and the follow-up to student contributions that pre-service teachers provide during science conversations. The use of dialogic practices like varied question types and follow-up are seen as opportunities to increase student

TABLE 9.2 EDAISI Science Talk Rubric

0 NOT PRESENT	1 INTRODUCING	2 IMPLEMENTING	3 ELABORATING
Academic Science Discourse			
A. Teacher does not use or draw attention to science discourse patterns (e.g., ways of providing evidence, making explanations, expressing judgments)	A. Teacher uses but does not explain science discourse patterns (e.g., ways of providing evidence, making explanations, expressing judgments)	A. Teacher explicitly models but does not give feedback on student use of science discourse patterns (e.g., ways of providing evidence, making explanations, expressing judgments)	A. Teacher explicitly models, guides, and provides feedback on student use of discourse (e.g., ways of providing evidence, making explanations, expressing judgments)
Instructional Conversations			
A. Teacher does not use questions to involve students in science activity	A. Teacher uses *closed* questions (yes/no, known-information, pre-specified)	A. Teacher uses *some open-ended questions* (indefinite, investigatory, and legitimate) to generate student talk on science topics	A. Teacher uses *mostly open-ended questions* (indefinite, investigatory, and legitimate) to generate student talk about science topics.
B. Teacher does not follow up on students' responses	B. Teacher provides few instances of *follow-up* of students' science talk	B. Teacher follows up on student science talk by revoicing and connecting student talk to talk of others	B. Teacher *and* students follow up on science talk by revoicing and connecting science talk to talk of others

science talk in small groups, pairs, and large-group formats. At the low end of the rubric (*Not Present*), the teacher provides no questions and does not follow up on the contributions students make. At the *Introducing* stage, the pre-service teacher uses mostly closed questions (i.e., yes/no; known answer questions) and follow-up to student contributions is done in a manner that is momentary and lacking deep connections to science learning. When pre-service teachers are *Implementing* instructional conversations, they use mostly open-ended questions that allow for elaborated student talk on science topics. The follow-up pre-service teachers provide connects the talk of various students. When *Elaborating* is implemented, the pre-service teacher uses mostly open-ended and investigatory questions that allow students to voice their scientific understandings. The follow-up teachers provide to student contributions *revoices* student talk in the discourse of science.

Literacy in Science. The Authentic Science Literacy and Science Vocabulary dimensions comprise the third ESTELL rubric. Authentic science literacy refers to the use of science-driven literacy functions and support within science activities, as opposed to disjointed literacy connections to science learning or the lack of attention to reading and writing tasks altogether. At the *Not Present* end of the rubric, authentic science literacy documents the lack of attention given to literacy tasks for doing science as well as those examples where reading or writing of any kind do not occur during a science lesson. *Introducing* levels of this construct involves the expectation of reading and writing tasks during science activities but science reading and writing that is not part of the scientific enterprise (e.g., writing poems about science phenomenon, reading narrative books about science phenomenon). *Implementing* and *Elaborating* involves explicit instruction about the reading and writing that scientists do. Pre-service teachers' attention to reading and writing tasks here are germane to science (e.g., writing science reports, reading tables and images). Elaborating also involves modeling expected literacy tasks for students while also providing opportunities for feedback to students in the use of science literacy tasks. Table 9.3 presents the rubric for the Literacy in Science ESTELL pedagogy.

Science Vocabulary, the second dimension of this rubric, attends to two types of science-related vocabulary – process inquiry words (e.g., observe, predict) and focal science concepts (e.g., erosion, adaptation) and the quality of instructional attention they receive. At *Not Present*, the science vocabulary of the lesson is not identified or addressed. At an *Introducing* level, the pre-service teacher provides limited instruction on key terms that may simply offer the definition of focal science concepts. For an *Implementing* score, the pre-service teacher provides instructional attention in a form that involves more elaboration than providing definitions (e.g., word maps, cognates) by providing multiple exposures and uses for key science terms. The *Elaborating* stage includes the *Implementing* requirements, but the pre-service teacher also checks for student accuracy and understanding in using these terms in their talk and writing.

Scaffolding and Development of Language in Science. The dimensions of this rubric include *Language Scaffolding* and *Content Scaffolding*. At one end of the rubric, *Language Scaffolding* is not attended to (*Not Present*) with regard to language

TABLE 9.3 EDAISI Literacy in Science Rubric

0 NOT PRESENT	1 INTRODUCING	2 IMPLEMENTING	3 ELABORATING
Authentic Science Literacy			
A. Teacher does not provide students with opportunities to use authentic literacy task	A. Teacher provides students with few opportunities to use authentic literacy task and does so without instructional attention to these literacy tasks (literacy tasks may supplant inquiry science – just reading science, writing definitions)	A. Teacher provides students with opportunities to use authentic literacy task and provides instruction on their use in science (e.g., reading the work of other scientists, writing scientific observations)	A. Teacher provides students with opportunities to use authentic literacy task and provides instruction on their use in science (e.g., reading the work of other scientists, writing scientific observations) as well as provides feedback on student use of literacy practices
Science Vocabulary			
A. Teacher does not use key science terms (e.g., erosion, adaptation) and if used, their use is inaccurate	A. Teacher accurately uses *1–4* key science terms (e.g., erosion, adaptation) and inquiry terms (e.g., observe, predict, model)	A. Teacher accurately uses *5–7* different key science terms (e.g, erosion, adaptation) and inquiry terms (e.g., observe, predict, model)	A. Teacher accurately uses *8+* different science terms and inquiry terms (e.g., observe, predict, model) and key science terms (e.g, erosion, adaptation)
B. Teacher provides no instruction on science terms	B. Teacher provides limited instruction on science and inquiry terms (oral definitions, pronunciation)	B. Teacher provides instructional activity on key terms that is not just momentary but may be written and discussed (e.g., student glossary, vocabulary word list)	B. Teacher provides substantive instructional attention to key terms (e.g., student glossary, written on word wall, connected to what students already know), checks for student accuracy in use of terms, and promotes students' use of key words in writing or talk

structures found in science instruction (e.g., metaphors, dual meaning words, nominalizations) and absence of pre-service teacher modification of their talk (e.g., appropriate wait time for student response, allowances for native language use, use of intonation to bring emphasis to concepts). At the *Introducing* level, the pre-service teacher is minimally attending to language structures that could impede ELLs' comprehension of or participation in science tasks. *Implementing* levels of this practice include explicit instruction about these language structures during science teaching as well as substantive modified teacher talk. At the *Elaborating* stage, the pre-service teacher provides explicit instruction on language structures common in science, but does so with consideration to ELLs' English language proficiency abilities. Table 9.4 presents the rubric for the *Scaffolding and Development of Language in Science* ESTELL pedagogy.

TABLE 9.4 EDAISI Scaffolding and Development of Language in Science Rubric

0 NOT PRESENT	1 INTRODUCING	2 IMPLEMENTING	3 ELABORATING
Language Scaffolding			
A. Teacher does not provide attention to language structures (e.g., figurative language, idioms, dual meaning words, nominalizations)	A. Teacher provides implicit attention to language structures (e.g., figurative language, idioms, dual meaning words, nominalizations) but not connected to science learning goals	A. Teacher provides explicit attention to language structures (e.g., figurative language, idioms, dual meaning words, nominalizations) but not connected to science learning goals	A. Teacher provides explicit attention to language structures (e.g., figurative language, idioms, dual meaning words, nominalizations) but not connected to science learning goals with opportunities for students to practice and provision of feedback
B. Teacher does not modify his/her talk (e.g., repetition, wait time, proper enunciation, rate of talk, native language use)	B. Teacher minimally modifies his/her talk (e.g., repetition, wait time, proper enunciation, rate of talk, native language use)	B. Teacher appropriately modifies his/her talk (e.g., repetition, wait time, proper enunciation, rate of talk, native language use)	B. Teacher appropriately modifies his/her talk (e.g., repetition, wait time, proper enunciation, rate of talk, native language use) considering the language proficiency of ELLs

0 NOT PRESENT	1 INTRODUCING	2 IMPLEMENTING	3 ELABORATING
Content Scaffolding			
A. Teacher does not use multisensory (gestures, manipulatives, hands-on, kinesthetic) or visual representations (word wall, semantic map, graphic organizers, charts) to amplify science content	A. Teacher uses either multisensory (gestures, manipulatives, hands-on, kinesthetic) or visual representations (word wall, semantic map, graphic organizers, charts) to amplify science content	A. Teacher uses multisensory (gestures, manipulatives, hands-on, kinesthetic) and visual representations (word wall, semantic map, graphic organizers, charts) to amplify science content	A. Teacher uses multisensory (gestures, manipulatives, hands-on, kinesthetic) and visual representations (word wall, semantic map, graphic organizers, charts) to amplify science content with considerations for ELLs' language proficiency level

The *Scaffolding Content* dimension addresses the multisensory (e.g., gestures, manipulatives, kinesthetic) and visual (e.g., graphic organizer, Venn diagram, charts) representations that pre-service teachers are encouraged to use with the intent of amplifying science concepts for ELLs. As would be expected, at the level *Not Present*, pre-service teachers do not implement either type of strategy. At the *Introducing* stage, pre-service teachers utilize either multisensory experiences *or* visual representations in their science lesson. At the *Implementing* level, pre-service teachers use both types of support. At the *Elaborating* stage, pre-service teachers take into account ELLs' English language proficiency in identifying the appropriate choice of scaffolding.

Contextualizing Science Activity. With this ESTELL practice, we look to gather information regarding how pre-service teachers are connecting science instruction to ELLs' prior experiences at home, in the community, and in the natural world, which includes two dimensions: *Personal/Home/Community* experiences and *Physical Environment and Local Ecology* experiences. The scale of the *Personal/Home/Community Experiences* construct is anchored at one end of the rubric with an absence of pre-service teachers' elicitation from or providing examples to ELLs of the ways in which science relates to prior experiences (e.g., observations of plant life); home knowledge regarding science phenomenon (e.g., medicinal aspects of plant life); or community experiences with science learning goals (e.g., knowledge from communal gardens). At an *Introducing* level, pre-service teachers mostly provide these connections to ELLs and these examples may not be completely visible for ELLs or the teacher may acknowledge ELLs contributions but doesn't incorporate them into the science activity; teachers may believe certain sociocultural experiences resonate with students, but in fact are still limited to teacher-driven examples at this level. The *Implementing* stage is differentiated from previous stages in that pre-service teachers mostly elicit these examples from ELLs and connects these student examples to the science learning goals; student examples are produced but mostly ad hoc in the unfolding of the lesson. At an *Elaborating* stage, pre-service teachers design science lessons to explicitly elicit examples from ELLs and ensure that these examples are connected to the science learning goals. Table 9.5 presents the rubric for the *Contextualizing Science Activity* ESTELL pedagogy.

The *Physical Environment and Local Ecology* dimension follows similar contextualizing moves by the teachers as those used in the *Personal/Home/Community* dimension. The distinction here is that instead of a focus on personal, home, and

TABLE 9.5 EDAISI Contextualizing Science Activity Rubric

0 NOT PRESENT	1 INTRODUCING	2 IMPLEMENTING	3 ELABORATING
Personal/Home/Community			
A. Teacher does not provide or elicit student science examples from home, community, or other sociocultural experiences	A. Teacher mostly provides student science examples from home, community, or other sociocultural experiences	A. Teacher mostly elicits student science examples from home, community, or other sociocultural experiences and incorporates these understandings into the science lesson	A. Teacher designs science lessons that build on and include home, community, or other sociocultural experiences of science learning goals that incorporate these understandings into the science lesson
Physical Environment and Local Ecology			
A. Teacher does not provide or elicit student science examples from local, physical, geographic, or ecological environment	A. Teacher mostly provides student science examples from local, physical, geographic, or ecological environment	A. Teacher mostly elicits student science examples from local, physical, geographic, or ecological environment	A. Teacher designs science lessons that build on and include students' local, physical, geographic, or ecological science understandings

community examples, this dimension addresses how pre-service teachers connect science learning goals with ELLs' experiences in their local environment and in the natural world around them (e.g., summer fog in the Bay Area, ubiquity of giant redwood trees, migration patterns of monarch butterflies, agricultural fields, etc.). The *Not Present* point on the rubric notes the absence of explanations regarding how science is present in and around the students' local ecology and physical environment. At an *Introducing* level, pre-service teachers provide explanations and connections that make science-related phenomena visible in the local ecology to ELLs, yet these examples may not be completely visible for ELLs or the teacher acknowledges ELLs' contributions but does not make them central to the science activity. At an *Implementing* phase on the rubric, the pre-service teacher elicits these examples from ELLs and connects these student examples to the science learning goals. At an *Elaborating* stage, pre-service teachers design science lessons to explicitly elicit examples from ELLs and ensure that these examples are connected to the science learning goals. In one lesson, a pre-service teacher had students observe a patch of grass near their home and sketch and write changes happening to that space over the course of a month. This was done to illustrate the concept of *habitat*. Such planned instruction regarding the local ecology garnered an *Elaborating* score on the rubric.

Promoting Scientific Thinking. This domain encompasses two dimensions: *Scientific Understanding* and *Developing Inquiry Skills*. At the *Not Present* stage of the first construct, pre-service teachers do not probe prior science knowledge or make evident the scientific process (inquiry cycle, scientific method). *Introducing* levels refer to probing prior knowledge or opportunities to understand how scientific processes are undertaken. At an *Implementing* level, the teacher elicits, models, and guides activation of ELLs' prior knowledge and understanding of the scientific process. At an *Elaborating* level, pre-service teachers make evident the scientific process by contrasting it to approaches taken in other subject areas and ensuring the activation of prior student knowledge that is closely related to the science learning goals. Table 9.6 presents the rubric for the *Promoting Scientific Thinking* ESTELL instructional practice.

The *Developing Inquiry Skills* domain accounts for pre-service teacher plans to help ELLs see how scientists study the natural world around them and make explanations based on evidence from their work. At a *Not Present* level, the pre-service teacher does not spend instructional time explaining the skills of scientific inquiry or the scientific method. At an *Introducing* level, pre-service teachers involve ELLs in the inquiry process but do not explain this process explicitly as part of the scientific method or processes for asking questions and answering them. The *Implementing* stage references pre-service teacher explanation and feedback of ELLs' understanding of the inquiry process. At a more evolved level of this construct, pre-service teachers facilitate student-led inquiry processes.

TABLE 9.6 EDAISI Promoting Scientific Thinking Rubric

0 NOT PRESENT	1 INTRODUCING	2 IMPLEMENTING	3 ELABORATING
Scientific Understanding			
A. Teacher does not provide or elicit students' prior science understandings	A. Teacher provides prior school-based science understandings	A. Teacher elicits prior school-based science understandings and makes connections with science learning goals of current lesson	A. Teacher elicits prior school-based science understandings and makes connections with science learning goals of current lesson with substantial opportunity for student reflection on connections
Developing Inquiry Skills			
A. Teacher does not provide instruction on scientific inquiry process or scientific method	A. Teacher leads scientific inquiry process or scientific method with little instructional attention to these processes	A. Teacher guides students through the scientific inquiry process or scientific method with instructional attention to these processes	A. Teacher guides students through the scientific inquiry process or scientific method with instructional attention to these processes and provides feedback on student use of these processes

Psychometric Properties

We tested the internal consistency of each domain of the EDAISI observation instrument using a classical test analysis approach to assess the quality and distinctiveness of each of the six EDAISI instructional practices. Our goal for the reliability of each dimension of the observation instrument was to reach a Cronbach's alpha greater than 0.70 (alpha > .70), which is generally considered to indicate acceptable reliability. The reliability results in Table 9.7 show a high degree of consistency among the EDAISI domains, all of which exceed acceptable levels of internal consistency. Table 9.7 shows the EDAISI reliability analysis of a subsample of observations from the larger data corpus.

Enactment of Amplified Science Instruction **169**

TABLE 9.7 EDAISI Reliability Analysis

	Number of Observations (n = 115)	Cronbach's Alpha
Collaborative Inquiry	112	0.782
Promoting Science Talk	110	0.771
Contextualizing Science Activity	113	0.729
Literacy in Science	115	0.791
Scaffolding and Development of Language in Science	113	0.804
Promoting Scientific Thinking	110	0.832

Qualitative Dimensions

The qualitative dimension of the EDAISI included *Ethnographic Fieldnotes* and *Post-observation Debrief* portions of the instrument. The inclusion of these qualitative elements addressed multiple methodological purposes, such as providing supporting evidence for the EDAISI scores and addressing extra-contextual information contributing to scores. Moreover, qualitative data that was compiled along with each observation as observational data sets were useful for multiple research purposes, including the development and refinement of related research instruments and tools (i.e., classroom demographic surveys, teacher surveys, scoring forms).

Ethnographic Fieldnotes. The classroom observation fieldnotes were referred to as written classroom observational records (Bogdan & Biklen, 2003; Mackey & Gass, 2012). Observers described the general lesson activities, time stamping each separate activity or every 15 minutes, teacher and students' roles during the lesson, and major tasks and procedures. In addition and if applicable, special notes, much like analytic memos (Saldaña, 2012), were made of specific or closely related ESTELL practices driving lesson segments. A fieldnote template graphic organizer was used by observers to complete fieldnotes. Observers were asked to write running notes describing teacher/student actions, teacher/student talk, grouping structures, and other relevant aspects of the classroom segmented by 15-minute increments. For example, we documented the environmental print in the classroom. In Figure 9.1 we provide a sample fieldnote collected during an observation of a fourth-grade Space Science lesson. This particular example exemplifies our attempt to capture the classroom ethos.

To create a complete picture of the context in which the ESTELL practices were implemented, observers used fieldnotes like the fieldnote example in Figure 9.1

DESCRIBE THE PHYSICAL ENVIRONMENT OF THE CLASSROOM (ROOM SIZE, CONFIGURATION AND "FEEL"; WHAT'S ON THE WALLS; PLACEMENT OF TABLES AND DESKS; AVAILABILITY OF BOOKS):
Classroom has whiteboard with Math terms. on opposite wall Key concepts wall and Science Guiding questions as well as images of the planets & moons as well as chart of Language of Argumentation, Guidelines for partner Reading and Scientific Discussion Guidelines. Students are in 4 groups with six students per group there are 2 computers in the class and a moveable chart paper cart. There are books in different baskets in the back of the room and to one side of the room.

FIGURE 9.1 Examples of EDAISI observational fieldnotes.

to contextualize science lessons. Observers also partially coded fieldnotes with observer comments related to relevant ESTELL practices and focal vocabulary on separate fieldnote columns.

Post-observation Debriefs. Each EDAISI observation was followed by an audio-recorded debrief conversation between the pre-service teacher and the researcher. The post-observation debrief elicited supplemental contextual information from pre-service teachers about classroom practices and background on target lessons, such as grouping norms, previous exposure of lesson topics and content, and how well the lesson addressed planned activities. Specific questions also focused on teachers' views about their role throughout the lesson, about their notion of inquiry as represented in the lesson delivered, and their command of science content covered in the lesson.

The following are sample questions from the post-observation debrief that were elicited following each observation:

- Have you taught other related lessons to your students? Yes/No. If yes, which ones?
- Did you group your students during the lesson? Yes/No. If yes, how and why?
- Did your role change during the lesson? Yes/No. If yes, how and why?
- How would you rate your content knowledge on this topic?
- Do you feel you had enough time to complete the lesson? Yes/No. If no, why not?
- Were there any unforeseen or unexpected occurrences in teaching this lesson?

Post-observation debriefs were transcribed with each recording lasting approximately 10–20 minutes. These debriefs usually occurred on school grounds in nearby classrooms or resource rooms immediately following an observation where pre-service teachers could speak candidly about their student-teaching experience while the target lesson was still fresh in their minds.

In the following section we present information about a sample of pre-service teachers involved in the research study and results that illustrate the ability of the ESTELL practices to distinguish both presence and level of integration of the ESTELL practices across two groups of pre-service teachers.

Demographics. We conducted this work across the teacher education programs at three universities. Each of the three teacher preparation programs offered both a general and bilingual credential. Across the programs, over half of the participating pre-service teachers were white (51 percent), Latino pre-service teachers comprised 32 percent of the sample, 5 percent were Asian, and 4 percent were multiracial (8 percent did not report). In addition, over 77 percent of the participants' ages ranged between 20 to 30 years of age. The gender makeup of the sample was 81 percent female and 19 percent male. Notably, only two participants majored in a science related field, while the majority (81 percent) majored in Education, Humanities, Liberal Studies, and Social Science.

We compared changes in pre-service teachers' science instruction that addressed the needs of ELLs across two conditions. One group of pre-service teachers in each of the three programs received support in integrating science, language, literacy, and culture using our intervention; the other did not. Within each program, pre-service teachers were assigned to either of the two conditions. The business as usual or non-intervention condition initiated their involvement in the study before modifications were made to the teacher education program. All teacher candidates in the intervention and non-intervention conditions were enrolled in a target science methods course and were invited to participate in the study.

Results

The quantitative dimensions of the EDAISI tool proved to be sensitive enough to distinguish between different levels of implementation and provided needed information about the efficacy of the intervention. The ESTELL intervention group scored higher on all six domains of the ESTELL pedagogy relative to the control group. There was a statistically significant difference between the ESTELL and control group on two instructional practices: Contextualizing Science Activity and Promoting Science Talk. These results suggest that the ESTELL intervention pre-service teachers were able to make more connections between students' home/community/personal and ecological experiences (Contextualizing Science Activity) and were more successful at integrating academic language or science talk into science instructional activities (Promoting Science Talk). Table 9.8 reports the scores on all six categories.

Although two of the ESTELL practices were higher and statistically significant relative to the control group (at a $p < 0.05$ level), it is worth noting that the Language Scaffolding scores for the intervention participants were higher as well, but only statistically significant at a $p < 0.10$ level.

Exemplifying EDAISI Scores

Qualitative data analysis was needed to describe classroom contexts in which the ESTELL practices were implemented and to dig deeper into how certain

TABLE 9.8 EDAISI Results (n = 228)

EDAISI Subscale	Condition	Mean	Standard Deviation	One-Way ANOVA
Collaborative Inquiry	ESTELL	1.622	0.412	
	Control	1.535	0.408	
Science Talk	ESTELL	1.515★	0.421	$F(1,227) = 3.45, p < .05$
	Control	1.380	0.472	
Literacy in Science	ESTELL	1.320	0.437	
	Control	1.207	0.444	
Scaffolding Language	ESTELL	1.387~	0.434	$F(1,227) = 3.45, p = .067$
	Control	1.260	0.435	
Contextualizing	ESTELL	0.945★★★	0.556	$F(1,227) = 3.45, p < .001$
	Control	0.572	0.477	
Scientific Thinking	ESTELL	1.321	0.482	
	Control	1.192	0.539	

Note: ★ = significant for $p < .05$; ★★★ = significant for $p < .001$

teacher moves mediate varied levels of implementation of the intervention. The qualitative data, including observational fieldnotes, teacher debriefs, and transcriptions of naturally occurring classroom interaction, provided us with vital contextual information for understanding and further triangulating the quantitative EDAISI scores. To exemplify the qualitative elements of the instrument, below we offer results of two pre-service teachers during an observation of their science teaching and the ethnographic elements that allowed us to see the nuances of ELL strategies implemented.

Maria. In Maria's fourth-grade student teaching placement classroom, she has three languages represented and ELLs at various levels of English proficiency. Science is taught sporadically and often out of a book where students read a passage about science phenomenon and then answer questions at the end of the chapter. Maria prepared her first science lesson to involve more student investigation and inquiry science. In the lesson she prepared regarding the phases of the Moon, her learning goal was for her students to know the reasons for the movement of Earth's moon. Maria offered effective forms of support for *Literacy in Science* and *Scaffolding and Development of Language in Science*.

In this initial observation, Maria's scores for the *Literacy in Science* construct were 3 for *Science Vocabulary* and 2 for *Authentic Science Literacy*. In a debrief session with Maria, she stated that her Spanish-speaking ELLs at lower levels of English proficiency required some native language support due to the number of new words introduced, hence the reason she called out the words that were Spanish-English cognates in the lesson. She wrote on the board both inquiry words (e.g., model/modelo, explore/explorar) and key science concepts (e.g., lunar/luna, space/espacio) and told students "use your Spanish to figure out some of the English words, what word in Spanish is similar to explore?" (Fieldnote, 5/6/10). Maria had students create a glossary of these words and added these sheets to students' Science Notebooks. Such attention to the science words needed to complete the model of the phases of the Moon she prepared was critical for the full participation of ELLs. There is an abundance of Spanish-English cognates in science terms but most significantly for ELLs, many of these cognates are high frequency words in Spanish and low frequency words in English, providing Spanish speakers with a built-in advantage in comprehension (Bravo, 2011).

In the lesson, Maria created a model of the phases of the Moon using a lamp in the center of the classroom to represent the Sun. After shutting out the light from her classroom, she used styrofoam balls to serve as models of the Moon so that students could see that the phases are caused by the Moon's changing position relative to the Sun as the Moon orbits the Earth. In this lesson, Maria had students collect data (images of the shadows on the styrofoam balls and location) in their Science Notebooks. They wrote explanations about why the phases of the Moon occur. We collected the notebook pages of students as part of our observation scheme and noted no feedback on students' science explanations. While this literacy event was authentic to the science discipline, without a model of the expected outcome or feedback on students' written explanations (an *Elaborating* score), the score for this type of instruction was at an *Implementing* phase.

With respect to Scaffolding and Development of Language in Science, Maria received a score of 1 for *Language Scaffolding* and 2 for *Science Content Scaffolding*. The Language Scaffolding subdomain was scored at an *Introducing* phase due to the absence of attention to language structures that are often problematic for ELLs. In the fieldnotes (5/6/10), the observer noted missed opportunities to address "linguistic blindspots" that interfere with ELLs' science understanding. First was the presence of many words that had multiple meanings, such as *force, mission, space*, and *land*, that were used by the pre-service teacher without instructional attention or warning to students about their presence in the lesson. A second missed opportunity to address language structures in this lesson was addressing collocations such as *shut off, get around, figure out*, and *Moon phase*. Collocations are words that often appear in a certain sequence and have a unique meaning together that is different from the meaning of the separate words. ELLs tend to read these words independently and may not understand their nuanced meaning when the terms' meanings are considered together.

Maria received a score of 2 (*Implementing*) for *Science Content Scaffolding*, which revealed that she employed multisensory experiences for her ELLs with the intent of amplifying their science learning and utilized visual representations to make abstract concepts more concrete. In Maria's Moon Phases lesson, the modeling of the phases of the Moon involved a kinesthetic activity where students rotated and orbited around a light source that represented the Sun in order to simulate the different phases of the Moon. This hands-on task employed manipulatives and gesturing. Both of these strategies are present in the rubric at the *Implementing* phase. Fieldnotes captured Maria's use of intonation in her voice to draw attention to concepts of rotation and orbit. While this was not an element of the rubric, in the debrief session following the observation, Maria describes adjusting her speech to emphasize these key words and to also help her ELLs learn the pronunciation of these words so they could fully participate in the lesson. Maria also employed visual representations such as T-charts and tables to represent data that was collected by the students. Having a place to capture data in a manner that is visually accessible is helpful for ELLs as it allows them to see abstract concepts in more concrete ways and to recognize relationships between different parts of an activity.

Maria's scaffolds were well positioned to assist ELLs in gaining access to the science learning goals. In the post-lesson debrief, the observer asked Maria if she made a conscious effort to consider the language levels of her ELLs when planning and implementing the scaffolds in her lesson. She spoke about "reaching all ELLs" and "using scaffolds that will help all ELLs and all students." For Maria to reach an *Elaborating* stage (score of 3), she would have had to think about the level of implementation for the scaffolds and the variety of scaffolds to best fit the needs of ELLs at various levels of English proficiency. In this respect, post-observation debriefs are critical methodological tools that provide much needed background knowledge about student language proficiency and teacher moves.

Juan. Bilingual pre-service teachers were also observed as part of their participation in a bilingual teacher certification program. Juan's pedagogical development informs our understanding of what it means to support and train bicultural/bilingual teachers (Grosjean, 2015) and for that matter, all new teachers. Juan's bicultural/bilingual background does not inherently give him the knowledge or disposition to recognize contextualized teacher moves, much less the knowledge of how such moves can be used in the teaching of science to bilingual children. When it comes to teaching science, bilingual teachers often need to develop new orientations toward contextualizing science activity not unlike any other teacher candidate.

When asked about his interest in becoming a teacher, Juan reported an interest in becoming a teacher so that he could redress underrepresentation of Latino male teachers in elementary school. He also wished to help those students who struggle getting through the K–12 educational system and who are often "kids who people write off." He identified with these children, having graduated from a continuation school himself.

> There is still a lack of males within – especially in the elementary level. A lack of Chicano males, or Hispanic, or Latino. At the same time I've always wanted to help young students – I graduated from a continuation school, so I know what it's like to struggle. And um kind of go against adversity. So I just wanna help those kids who people write off. Or those kids who definitely need the help. (G., Interview #1)

Here Juan expresses a teaching for educational equity stance at the onset of his enrollment in the credential teacher education program by articulating a focus on providing all students a chance to gain greater access to quality education. Despite this orientation toward teaching, when asked about his understanding of what it means to be a good science student and how he thinks scientists do science, Juan relied on traditional conceptions of classroom learning to describe "a good science student," despite describing what scientists do in a very different way. He described "a good science student" as someone who is orderly, shows effort, does some talking in class, tries their best, stays on task, and follows class procedures. On the other hand, Juan described the work that scientists do as people who actively question, test, hypothesize, theorize, and "dig for facts" on a range of problems they want to understand. Based on participant interviews conducted at the onset and again at the end of Juan's matriculation in the teacher education program, we saw little change in how he conceptualized good science students and the work of scientists over the duration of his teacher education program. However, when it came to understanding how to contextualize science lessons, Juan shifted his understanding of using students' prior science knowledge. He initially described student science background as dependent on their home circumstances and potentially very limited or not present. However, at the end of the teacher education program, Juan expanded his perceptions of the sources of student science background knowledge and made this knowledge more likely to be leveraged by teachers. At the end of the program, Juan stated that students' science background knowledge can come from home, popular media, their peers, prior schooling, and even their experiences playing outside where they play in dirt and "tasted dirt."

Despite Juan's seemingly contradictory orientation between what it means to be a good science student and what it means to do science, his development of contextualizing science corresponds to his support of applying student-generated out-of-school connections to students' in-school science learning. The following excerpt (see Figure 9.2) is taken from one of Juan's pre-service observations teaching a life sciences lesson (taught in Spanish) to a third-grade bilingual class where students engage in discussions on animal structures and their functions for growth, survival, and reproduction. The lesson began by Juan asking his students "What is a vertebrate?" in Spanish. As the teacher sits with students huddled around a projector flashing different images of animals, the students engage in a discussion about warm-blooded and cold-blooded animals and animal reproduction differences. As Juan notes that reptile eggs are joined together by a gelatinous substance, he begins to associate this example with other possibly familiar substances like gelatin dessert and hair gel which is taken up unexpectedly by a student noting that the reptile eggs look like marshmallows (in Spanish).

This brief exchange between Teacher Juan and his third-grade students illustrates how Juan is beginning to draw on student connections to science activities by both offering what may be familiar examples to students (i.e., dessert gelatin, hair gel) and also by validating student contributions (i.e., "The white eggs look like marshmallows"). In accordance with the EDAISI rubric, Juan's implementation of *Contextualizing Science Activity* practices is emerging (Level 1 in the rubric), because while he acknowledges student contributions as relevant, he doesn't incorporate student contributions to extend their science understandings. This student contribution was a missed opportunity that could have led

Interaction	Comment
1. **Teacher:** *Los huevecillos están unidos por una sustancia gelatinosa.* (The eggs are joined by a gelatinous substance.)	Teacher observation
2. **Student:** *Guac* (Yuk)	
3. **Teacher:** *Como la gelatina. Pero no de la gelatina que nos comemos o que nos ponemos en el pelo es de otra gelatina natural que ellos usan para quedarse unidos.* (Like gelatin. But not the gelatin that we eat or that we put on our hair, its from another natural gelatin that they use to remain joined together.)	Teacher offers examples
4. **Student:** *¿Maestro?* (Teacher)	
5. **Teacher:** *¿Si?* (Yes?)	
6. **Student:** *Los huevos blancos parecen bombones.* (The white eggs look like marshmallows.)	Student observation
7. **Teacher:** *Si, parecen bombones. Vamos a seguir. Los huevos del reptil son blandos. ¿Están duros?* (Yes they look like marshmallows. Let's continue. Reptile eggs are soft. Are they hard?)	Teacher accepts observation without expansion

FIGURE 9.2 Classroom observation of teacher Juan.

to additional discussions comparing and contrasting texture and color between reptile eggs and marshmallows. We clearly see here a recognition by a novice teacher of making connections to student experiences in reference to science activities (line 3) and again in partially validating a relevant student contribution (line 7).

Conclusion

The ESTELL multiyear study contributes to a body of sociocultural research on achievement and equity in education that aims to support the linguistic needs of a vulnerable population of students in academic courses – ELLs as they learn science content. Our approach views the teaching of science as teaching the language of science that must be used to address the teaching and learning of complex content, while simultaneously drawing attention to students' local cultural context to help facilitate access to such content. The ESTELL project tested the effectiveness of a model that integrated language, literacy, culture, and science to facilitate students' science understandings and English language development.

In order to understand and address the complexity of teaching integrating language and literacy in science, we developed an observation tool to disentangle different aspects and degrees of implementation of the ESTELL strategies. The EDAISI helped us capture whether the ESTELL practices that pre-service teachers were introduced to in their science methods course were utilized as they planned and delivered science instruction in classrooms where ELLs were present. The subscales on the rubrics provided further detail as to the level of implementation of these practices. Yet, without the fieldnotes and observation debrief, we would not have been able to document the adaptations to a lesson or the nuances of considerations that pre-service teachers employed in their delivery of the science lessons. The ethnographic observations allowed us to tease apart scaffolds pre-service teachers were implementing from what some would consider simply "good teaching" in tasks that were deliberately structured to support the ELLs in the classroom. These teacher moves included attention to ELLs' native language (e.g., bilingual glossaries, cognate list) and the presence of "linguistic blindspots" that would be particularly problematic for ELLs (e.g., collocations, dual meaning words).

While successful in capturing some of the nuanced ways that pre-service teachers scaffold the science learning of ELLs, EDAISI and ESTELL have limitations that must be considered. First, the training of the observers is time intensive. Learning to understand and to capture the various dimensions of this tool all at once is challenging. We found it easier to understand the different domains by focusing on one or two at a time. A second limitation is the scoring guide, which captures implementation of the ESTELL practices every 15 minutes. Some of the practices seemed more appropriate to implement at specific points in a lesson and less so in others (e.g., previewing science vocabulary, probing prior home/school/community knowledge at onset). While our expectations were not that all ESTELL practices be instantiated in every lesson, we did have a goal that all lessons should attempt to integrate one or two of the practices. The ESTELL instructional practices represent a group of practices that are potentially useful in every science lesson to more successfully support ELLs, yet each ESTELL instructional practice is activated and used differently based on classroom schedules, the development of scientific ideas, the unfolding of inquiry activities, and student backgrounds. A third limitation of this instrument is the absence of considerations of vocal affect or how teachers modulate their speech (e.g., use intonation, exaggerated pronunciation) to scaffold language and content learning. Simultaneously learning a second language and learning science content can be an anxiety-ridden experience for ELLs (e.g., lack of science background language, low levels of English proficiency). Thus, additional scaffolds of how to minimize anxiety (e.g., time on task, game-like structures for sharing findings) should also be considered as part of this approach to making science learning more accessible for ELLs.

The EDAISI approach offers a productive tool for supporting teacher development in the use of effective pedagogical practices in science for ELLs. Master teachers (teachers of record where the pre-service teachers conducted their practicum experience) noted that the EDAISI tool was helpful in guiding areas for reflection on the part of the pre-service teacher after science lesson delivery. This process offers an alternative approach from value-added models (VAM) for evaluation processes that are increasingly showing gaps in validity and reliability in assessing teacher practices and student learning (AERA, 2015). The EDAISI, in contrast to VAM approaches, offers a process that resembles formative assessment in how it can help guide science instruction with special considerations to the needs of ELLs and opportunities to reflect on and incorporate improvements to subsequent lessons.

References

AERA. (2015). AERA Statement on use of Value-Added Models (VAM) for the evaluation of educators and educator preparation programs. *Educational Researcher, 44*(8), 448–452.

Bogdan, R. C., & Biklen, S. K. (2003). *Qualitative research for education: An introduction to theories and methods.* Boston, MA: Pearson.

Bravo, M. (2011). Leveraging Spanish-speaking ELs' native language to access science. *AccELLerate!, 21,* 21–23.

Bravo, M. A., Mosqueda, E., Solís, J. L., & Stoddart, T. (2014). Integrating science and diversity education: A model of pre-service elementary teacher preparation. *Journal of Science Teacher Education 43,* 1–15.

Bunch, G. C., Kibler, A., & Pimentel, S. (2012). Realizing opportunities for English learners in the Common Core English Language Arts and Disciplinary Literacy Standards. *Paper presented at the Understanding Language Conference at Stanford University.* Stanford, CA.

Cervetti, G. N., Pearson, P. D., Barber, J., Hiebert, E. H., & Bravo, M. A. (2007). Integrating literacy and science: The research we have, the research we need. In M. Pressley,

A. K. Billman, K. Perry, K. Refitt, & J. Reynolds (Eds.), *Shaping literacy achievement* (pp. 157–174). New York, NY: Guilford.

Doherty, R. W., Hilberg, R. S., Epaloose, G., & Tharp, R. G. (2002). Standards performance continuum: Development and validation of a measure of effective pedagogy. *Journal of Educational Research, 96*, 78–89.

Goldenberg, C. (2008). Teaching English language learners: What the research does – and does not – say. *American Educator, 2*, 8–23.

Grosjean, F. (2015). Bicultural bilinguals. *International Journal of Bilingualism, 19*(5), 572–586.

Ku, Y. M., Bravo, M., & García, E. E. (2004). Science instruction for all. *NABE Journal of Research and Practice, 2*(1), 20–44.

Mackey, A., & Gass, S. (2012). *Research methods in second language acquisition: A practical guide*. New York, NY: Wiley-Blackwell.

Reyes, I. (2009). English language learners' discourse strategies in science instruction. *Bilingual Research Journal, 31*(1–2), 95–114.

Saldaña, J. (2012). *The coding manual for qualitative researchers* (No. 14). Thousand Oaks, CA: Sage.

Solís, J. L. (2005). Locating student classroom participation in science inquiry and literacy activities. In J. Cohen, K. McAlister, K. Rolstad, & J. MacSwan (Eds.), *ISB4: Proceedings of the 4th International Symposium on Bilingualism* (pp. 2143–2151). Somerville, MA: Cascadilla.

10
CAPITALIZING ON THE SYNERGISTIC POSSIBILITIES BETWEEN LANGUAGE, CULTURE, AND SCIENCE

Jorge L. Solís, Marco A. Bravo, & Eduardo Mosqueda

Introduction

Our efforts to provide pre-service teachers with approaches that integrate science, culture, and language materialized in the development of a restructured framework for teacher education programs (Stoddart, Solís, Tolbert, & Bravo, 2010). This work increased the coherence between what took place in pre-service teacher's practicum experiences and in the courses they enroll in as part of their teacher education program by tying together these experiences with a common set of pedagogies. The new framework explicitly and systematically articulated the Effective Science Teaching for English Language Learners (ESTELL) instructional practices in elementary science contexts and prepared teacher candidates to teach science to English Language Learners (ELLs[1]). This work involved redesigning the content and delivery of the science methods course that is a part of our teacher preparation programs. Two of the authors of this chapter took the lead in developing the observational protocol for observing the science methods courses and then conducted the observations in these courses along with other colleagues. The collaborative work on the science course framework involved science and language educators in restructuring the science methods course to focus on the "sweetspots" between these disciplines – where language and culture can be authentically addressed as part of authentic scientific practices (Buxton, 2006; Lee, Quinn, & Valdes, 2013; Lynch, 2001). This chapter explains the process undertaken by our research team to construct an intervention course for pre-service teachers where they learned research-based instructional approaches for leveraging cultural and linguistic knowledge in the service of ELLs' science learning (August, Branum-Martin, Cardenas-Hagan, & Francis, 2009; Goldenberg, 2013; Lee & Luykx, 2006; Lynch, 2001). We provide qualitative exemplars of how the ESTELL practices were integrated into teacher education science methods courses. Moreover, this chapter addresses the following research question as part of the larger ESTELL study: How do teacher education science methods faculty implement the ESTELL instructional practices in their ESTELL-infused courses?

We also describe the contributions and challenges shared by the four ESTELL project science methods instructors in implementing this new model of science education. State certification course standards, accountability assessments, and science educators' pedagogical orientations were all elements that required attention as we supported instructors in enacting the framework incorporating ESTELL practices for pre-service teachers. Observations of the science courses along with instructor reflections support the claim that science methods faculty successfully drew from the ESTELL science methods course framework to prepare pre-service teachers to teach science to ELLs. In our work with teacher educators, we drew on previous related analysis that showed the possibilities and limitations of promoting more inclusive science pedagogy with novice teachers (Bravo, Mosqueda, Solís, & Stoddart, 2014).

Finally, we present results that highlight the impact of the redesigned ESTELL intervention course on pre-service teachers' efficacy in teaching science with considerations for ELLs. A survey administered at the onset and end of the science methods course offers some insights as to how the pre-service teachers in the intervention felt about their instructional skills to teach science to ELLs. Pre-service teachers who did not experience the redesigned science methods course served as a comparison to the intervention group.

University Science Methods Courses: Planning the Model of Integration

The research team devoted to the redesign of the science methods course included experts in science education, culturally responsive pedagogy, and second language acquisition. Given that three universities were involved in teaching the redesigned course, we drew from science faculty across these campuses. Science faculty expertise included specializations in science education and assessment, bilingual education in elementary school, language and literacy development in science, and culturally responsive pedagogy. We also wanted to include research personnel who would be observing the pre-service teachers at their placement as they enacted the type of science instruction modeled for them in the science course. These observers were advanced doctoral students with science education background and a postdoctoral researcher with an educational linguistics background. This varied expertise from faculty and graduate researchers allowed us to find areas of natural convergence between the ESTELL practices and science education. Below we present the planning undertaken to identify areas of convergence and provide exemplars of such convergence included in the redesigned science methods course.

Areas of Convergence: ESTELL Course Activities and Scientific Practices

A science methods course matrix outlining ESTELL activities was constructed by science methods faculty to both target specific activities and materials across sites and to capture how ESTELL instructional practices for supporting ELLs were relevant to scientific practices. Three areas of convergence were identified: (1) *Nature of Science* and *Facilitating Collaborative Inquiry*; (2) *Inquiry Science* and *Contextualization/Scientific Thinking*; and (3) *Discourse of Science* and *Literacy in Science* and *Scaffolding and Development of Language in Science*. Faculty then co-constructed *anchor lessons* that were structured around the areas of convergence that would be implemented in the science methods course intervention. The following list provides a series of science topics and lessons in which the ESTELL practices were embedded:

- Schoolyard Investigation (Big Ideas: Inquiry, Ecological Diversity)
- Skulls Lesson (Big Ideas: Structure and Scale, Diversity)
- Moon Investigation (Big Ideas: Systems, Interrelationships)
- Electricity and Magnetism Lesson (Big Ideas: Energy, Transfer and Conservation)
- Arthropod Lesson (Big Ideas: Diversity, Systems and Interrelationship)

Each of these ESTELL anchor lessons integrated the three themes: (1) Nature of Science and Facilitating Collaborative Inquiry; (2) Inquiry Science and Contextualization/Scientific Thinking; and (3) Discourse of Science and Literacy in Science and Scaffolding and Development of Language in Science.

Linking Nature of Science and Facilitating Collaborative Inquiry

To help pre-service teachers present science as a process of discovery rather than as a collection of facts, the Moon investigation lesson was developed to include activities that would allow children (and pre-service teachers) to see how scientists do their work. Pre-service teachers were asked to keep a Moon notebook, making daily observations. By focusing lessons on science practices, our hope was that pre-service teachers would experience scientific habits of mind and in turn implement them as they guided science investigations in their classrooms. Two nature of science dispositions targeted in the Moon investigation lesson were "scientists work with other scientists" and "scientists investigate questions and problems." Both nature of science dispositions were integrated with the *Facilitating Collaborative Inquiry* ESTELL practice. *Facilitating Collaborative Inquiry* emphasizes collaboration among students and the teacher, but encourages greater interaction among students, allowing students to share their ideas with each other in order to articulate and sharpen their thinking. In the intervention course, pre-service teachers were asked to work in small teams to compare their Moon observations and share their results with the rest of the class. This notion of collaboration parallels the nature of science goal of having students understand that scientists do not sit in labs to work in isolation, but instead work collaboratively with other scientists.

The second subdomain of this ESTELL practice, *Authority*, similarly intersects with the practice of "scientists investigate questions and problems" rather than find answers about the science phenomenon under study in a science text. The ESTELL *Authority* subdomain focuses on how pre-service teachers present scientific knowledge as either one that is shared and challenged or as student-generated ideas. In the context of supporting ELLs in science, teacher candidates were encouraged to provide explicit attention to how participant structures for inquiry were organized and how ELLs' comprehension of science language and content was supported throughout a lesson. While this may appear as "just good teaching," support of ELLs in content areas like science requires particular attention to cultural and linguistic differences that may emerge (de Jong & Harper, 2005). This however does not mean that inquiry is eclipsed by teacher-directed scaffolding, but rather that ELLs receive support in accessing content and language where appropriate (e.g., demonstration and modeling of tasks, modification of speech, use of gestures and visuals).

As pre-service teacher candidates shared their observations of the Moon, others were encouraged to challenge and comment on how the phases of the Moon could be explained by the data that was collected by the groups. Such authentic considerations for the nature of science could help pre-service teachers move from initial understandings of the phases of the Moon to not only a stronger conceptual understanding of this phenomenon but also to promote teaching science as a process of discovery that takes place while working with others. Promoting authentic inquiry-driven science activities requires rethinking traditional didactic notions of teaching academic language to ELLs (Bruna, Vann, & Escudero, 2007; Bunch, Lotan, Valdés, & Cohen, 2005; Weinburgh, Silva, Smith, Gioulx, & Nettles, 2014). *Facilitating Collaborative Inquiry* directly addresses pedagogical considerations for ELLs by promoting varied and explicit grouping structures during inquiry activities including the use of differentiated instruction and support. Teachers are asked to plan for engaging students with different and varied language proficiencies and academic skills. Moreover, higher levels of implementation (the EDAISI instrument, as described in Chapter 9 of this volume) of the collaboration and authority promote student-driven activities that are not the norm for ELLs in the classroom (Solís, 2016). Most ELLs are not able to access science content because they often don't have opportunities to talk and write during science classroom lessons. *Facilitating Collaborative Inquiry* frames the uses of purposeful grouping structures, explicit communication of student tasks and roles in group work, and varied teaching structures as a means to both advance inquiry activities and ensure all students are involved in those activities. Collaborative grouping structures are critical spaces to provide appropriate science-driven language feedback to ELLs.

Inquiry Science and *Contextualization/Scientific Thinking integration.* The cycle of science inquiry involves probing what you already know, planning an investigation to answer a question, gathering and analyzing data regarding the question posed, reflecting on what was learned from the investigation, and proposing an explanation given the results attained and potentially posing new questions (Buxton, 2006; Chinn & Malhotra, 2002; Hapgood, Magnusson, & Palincsar, 2004). In the *Contextualization* ESTELL practice, pre-service teachers were asked to probe what students already know related to their personal/home/community as well as their local ecology in order to frame the initial science lesson inquiries. Contextualizing instruction is considered here as both a way to elicit relevant prior knowledge and also as a way to expand on previous academic and cultural knowledge that students bring to the classroom (Baquedano-López, Solís, & Kattan, 2005; Buxton, Salinas, Mahotiere, Lee, & Secada, 2013; Hammond, 2001; Tharp & Dalton, 2007). Similarly, the *Scientific Thinking* practice prompted pre-service teachers to assist K–5 students in thinking logically and critically and also asked pre-service teachers to consider alternate explanations that could change theirs and students' initial perspectives. Strategies for supporting students in developing their scientific thinking and explanations were modeled. This parallels the goals of inquiry-based science.

An example of the convergence between Inquiry Science and the ESTELL practice of *Contextualization* and *Scientific Thinking* was exemplified in the planning of the Arthropod lesson. Science methods faculty constructed an experience for pre-service teachers that would probe their prior knowledge from their homes and communities to list the various arthropods that can be found in the local ecology. All of the responses would be acknowledged, including prospective ecological roles of these organisms or pre-service teachers' feelings of uneasiness with particular organisms such as spiders. Teacher candidates would then move through an inquiry cycle by posing a question about local arthropods, investigating, observing and recording observations, making explanations based on evidence gathered, and finally posing a new question if necessary. Contextualization was addressed in the methods course by having methods course instructors both model ways of eliciting and integrating student knowledge and also implementing an anchor lesson, like the Arthropod lesson, where teacher moves could be highlighted.

Discourse of Science and *Literacy in Science/Scaffolding Development of Language in Science integration.* There are specialized ways in which language and literacy are integrated in the context of science. Such discourse practices include specialized ways of talking and writing about the natural world around us (Cervetti, Pearson, Barber, Hiebert, & Bravo, 2007; Lemke, 1990). The specialized language of science also has its own vocabulary (Bravo & Cervetti, 2008) and presents arguments in specific ways (Osborne & Patterson, 2011). Learning the classroom discourse of science is important for all students and especially ELLs who may have less access to disciplinary English language production and reception functions outside of the classroom (Lee, Quinn, & Valdés, 2013). Given this unique way of using language in science, the research team set out to bring instructional attention to the specialized ways in which reading/writing (e.g., reading informational texts, writing observations), talk (e.g., providing scientific explanations and arguments), and vocabulary (e.g., articulating inquiry terms and key concepts) take place in the context of science.

In the Skulls lesson, the methods instructors emphasized such science discourse practices in ways that helped pre-service teachers organize data from their investigations and observations in written form. The specific tasks included making inferences about the categorization of skulls as *herbivore, omnivore*, or *carnivore* based on observations of the structure of each skull and the size/type of teeth. The instructor applied scientific explanations strategies to communicate ideas and model for students that a scientific explanation seeks to answer a specific question. For example, how are teeth adapted for certain types of food? Instructors also emphasized the ways in which scientific explanations detail how something in the world works or why something happens, and must be supported by evidence. The evidence provided could be in the form of firsthand experiences, such as observation and investigations of the various skulls or from reading and carefully weighing the work of others who have conducted investigations about skulls. An exemplary scientific explanation ties the evidence together in a way that answers the question posed and provides reasons for the conclusions that are drawn based on an understanding of the related scientific principles. Pre-service teachers practiced using prompts that generated scientific explanations to scaffold how they would support scientific explanations with children in the classroom.

In this lesson, pre-service teachers are expected to write their explanation of why certain skulls would be categorized as an *herbivore, carnivore,* or *omnivore* and feedback on their work emphasizes the strength of their evidence and requests rewrites as necessary. Feedback should also address the choice of vocabulary used to construct their explanations. For example, if students use words such as *saw* or *felt*, the instructor would remind students that scientists use the term *observe* to capture the use of all of their senses to explain a concept or idea. ESTELL promoted the use of explicit attention to scientific discourse for speaking and writing. This precision with vocabulary was explained by the methods instructors as "the way scientists talk." Attention to other vocabulary would include terms such as *herbivore, omnivore, carnivore, paleontology, model*, and *inference*. Pre-service teachers were reminded that students acquire and employ these terms when they hear them and are expected to use them in their talk and writing.

In the intervention science methods courses, reading in science focused on reading and writing material germane to the science discipline – expository texts (e.g., procedural, descriptive, comparative). The goal was to draw attention to literacy models that are part and parcel of science. Literacy in science is often only implicitly addressed and can thus serve as a barrier to ELLs' full participation. The literacy practices of science were explicitly modeled for pre-service teachers and scaffolds for making these practices accessible to ELLs were presented. Scaffolded ESTELL anchor lessons illustrated authentic literacy and methods instructors provided opportunities for teacher candidates to reflect on how anchor lessons could be modified to engage students from different language abilities and academic backgrounds. The hope was that these science investigation experiences where instructors modeled ESTELL practices in university teacher education courses would provide the teacher candidates with tangible models for supporting ELLs in science by showing pre-service teachers multiple models that attend to language skills while learning the discourse of science.

Science Methods Course Implementation

In implementing the ESTELL-infused science methods course across multiple sites, several logistical and methodological challenges emerged as well as trends related to how the methods instructors were *taking up* the ESTELL practices in their respective courses. Instructors needed a certain degree of flexibility to adapt their traditional course while simultaneously adhering to ESTELL practices and site-specific responsibilities (e.g., signature assignments, time frame of course). All of the courses were observed using a modified version of the ESTELL Dialogic Activity in Science Instruction (EDAISI) (explained in Chapter 9, this volume). The results from the instructor observations revealed particular trends in the attention to the practices that methods instructors provided. Science teachers' epistemological beliefs provide insight into how teachers view the nature of learning and knowledge in the classroom (Hashweh, 1996; Luft & Roehrig, 2007). Such beliefs include views about the role of teachers and of students in the classroom, beliefs about how students acquire science concepts, and how mediating factors like language and culture influence science learning (Solís, Kattan, & Baquedano-López, 2009). In this respect, the implementation of ESTELL practices in the science methods course illustrates how each instructor expressed particular epistemological stances related to science teaching.

Course Implementation Logistics

Faculty collaborators teaching the ESTELL-infused science methods course committed to using ESTELL course activities, readings, and assignments incorporating ESTELL practices over the course of an academic term, which was most commonly done during a semester-long course. For a semester course, the class met once a week for approximately two hours and thirty minutes for a total of 15 weeks. For many teacher candidates, science was not a subject area that was taught regularly in the classrooms where they carried out their field experiences. Pre-service teachers in this circumstance had to wait until the following semester when they taught science and their Cooperating Teacher (CT) was more inclined to include science as part of the curriculum. The time lapse between when they experienced the redesigned science course and when they had an opportunity to enact a lesson with attention to ELLs was not optimum.

Another logistical variable dealt with in implementing the ESTELL pedagogy with fidelity across courses was the presence of *signature assignments* (common assignments completed across cohorts), state-required assessments, and course registration logistics. These variables took precedence over the redesigned course content. For instance, in one course, considerable time was spent on explanations of the signature assignment that needed to be completed, submitted, and passed in order to receive a passing grade for the course. Significant time was cut from the Skulls lesson, which in turn did not allow the pre-service teachers to have a full science inquiry experience.

Finally, we noted that science materials used in the lessons were not fully available across all sites. One instructor, for instance, had a personal collection of skulls that had been used over the years that was not available at the other science methods course sites. Similarly, instructors brought significant resources from other lessons to compensate in cases where some materials were not available. Overall, despite these challenges, we agreed that each science and ESTELL convergence received adequate attention as reflected in pre-service teachers' demonstrated efficacy within the intervention course as compared to the control group (described further in Chapter 9, this volume).

Methodological Variables in Course Implementation

In translating the K–5 classroom observation instrument (EDAISI) to the university context, the research team was able to create a tool that could capture how the methods faculty integrated the ESTELL pedagogy into their university classroom setting. However, when it came to systematically scoring every 15 minutes, as is the case with the EDAISI, results seemed a bit skewed.[2] Methods instructors spent time at the beginning of class on course logistics (due dates for assignments) and would come back to these during the lesson as well. Because observations of science methods courses needed to capture complete sessions, overall scores for each science methods course observation resulted in a range of high and low ESTELL scores over the duration of an observation.

Additionally, in some cases, the teacher education program followed a cohort model, which meant that students in all science methods courses enrolled in the same section of courses throughout the program. For example, bilingual credential candidates completed the science methods course following a different sequence of courses than the mainstream candidates. Alignment of courses meant that we also needed to consider what other courses pre-service teachers were taking before and after the redesigned science methods course. We had to carefully consider whether pre-service teachers were introduced to language and literacy methods for diverse learners before and whether they were advancing to the next phase of the teacher education program. These were questions that had to be taken into account as we analyzed the results from the ESTELL intervention.

Faculty Epistemological Stances

Observing faculty as they taught the redesigned science methods course, coupled with interviews conducted with the faculty, revealed that each of the four instructors approached the redesigned course from a particular theoretical perspective on learning, which impacted and supported the degree to which they rigorously implemented each ESTELL practice (Lee, Penfield, & Maerten-Rivera, 2009; O'Donnell, 2008). To understand these trends, it is first helpful to understand the approach that was taken to the observation of the science methods courses.

Methods course observations. Four teacher education courses across three sites implementing the reform pedagogy were observed using an adapted version of the EDAISI observation instrument. In addition, qualitative participant observation fieldnotes and audio recordings were collected for each observation. Additional firsthand instructor oral reflections were also collected. In particular, the focus of these observations captured:

- Adherence to *planned ESTELL related activities* such as core ESTELL-related course components, activities, topics, and materials in each course (e.g., activities/topics, course readings, curriculum materials, review/attention to course assignments)
- Adherence to core *pedagogical knowledge and skills* such as how consistent and to what extent each course discussed pedagogical science knowledge, curricular knowledge, and subject-matter knowledge
- Adherence to *ESTELL instructional practices* including explicit or implicit attention to the six pedagogical practices and their subdomains including the performance and/or discussion of these practices (i.e., Facilitating Collaborative Inquiry, Literacy in Science, Scaffolding and Development of Language in Science, Contextualizing Science Activity, Promoting Complex Thinking, Promoting Science Talk)

Adherence here refers to how consistently each course addressed these three areas and to what extent participants were exposed to ESTELL anchor lessons, target activities and materials, pedagogical knowledge, and ESTELL practices. All of the areas concerning the observation were documented as either present or not present and, if appropriate, the extent of pre-service teacher engagement during an observation. Examples of these occurrences included attention to particular assignments, discussion of a particular science lesson template such as the 5E model (Engage, Explore, Explain, Elaborate, Evaluate), and school curricular materials such as FOSS (Full Option Science System) including Spanish language adaptations.

Course adherence to the ESTELL activities was documented through an inventory of their presence and non-presence throughout the duration of the course observations that usually lasted 2.5–3 hours. The methods course observation instrument adapted the EDAISI instrument by taking an inventory of contextual information surrounding each observation and, more significantly, by allowing methods course observations to capture discussions of ESTELL/science convergence (i.e., "meta-discourse" on these practices) as well as the implementation of these practices during each observation. Each ESTELL practice was scored every 15 minutes including the performance or modeling of an ESTELL/science convergence and meta-discourse on the convergence. These two aspects of the ESTELL framework within teacher education courses were conceptualized as (1) performance of an ESTELL/science convergence domain and (2) meta-discourse about an ESTELL/science convergence. Performance of an ESTELL domain refers to the level of implementation, modeling, or carrying out of a particular ESTELL instructional practice by the university instructors. Meta-discourse of an ESTELL domain refers to the level of attention beyond its enactment including reflection on and discussion about teaching through a particular ESTELL instructional practice by university instructors and pre-service teachers. The following observational examples draw from approximately 60 hours of observations across the four participating faculty collaborators. The examples focus on lessons where instructors were fully implementing all ESTELL instructional practices. While not expected or required, ESTELL instructional practices are all potentially activated and present in any given lesson. All ESTELL instructional practices were observed across all sites at varying levels of implementation. Table 10.1 describes the EDAISI domains that each of the instructors whose teaching is analyzed in this chapter implemented at higher levels during their methods courses.

ESTELL instructors all implemented the reform pedagogical practices in their methods courses. Of note here is how all instructors had the most difficulty in modeling and reflecting on *Contextualizing Science Activity* and *Scaffolding and*

TABLE 10.1 Highest levels of implementation by instructor

EDAISI Domains	Instructor A	Instructor B	Instructor C
Facilitating Collaborative Inquiry			•
Promoting Science Talk	•	•	•
Literacy in Science	•	•	
Scaffolding and Development of Language in Science			
Contextualizing Science Activity			
Promoting Scientific Thinking	•		•

Development of Language in Science. All focal instructors scored high in *Promoting Science Talk.*

Instructor A: Pragmatic, curricular-based epistemology. Instructor A scored high in the *Promoting Scientific Thinking, Science Talk,* and *Literacy in Science* domains; this instructor also scored the highest in *Promoting Scientific Thinking* compared to other instructors. Instructor A followed a more pragmatic approach to teaching science methods to teacher candidates, placing emphasis on school-based curricular requirements (i.e., following the 5E inquiry activities) to model and discuss ESTELL practices. Instructor A often referred to classroom dynamics and her own classroom teaching experience with K–8 students to highlight ESTELL practices. The following lesson focuses on one of the ESTELL anchor lessons that is used across ESTELL sites, referred to as the "Skulls lesson," where students discuss structure, scale, and biodiversity by examining their own teeth and that of different organisms (see Appendices A and B). While all instructors collaborated on sharing ESTELL anchor lessons such as this lesson, each anchor lesson was implemented within the resources and constraints available at each site and interpreted through varied epistemological viewpoints by each instructor.

The following observation (Fieldnotes, 10/15/2009) highlights the dual levels that ESTELL science methods instructors engaged regarding the performance and the meta-discourse around the ESTELL practices. These two levels are significant, simultaneous contexts that teacher candidates needed to attend to and that instructors managed in their classrooms to bring attention to the natural convergences between science and the ESTELL practices. Instructor A begins this lesson by reviewing the previous week's lesson on biodiversity and then asking teacher candidates about the benefits of doing this kind of lesson for ELLs. As teacher candidates resume with their biodiversity investigation, Instructor A rotates through each small group. Afterward, teacher candidates share results with others of their investigations of the soil composition, description of their school sites, and human impact on this context.

Instructor A recaps and relates the lesson to how it can be implemented with children and possible next steps and real-world writing opportunities. Upon finishing the final activity (that takes over an hour to complete), Instructor A transitions into reviewing *Contextualizing Science Activities* (in reference to the previous biodiversity lesson) and other ESTELL practices before introducing the Skulls lesson. Teacher candidates complete a brief pair-share where they examine an ESTELL lesson plan outline of the previous lesson on biodiversity and discuss the connections to the lesson just completed. The instructor rotates through each pair once again and addresses questions about ELL methods including differentiated instruction. Instructor A then asks the whole class for any comments about ESTELL instructional practices before re-introducing the 5E lesson model (i.e., Engage, Explore, Explain, Elaborate, and Evaluate) (Bybee, Taylor, Gardner, Van Scotter, Powell, Westbrook, & Landes, 2006). Instructor A completes a class discussion on the "elaborate" step of the 5E model before introducing a lesson based on the 5E lesson model. The following transcript is an excerpt describing what occurs during this stretch of time where the instructor focuses on ELLs and language associated with the Skulls lesson. Teacher candidates take out their lab books as the instructor conducts a mini-lesson on teeth. The instructor asks student to pair-share favorite foods and chewing action in the mouth when they eat different foods and to record these observations in their notebooks. The instructor then models a lesson to the teacher candidates as if teaching children about teeth. As she wraps up her mini-lesson she engages teacher candidates in sharing their observations of their own teeth. As she begins this lesson she asks students the following question:

> **Instructor A:** I want you to think of your favorite food. Got it? Aww, see mine is popcorn. It's just right there. Okay? So, I want you to think of your favorite food. And in thinking of that, I want you to feel it in your mouth. Okay? Taking that bite, got it? Feel it? Okay? Now, could you turn to your neighbor? And could you tell them your favorite food? And could you describe what it feels like as you are putting it into your mouth and chewing it. So—okay? Describe it! [Teacher A, Line 182, Time 1:18:10]

Next, Instructor A asks teacher candidates to write down all the verbs that describe the actions or work that their teeth accomplish when eating the different foods. Providing a brief meta-discursive move about teaching this lesson with children, the instructor notes that any language would be accepted including English, Spanish, or Vietnamese. The following excerpt precedes the brainstorming of words by teacher candidates that also involves thinking about connecting the lesson to children. While brief and not actually modeling the creation of a word wall, the instructor effectively uses the impending brainstorming session as an opportunity to point to an instructional adaptation for teaching this lesson later with children.

> **Instructor A:** So just say a word and go. And of course, what would you do with kids?
>
> **Student:** Write it on the board.
>
> **Instructor A:** You would write it up on there, and you would have a word wall on the word chart, but we're not gonna take the time. Go Rebecca, go.

Teacher candidates quickly take turns uttering a word that comes to mind related to eating. Here language knowledge and cultural expressions intersect to make sense of a science inquiry activity. Teacher candidates identify a range of words describing what their teeth do when eating certain foods, including words such as grind, gnaw, break, chatter, nibble, masticate, chomp, clench, crunch, mash, puncture, and shatter. In the context of bilingual science methods courses, instructors also urged teacher candidates to similarly identify a range of related words in Spanish such as *masticar/ masticate, comer/eat, morder/bite, picar/poke at*, and *romper/rip*.

The second part of this segment illustrates how Instructor A manages to engage teacher candidates in inquiry while also scaffolding pedagogical adaptations for the teaching of this lesson with elementary school children. Instructor A engages students in a discussion focused on student observations of their teeth before discussing later the characteristics of the teeth of other animals. The teacher asks students if they noticed anything unusual about their teeth. Some students mention that they are all different and another notes that her teeth in the back are "whiter." This student observation sends students back to reexamine the color of their own teeth (with their mirrors), with some students reporting different patterns. The following exchange describes this sharing of observations, with the teacher facilitating the sharing of varied teeth patterns and colors.

> **Student 1:** The teeth in the back are whiter than (inaudible)
>
> **Instructor A:** Huh, that's interesting.
>
> **Student 2:** Really?
>
> **Instructor A:** Ooh, I like that. People are saying really, and they're looking back. Yeah. Not mine. Mine are golder in the back than they are in the ... ((laughing))
>
> **Student 3:** ((laughing)) Um, there is a gradual change from front to back. Start off with a single, um, blade, if you will. And the premolars, they change to having two blades. And then the molars, you know, it's kind of like the Central Valley.
>
> **Student 4:** They're also symmetrically, starting in the middle, they're sort of the same, and as you go out, they're also the same.

This discussion continues with students sharing how many teeth they have including some reporting 28, 26, and 30 teeth. This is where a student notes how K–5 children might have fewer teeth than the adults in the room. This example illustrates how science inquiry activities can work together to promote contextualized learning opportunities. In this case the *Contextualizing Learning* ESTELL practice connects with teacher candidates' familiarity with K–5 children. A student notes that "kids expect to have ...," both noting that the number of teeth reported by the teacher candidates might be different than those numbers reported by K–5 children, but also in so doing bidding for some clarification on how many teeth children might report having. Instructor A talks about modifying lessons for children by using clue charts where students refer to or write colorful and vivid definitions, examples, synonyms, antonyms, and uses of key science terms. Of note here is also how this exchange shifts with an observation by the teacher candidate and not the instructor.

> **Student 5:** Some have less.
>
> **Instructor A:** Some have less, some have more, yup.

Student 6: Kids expect to have (inaudible)

Instructor A: Yup. Alrighty, there we go. Cool. Excellent. Yeah. One of the things that we could have done on this, also, is that we could have set up a clue chart right after our vocabulary. We could have done a clue. So what do you know about your teeth first? What do you think you know about your teeth? We – definitely would have been a beautiful place to do that. In fact, it was in my lesson plans, but I forgot it. So, um, it happens. Um, so, we're now – we've gone through. You've got some questions that you're wondering about your teeth, things that you have noticed about your teeth. So we're going to move from that "explore" stage into an "explain" stage.

Instructor A attended to ESTELL practices by consistently contextualizing science experiences for teacher candidates by expressing a pragmatic orientation to teaching science methods. She shows this orientation by treating teacher candidates as classroom teachers already and explicitly providing practical, classroom-based scenarios that could assist teacher candidates in making sense of ESTELL practices. In this exchange Instructor A promotes discussion of teacher candidate observations by continually referencing the K–5 classroom scenarios that could be used (i.e., setting up a clue chart, signaling transitions between phases of inquiry process).

Instructor B: A focus on language use in science activities. Instructor B scored the highest in the *Science Talk* and *Literacy in Science* domains. Observations of Instructor B showed a systematic use of ESTELL practices while regularly attending to language development themes, particularly for ELLs. Instructor B, similar to the other ESTELL instructors, supports ESTELL practices through a particular epistemological lens. Her orientation to teaching science methods and creating science experiences for teacher candidates enacts a preference for explicitly teaching aspects of the language of science as part of her science teaching philosophy. This epistemological stance mediates her interpretation and implementation of ESTELL practices that for the most part aids in regularly addressing all six ESTELL practices with some more limited development of collaborative inquiry activities, for example. The following ESTELL methods course observation example depicts how Instructor B frequently displayed her preference for supporting the language of science as vocabulary development; that is, how she interpreted promoting ESTELL practices by attending to aspects of language use in science. In many cases, attending to the language of science translated into explicitly pointing out, discussing, and sharing specific science vocabulary with and between teacher candidates.

This Skulls lesson begins with Instructor B reminding students about the big ideas discussed in the previous class session on Arthropods, including asking students for some ideas on K–5 classroom applications. Instructor B then moves on to introduce a new lesson by projecting slide images of different skulls that will address "diversity of life" and "evolution and systems" through an inquiry activity. Instructor B asks students to write in their science notebooks and describe or list action verbs associated with eating. Instructor B notes that words in another language could also be used. At this point, Instructor B has students work in groups creating a common list of action verbs for their teeth. Instructor B moves from group to group asking students questions like, "How many different types of words did you find?" Each group then shares some ideas with Instructor B, providing some additional pedagogical considerations – e.g., show "little kids" how to do these with physical action. Instructor B tells students that after they use this with students, the list of common action verbs can be placed on a word wall. Instructor B notes that this activity is one way to encourage ELLs and other students to respond in different languages with their peers. Instructor B then provides a list of more than twenty action verbs on a slide (e.g., bite, break, chew, chomp, crack, crunch, crush, cut, gnaw, rip, shred, stab, tear) that could be used with children as she engages teacher candidates on constructing learning objectives for this lesson on skull models (i.e., structure and function of human teeth, value the nature of paleontologist's work).

At this point, Instructor B tells students that the goal of the next five-minute activity is to create a map of their teeth in pairs as she passes a datasheet to record their observations and a mirror. At one point, as Instructor B walks around to each pair, she notes that "this is a time to listen to the stories of students about their teeth like the tooth fairy." She also reminds students to identify different types of teeth by showing a slide of a human mouth that identifies the location of canines, molars, incisors, premolars, and molars. After pairs complete writing their observations, they are asked to share what different types of teeth are used for eating by humans. Instructor B notes that this part of the skull models lesson could be further contextualized when teaching this lesson with children by asking children to bring food from home to examine how different types of teeth are used with different foods, particularly when children may eat foods more common in other countries. Resuming the in-class activity, Instructor B asks groups of students to select four different foods (i.e., raisins, corn, cheese, nuts, dried mango, carrots, turkey jerky) from the front of the classroom to investigate how different foods work with different types of teeth as they complete their observations.

The following exchange illustrates Instructor B's frequent focus on science vocabulary as she models and discusses ESTELL practices. The ten-minute activity begins by students first predicting how each food might interact with different types of teeth and then trying out each of the selected four snacks. Here, Instructor B provides some commentary again on teaching this lesson to children by noting that this part of the activity would be a good opportunity to check and see if children are using science vocabulary like incisors, molars, and canines and noting the class reading on promoting science talk with children. In this exchange Instructor B repeatedly requests that students practice using terms used to identify different types of teeth.

> **Instructor B:** Think about the levels of communication that was presented in our readings when you are working on this as a group. Did you like the corn?

Student: It's funny how when you eat, you never really pay attention to what teeth you're using until you get to this class.

Instructor B: And this is the time you want students to reinforce the vocabulary. Are they using the incisor, the academic language here?

Instructor B is facilitating both teacher learning contexts (making sense of eating snacks in the moment) and the potential K–5 learning contexts (where teacher candidates will be teaching in the future). After each group has tested each type of food, the class comes back together to discuss their observations. Instructor B also notes that this could be a good time to discuss with children the importance of children caring for their own teeth. As teacher candidates share their observations, Instructor B facilitates a class discussion on the observations by having students comment on each other's observations and even some contrasting findings. Instructor B again informs teacher candidates that it is important to encourage the use of key science vocabulary as they ask children to share their own observations and perhaps even things they still wonder about related to their teeth.

Instructor B: How about our, the dried mango? Who had dried mango— Oh you did? Katie, or Kathleen?

Student K: We, I think we all agreed that we used our incisors for dried mangos because they are kind of soft and flat and you just kind of nibble off a piece and chew it with your molars.

Instructor B: Ok, good. Any other? Dried mango?

Student: Same thing.

Instructor B: Same thing, ok. And you may want to encourage students to use the vocabulary, the verbs earlier that you have generated. Let's see, so you may want to have, make sure you spend enough time for each food, each group to share, to communicate their experiences here. And questions that students are still wondering about. What do you think, are there questions that came up while you were doing this task? Questions related to the functions of teeth?

A student interjects a statement about how, in fact, mangoes interact with her teeth unexpectedly. Instructor B repeats again a contextualizing opportunity where children can bring foods from home to complete the testing of food activity with teeth; she goes on to demonstrate how some foods are eaten differently, like fresh mangoes in the Philippines. Instructor B provides several additional resources online where teachers could promote investigations into what different animals might eat based on the types of teeth they possess (which is the focus of the ensuing activity with animal skulls). She concludes by noting that teachers can scaffold both language and content in a lesson like this activity with children. Several teacher candidates agree, with one exclaiming that her second-grade students would love doing this lesson.

Instructor C: Reformist epistemological focus. Instructor C implemented *Facilitating Collaborative Inquiry, Science Talk,* and *Promoting Scientific Thinking* at high levels regularly; Instructor C also scored the highest in *Facilitating Collaborative Inquiry* compared to other instructors. The instructor's disposition toward science instruction was guided by a reformist, social justice stance on science education (Calabrese Barton, 2003). Instructor C approached the development of the ESTELL-infused course with the premise that traditional approaches to science education marginalize culturally and linguistically diverse students, including ELLs. For this reason, Instructor C took on a reformist or critical approach to teaching the science methods course. Throughout our observations of this science methods course, there were numerous references to the critical need to attend to sociocultural contexts, avoiding breakdowns in comprehension by ELLs, and taking stock of teacher candidate's pedagogy for science teaching as distinct from didactic and transmission approaches to teaching.

The following segment describes how Instructor C approached teaching the ESTELL science methods course from a reformist and socio-constructivist viewpoint. The lesson was part of a Sun-Earth-Moon investigation examining the seasons on Earth (Fieldnotes, 10/7/2009). Fieldnotes capture a brief discussion about a state evaluation assignment for pre-service teachers before the instructor shifts attention to the use of "centers"[3] and scaffolding moves in the classroom. The instructor stresses the importance of making connections to children's homes, particularly those of ELLs, and provides a short video clip of a teacher making those contextualizing connections. This framing note is followed by the instructor providing teacher candidates with hard copies of the ESTELL lesson outline. The instructor initiates modeling a stage in the science inquiry strategy by posing a question, "Why do you think it's hotter in the United States in June than in December?" Students share their individual responses to this question with the instructor eventually asking the entire class if the majority opinion expressed by students should determine the consensus response to the question. After some student disagreement over whether or not scientific knowledge should be determined by majority consensus, another student explains that previously there was majority consensus on the world being flat.

After further discussion about how knowledge is examined in science, Instructor C explains to teacher candidates that this lesson will focus on explanations for the seasons on Earth. Students are then asked to again write their individual explanations for the causes of the seasons. Instructor C then plays a video clip from "A Private Universe" (Shapiro, Whitney, Sadler, & Schneps, 1987) that problematizes traditional science education and how knowledge about the seasons and phases of the Moon are not well understood by even advanced, post-secondary science students. After the video ends, Instructor C repeats the importance of learning centers in K–5 classrooms to address misconceptions in science that can go unattended. The use of "centers" here refers to the use of simultaneous, student-driven, and rotating in-class activities where children can experience different aspects of an inquiry project. The instructor punctuates this point by emphasizing that deeper learning uses less time in the long run because it is more effective than a traditional, teacher-centered approach to science teaching referring back to misconceptions expressed by college graduates unable to explain changing seasons on Earth.

As the instructor begins to provide this meta-discourse about effective science teaching, the students are directed to move on to a focal inquiry activity about the seasons. Teacher candidates then break up into two groups (or centers). One group works with thermometers, a flashlight, and a globe and another group works with a computer program and logoprobes. After clarifying student roles within groups, both groups are tasked with using their available tools and materials to *investigate* the question about the seasons. The instructor demonstrates how to use each probe and temperature readout with both groups – noting affordances, limitations/support for ELLs, and gaining scientific accuracy – and ensuring students *record their observations*. The instructor rotates through each group asking students for their *hypothesis* of where temperatures will be higher or lower depending on their angle to the light and explaining its relevance to seasonal change and trends. Instructor C asks questions to groups like, "Where would it be summer?" and "Did you find a difference in temperature?" and states, "Think about how kids react from seeing it on the computer (log of temperature changes)." The activity is sustained by Instructor C consistently asking teacher candidates for their *explanations based on evidence* from the data and models by asking questions like, "What do you think this light represents?" Before students switch groups, Instructor C emphasizes again that students need to "think about what causes the seasons based on the ... location of the light ..." This modeling of the inquiry cycle, as evidenced by the italicized words/phrases, illustrates how instructors addressed both scientific practices and ESTELL instructional practices.

After both groups collect their results and share them with each other with some variability in the data collected, Instructor C breaks frame in the lesson to discuss how the lesson addresses the ESTELL practice to "take a moment to take it apart." The instructor asks students for suggestions on improving the lesson and which particular ESTELL themes were highlighted in the lesson as teacher candidates referenced back to the ESTELL lesson outline handout.

> **Instructor C:** So, which one are we highlighting today?
> **Students:** ((inaudible)) talk
> **Instructor C:** Promoting science talk?
> **Students:** ((examine lesson outline handout))
> **Instructor C:** And how did we do that?
> **Students:** I think through direct and indirect light…
> **Instructor C:** Good and the way we were doing the activity ((inaudible)) in that you actually had a chance to use some of that terminology right

when you were actually doing it. Ahh I was talking to this group about if the teacher in the video [Private Universe] had an activity like this where students get to use a flashlight and draw the indirect light versus the direct light if that would of helped the girl in making more sense of that 'cuz it looked to me that she was using a more transmissive approach where she was just kind of telling them maybe using transparency or whatever but just telling them the information instead of having them aah do something with that knowledge

Students: ((nodding))

In this exchange, teacher candidates reflect on the pedagogical approach framing the rotating small group activities ("centers" or learning centers) and the role students took on during their small group work in promoting science talk. Learning centers play a particular significant role in linguistically diverse classrooms where teachers can provide differentiated instruction to ELLs balanced with authentic content instruction (Bunch et al., 2005; Martin & Green, 2012). Science talk becomes a converging idea for this instructor's approach to teaching science and the ESTELL practices. Here, the instructor repeats the importance of science talk where the teacher candidates "actually had a chance to use some of that terminology right when you were actually doing it" as opposed to what occurred in the "Private Universe" video where the teacher was "just kind of telling them" how light and indirect sunlight worked. The instructor uses these post-model lessons in class reflections to help teacher candidates reflect back on their science experiences while still pointing out specific features of an ESTELL lesson that made it especially supportive of ELLs. The following closure statements by Instructor C once again illustrate his reformist stance in a discussion regarding manipulatives (i.e., flashlight, probes).

Instructor C: So one of the things by having these kind of manipulatives, you know, you essentially get students to use the scientific language and the scientific talk, the scientific discourse, aah, you know they have no choice given these manipulatives you are encouraging to use those words and as they are explaining what's going on with one another you know they are engaging in scientific talk. But if you are the only one doing the scientific talk then the students are in a more passive role.

With this description, Instructor C helped the pre-service teachers see the benefit of discussion linked to investigation using manipulatives and *realia* (authentic physical objects), the need to allow *all* students a chance to build their scientific knowledge through discussion about the ideas and concepts they are investigating throughout the inquiry cycle.

Conclusion

This chapter provides a new analysis of teachers learning a reform science pedagogy focused on supporting ELLs (i.e., ESTELL instructional practices) by examining how science methods faculty scaffold these practices for pre-service teachers. Vignettes depicting teaching and learning episodes from science methods courses illustrate how university faculty and teacher candidates attend to science teaching for ELLs by addressing aspects of culture and language; these examples in particular focus on the convergence of ESTELL instructional practices and scientific practices as conceptualized by science methods instructors. Previous analysis on the development of the ESTELL methods course activities and how meaningful faculty collaborations unfolded during the course of this research project show potential for the approach (Bravo, Mosqueda, Solís, & Stoddart, 2014; Rodriguez, Houle, Quita, & Victorine, 2011).

Despite some differences in how science methods instructors appropriated ESTELL instructional practices in their courses (see Table 10.1), this analysis suggests that their particular epistemological stances enabled these instructors to implement ESTELL practices in their teaching. This chapter shows how teacher candidates were exposed to and acquired the ESTELL instructional practices, which led us to investigate how teacher candidates come to support these practices in their own teaching (described further in Chapter 9, this volume). Science methods faculty drew from familiar pedagogical frameworks in making sense of the ESTELL instructional practices connecting to practical-pragmatic (Instructor A), language-focused (Instructor B), and critical-reformist (Instructor C) approaches to teaching science methods. Individual instructors re-interpreted the ESTELL instructional practices as they adapted both the ESTELL practices and their own usual teaching approaches. One pattern we noted was that instructors were consistently able to address *Promoting Science Talk* at higher levels of implementation than the other EDAISI domains. This domain draws special attention to explicit modeling of and giving feedback to children on their use of practices that provide evidence, make explanations, or propose methods of inquiry during science lessons, in line with the nature of science practices outlined in the anchor lessons.

Science methods faculty who may want to incorporate ESTELL instructional practices and activities in their own classrooms need to carefully consider how to adapt existing course requirements while also identifying where their pedagogical approach and the ESTELL practices may already have strong areas of convergence. ESTELL instructional practices offer a pedagogical orientation, not a blueprint, for reforming existing science methods instruction. An additional benefit of our research and development effort was faculty recognizing the value of this collaboration as a professional development opportunity as they established an environment of trust and respect (Rodriguez et al., 2011). This foundation led faculty collaborators to engage in discussions where they made changes to their existing course syllabus by reaching a consensus on what would be core ESTELL activities and materials shared across the three sites. This, in turn, led to discussions on where individual courses would have some flexibility to address institutional requirements of the course as well as credential requirements while still adhering to the ESTELL practices and common activities.

Our findings from observing the ESTELL science methods courses show how university faculty capitalize on the synergistic possibilities between language, culture, and science teaching. Future research will examine the relationship between the implementation of ESTELL instructional practices within each course/instructor and clinical teaching practices at each site as well as the continuation of the ESTELL instructional practices into the graduates' first year of teaching. Part of this analysis also includes examining case study student achievement data comparing treatment and control group participants and their students. This analysis will necessarily involve describing how teacher candidates' backgrounds (e.g., academic training, monolingual/bilingual skills, prior experiences in the classroom) may help shape how science methods instructors adapt the ESTELL instructional practices. Moreover, a secondary analysis of how methods instructors address ESTELL instructional practices holistically (instead of tracking how they unfolded every 15 minutes) may allow a different lens for examining how these practices are enacted in each ESTELL university course; again, university courses are much lengthier than K–5 classroom lessons and most observations of science methods courses showed high levels of implementation, however short-lived, during each 2–3 hour observation. Unpacking these segments qualitatively will provide richer detail on how teacher candidates and science methods faculty work together to make sense of effective science teaching for ELLs. Related to these differences between university and K–5 classrooms, we also wish to examine how instructors in university contexts can approximate and simulate the teaching of ELLs with novice teachers. Finally, more attention needs to be paid on how to consider and value both scientific experiences and meta-reflections of teaching science (meta-discourse of teaching) in teacher education courses. These two types of activities build on each other and are contexts for each other, particularly with respect to showing specific pedagogical moves, which are often not noticed by novice teachers without explicit guidance.

Notes

1 "ELL" refers to how local districts identified children at varying levels of English language proficiency and diverse academic backgrounds. This single descriptor does not address the evolving nature of students' native language and biliteracy skills.
2 We acknowledge here important differences in how lessons unfold, the use of science materials, and the nature of meta-cognitive references between K–5 classrooms (reflected in the EDAISI) and university coursework.
3 Instructor C talks about "centers" as a grouping structure for organizing class activities where children take on more responsibility for their learning and inquiry processes.

References

August, D., Branum-Martin, L., Cardenas-Hagan E., & Francis, D. J. (2009). The impact of an instructional intervention on the science and language learning of middle grade ELLs. *Journal of Research on Educational Effectiveness, 2*, 345–376.

Baquedano-López, P., Solís, J. L., & Kattan, S. (2005). Adaptation: The language of classroom learning. *Linguistics and Education, 16*(1), 1–26.

Bravo, M. A., & Cervetti, G. N. (2008). Teaching vocabulary through text and experience in content areas. In A. E. Farstrup & S. J. Samuels (Eds.), *What research has to say about vocabulary instruction* (pp. 130–149). Newark, DE: International Reading Association.

Bravo, M. A., Mosqueda, E., Solís, J. L., & Stoddart, T. (2014). Possibilities and limits of integrating science and diversity education in preservice elementary teacher preparation. *Journal of Science Teacher Education, 25*(5), 601–619.

Bruna, K. R., Vann, R., & Escudero, M. P. (2007). What's language got to do with it?: A case study of academic language instruction in a high school "English Learner Science" class. *Journal of English for Academic Purposes, 6*(1), 36–54.

Bunch, G. C., Lotan, R., Valdés, G., & Cohen, E. (2005). Keeping content at the heart of content-based instruction: Access and support for transitional English learners. In J. Crandall & D. Kaufman (Eds.), *Content-based instruction in primary and secondary school settings* (pp. 11–25). Alexandria, VA: Teachers of English to Speakers of Other Languages.

Buxton, C. A. (2006). Creating contextually authentic science in a "low-performing" urban elementary school. *Journal of Research in Science Teaching, 43*(7), 695–721.

Buxton, C. A., Salinas, A., Mahotiere, M., Lee, O., & Secada, W. G. (2013). Leveraging cultural resources through teacher pedagogical reasoning: Elementary grade teachers analyze second language learners' science problem solving. *Teaching and Teacher Education, 32*, 31–42.

Bybee, R. W., Taylor, J. A., Gardner, A., Van Scotter, P., Powell, J. C., Westbrook, A., & Landes, N. (2006). The BSCS 5E instructional model: Origins and effectiveness. *Colorado Springs, CO: BSCS, 5*, 88–98.

Calabrese Barton, A. (2003). *Teaching science for social justice*. New York, NY: Teachers College Press.

Cervetti, G. N., Pearson, P. D., Barber, J., Hiebert, E. H., & Bravo, M. A. (2007). Integrating literacy and science: The research we have, the research we need. In M. Pressley, A. K. Billman, K. Perry, K. Refitt, & J. Reynolds (Eds.), *Shaping literacy achievement* (pp. 157–174). New York, NY: Guilford.

Chinn, C. A., & Malhotra, B. A. (2002). Epistemologically authentic inquiry in schools: A theoretical framework for evaluating inquiry tasks. *Science Education, 86*(2), 175–218.

de Jong, E. J., & Harper, C. A. (2005). Preparing mainstream teachers for English-language learners: Is being a good teacher good enough? *Teacher Education Quarterly, 32*(2), 101–124.

Goldenberg, C. (2013). Unlocking the research on English learners: What we know – and don't yet know – about effective instruction. *American Educator, 37*(2), 4–12.

Hammond, L. (2001). Notes from California: An anthropological approach to urban science education for language minority families. *Journal of Research in Science Teaching, 38*(9), 983–999.

Hapgood, S., Magnusson, S. J., & Sullivan Palincsar, A. (2004). Teacher, text, and experience: A case of young children's scientific inquiry. *The Journal of the Learning Sciences, 13*(4), 455–505.

Hashweh, M. Z. (1996). Effects of science teachers' epistemological beliefs in teaching. *Journal of Research in Science Teaching, 33*(1), 47–63.

Lee, O., & Luykx, A. (2006). *Science education and student diversity: Synthesis and research agenda*. New York, NY: Cambridge University Press.

Lee, O., Penfield, R., & Maerten-Rivera, J. (2009). Effects of fidelity of implementation on science achievement gains among English language learners. *Journal of Research in Science Teaching, 46*(7), 836–859.

Lee, O., Quinn, H., & Valdés, G. (2013). Science and language for English language learners in relation to Next Generation Science Standards and with implications for Common Core State Standards for English language arts and mathematics. *Educational Researcher, 42*(4), 223–233.

Lemke, J. L. (1990). *Talking science: Language, learning and values*. Westport, CN: Ablex.

Luft, J. A., & Roehrig, G. H. (2007). Capturing science teachers' epistemological beliefs: The development of the teacher beliefs interview. *Electronic Journal of Science Education, 11*(2), 38–63.

Lynch, S. (2001). "Science for all" is not equal to "one size fits all": Linguistic and cultural diversity and science education reform. *Journal of Research in Science Teaching, 38*(5), 622–627.

Martin, S., & Green, A. (2012). Striking a balance. *Science Teacher, 79*(4), 40–43.

O'Donnell, C. L. (2008). Defining, conceptualizing, and measuring fidelity of implementation and its relationship to outcomes in K–12 curriculum intervention research. *Review of Educational Research, 78*(1), 33–84.

Osborne, J. F., & Patterson, A. (2011). Scientific argument and explanation: A necessary distinction? *Science Education, 95*, 627–638.

Rodriguez, A., Houle, M., Quita, I., & Victorine, A. (2011). Meaningful collaboration: Establishing a science methods course with a focus on English learners in three different universities. Conference presentation, annual meeting of the National Association for Research in Science Teaching, April 5, Orlando, FL.

Shapiro, I., Whitney, C., Sadler, P., & Schneps, M. (1987). *A Private Universe*, documentary produced by the Harvard-Smithsonian Center for Astrophysics. Science Education Department, Science Media Group. ISBN, 1-57680.

Solís, J. (2016). English language and disciplinary literacy development in science. In E. G. Lyon, S. Tolbert, J. L. Solís, T. Stoddart, & G. C. Bunch (Eds.), *Secondary science teaching for English Learners: Developing supportive and responsive learning contexts for sense-making and language development* (pp. 131–156). New York, NY: Rowman & Littlefield Publishers.

Solís, J. L., Kattan, & Baquedano-López, P. (2009). Locating time in science classroom activity: Adaptation as a theory of learning and change. In K. R. Bruna and K. Gomez (Eds.), *Talking science, writing science: The work of language in multicultural classrooms* (pp. 139–166). New York, NY: Routledge.

Stoddart, T., Solís, J. L., Tolbert, S., & Bravo, M. (2010). A framework for the effective science teaching of English Language Learners in elementary schools. In D. W. Sunal, C. S. Sunal, & E. L. Wright (Eds.), *Teaching science with Hispanic ELLs in K-16 classrooms* (Vol. Research in Science Education, pp. 151-182). Charlotte, NC: Information Age Publishing.

Tharp, R. G., & Dalton, S. S. (2007). Orthodoxy, cultural compatibility, and universals in education. *Comparative Education, 43*(1), 53–70.

Weinburgh, M., Silva, C., Smith, K. H., Groulx, J., & Nettles, J. (2014). The intersection of inquiry-based science and language: Preparing teachers for ELL classrooms. *Journal of Science Teacher Education, 25*(5), 519–541.

Appendix A – Syllabus Excerpt and Assignments

TABLE 10.2 Syllabus Excerpt/Schedule and Assignments

Week 1	• Overview: Course Syllabus and ESTELL Project • In-Class Activity. Pre-Survey for Student Teachers: ESTELL Project (45 minutes) • Sign-up for course projects/assignments Assignment: 1. Download CA Science Content Standards and bring to class (your grade level standards only) 2. Read "The Nature of Science and Science Inquiry" article, pp. 21–29 only (PDF, iLearn) 3. Read "The Many Levels of Inquiry" by Banchi & Bell (PDF, iLearn)
Week 2	• What is Science?/Science Inquiry Continuum • ICAR to be modeled using assigned readings – ESTELL: Promoting Science • Talk In-Class Activity: Buoyancy • Intro to Science Lesson Planning/Looking at CA Science Standards • ESTELL Framework Assignment: 1. Read "BSCS 5E Instructional Model," pp. 29–32. NSTA, 2007. (PDF, iLearn) 2. Read (Optional Textbook) Chapter 7: Designing Lessons: Inquiry Approach to Science Using SIOP Model, pp. 95–106. Fathman & Crowther, Eds.
Week 3	No Class
Week 4	• Planning for Instruction/Developing Lesson Plan • 5E Learning Cycle Model (LCM)/Science Inquiry discussion leaders (ICAR) – Chapter 7 and NSTA articles • In-Class Activity: Properties of Matter • ESTELL: Promoting Inquiry Skills Assignment: 1. Read "Schoolyard Inquiry for English Language Learners," pp. 47–51, by Westervelt. Science Teacher. (PDF, iLearn) 2. Read (Optional Textbook) Chapter 2: Learners, Programs and Teaching Practices, pp. 9–18. Fathman & Crowther, Eds.
Week 5	• Learning Theories: How Do Students Learn Science? ESTELL: Contextualizing Science Activity • In-Class Activity: Schoolyard Investigation discussion leaders (ICAR) – Westervelt and Chapter 2 articles Assignment: 1. Read "Four Strands of Science Learning" (Chapter 2), by Michaels et al. (PDF, iLearn) 2. Read "Outdoor Classrooms – Planning Makes Perfect," pp. 44–48, by Haines. Science and Children. (PDF, iLearn)

(continued)

TABLE 10.2 Syllabus Excerpt/Schedule and Assignments (*continued*)

Week 6	• Big Ideas in Science (National and State Science Standards)
	• In-Class Activity: Continuation of Schoolyard Investigation
	• Planning & Designing Scientific Investigation/COMIC-E science processes
	• Discussion leaders (ICAR) – Michaels and Haines articles
	Assignment:
	  1. Read "Sheltered Instruction Techniques for ELLs," pp. 34–38, by Pray & Monhardt. Science and Children. (PDF, iLearn)
	  2. Read (Optional Textbook) Chapter 4: Strategies for Teaching Science to English Learners, pp. 37–59. Fathman & Crowther.

Week 7	• Planning and Teaching for Diversity/Cross-Cultural Science
	• In-Class Activity: Arthropod discussion leaders (ICAR) – Pray and Fathman articles
	• Revisit ESTELL Framework and Unit Planning
	Assignment:
	  1. Read "Integrating Oral Communication and Science Instruction," by Freeman & Taylor. In Integrating science and literacy instruction: A framework for bridging the gap.
	  2. Read "Science Conversations for Young Learners," pp. 43–45, by Sander & Nelson. Science and Children. (PDF, iLearn)

Week 8	• Promoting Complex Thinking and Inquiry Skills
	• Promoting Science Talk In-Class Activity: Investigating Skulls of Herbivores, Omnivores & Carnivores
	• Discussion leaders (ICAR) – Freeman & Sander articles
	Assignment:
	  1. Read Carr, Sexton, & Lagunoff, 2007. "Scaffolding Science Learning" (Chapter 5, pp. 55-75). In Making Science Accessible to English Learners. (PDF, iLearn)
	  2. Read "The Science Representation Continuum," pp. 52–55, by Olson. Science and Children. (PDF, iLearn)

Week 9	• Student Assessment in Science/Scaffolding Language & Literacy in Science
	• In-Class Activity: Electricity
	• Discussion leaders (ICAR) – Carr & Olson articles
	Assignment:
	  1. Bring a science textbook, science kit, or other science resource being used in your respective field placements. Bring the accompanying teacher's manual if available. [Examples: FOSS, GEMS, AIMS, Delta Science Modules, etc.]
	  2. Read "Criteria for Selecting Inquiry-Centered Science Curriculum Materials," pp. 63–75. In Science for All Children.

Week 10	• Forms of Assessment in Science In-Class Activity: Science Curriculum Evaluation • Revisit SST – (Subject-Specific Task) Assignment: 1. Read "Seamless Assessment," pp. 41–45, by Volkmann & Abell. Science & Children. (PDF, iLearn) 2. Read (Optional Textbook) Chapter 5: Strategies for Assessing Science and Language Learning, pp. 61–75. Fathman & Crowther.
Week 11	No Class Reminders: (a) Work on your SST or Unit Plans, (b) visit this website and view the video segment: A Private Universe: Seasons & Phases of the Moon – www.learner.org/resources/series28.html (scroll down the page and click the icon: VoD)
Week 12	• Continue Assessment in Science In-Class Activity: Sun-Earth-Moon Investigation • Private Universe (video segment) • Discussion leaders (ICAR) – Volkmann & Fathman articles Assignment: 1. Read "Teaching for Conceptual Change in Space Science," pp. 20–23, by Brunsell & Marcks. (PDF, iLearn) 2. Read "More Than a Human Endeavor: Teaching the Nature of Science," pp. 43–47, by Olson. Science and Children. (PDF, iLearn)
Week 13	• Continue Moon Investigation • Misconceptions (or Alternative Frameworks) in Science • Whole Class Discussion & Application – Brunsell and Olson articles • Sharing Science Unit Plans (2 groups) Due: SST (Task 1 Form and Task 2)
Week 14	• Environmental Education: Project WILD/Project WET Sharing Science Unit Plans (3 groups)
Week 15	• Sharing Science Unit Plans (2 groups) Assessment and Reflection • Post-Survey for Student Teachers: ESTELL Project

Appendix B – Suggested Science Lesson Plan Format

Lesson Title:
Grades:
Big Ideas/Unifying Themes:
Process Skills:
Vocabulary:
Intended Learning Outcomes:
At the end of this lesson, students should be able to:
There are three types:

1. Content knowledge (content-specific knowledge described in the curriculum)
2. Skills and processes (COMIC-E, investigative skills, use of equipment, etc.)
3. Socially/culturally relevant critical thinking (attitudes, social relevance, social action)

Instructional Resources/Materials/Technology – What materials will the teacher and the students need to make this a successful science lesson? Include examples of science content-based children's literature/picture books and relevant websites. Discuss appropriate technology integration to enhance and extend science concepts and processes.

CA Frameworks/Standards:

- Lesson Development (or Procedures): This section details, in a step-by-step manner, the sequence of teaching that is planned in the lesson. Follow the 5E Learning Cycle Model in Science Inquiry (Engagement, Exploration, Explanation, Evaluation, Extension) in introducing and presenting the science concepts, processes, and applications to real-life situations.
- Include what you will say to move the children from one phase of the lesson to the next. If you intend, for example, to have them deepen their understanding through discussion and hands-on activities, you must include the prompts (questions) to scaffold the discussion.
- Identify and describe briefly the level/s of inquiry addressed in the lesson or sequence of activities (i.e., Structured Inquiry, Guided, Open/Full Inquiry).
- Include Assessment Plan (i.e., KWL, concept mapping, rubrics, journals, student demonstrations, quiz, worksheets, direct student observations, etc.).

TABLE 10.3 Lesson development framework

Approx. Time	Lesson Development (Content)	ESTELL Framework
5-10 min.	I. Introduction [Engagement: Attention-Activator, Brainstorming, or Discrepant Event/Demo]	
25-35 min.	II. Development [Exploration & Explanation: Hands-on Minds-on Activity or Learning Centers, Interactive Mini-Lecture/ PowerPoint Presentation	
10-15 min.	III. Closure/Evaluation [Review of information & experiences, Question & Answer session, Demo if needed, Homework] IV. Extension [Application]	

PART IV
CONCLUSIONS

11
CROSSCUTTING FINDINGS AND RECOMMENDATIONS FOR RESEARCH AND PRACTICE IN TEACHING SCIENCE WITH EMERGENT BILINGUAL LEARNERS

Martha Allexsaht-Snider, Cory A. Buxton, Yainitza Hernández Rodríguez, Lourdes Cardozo-Gaibisso, Allan Cohen, & Zhenqiu Lu

In this concluding chapter we highlight the key findings and discuss recommendations for research and practice based on the collective work represented in this volume. We describe contributions, challenges, and recommendations that emerge from this work in relation to teacher preparation and teacher professional learning designed to improve the science learning experiences and opportunities for emergent bilingual learners. This chapter also explores several other important topics that the three projects in this volume have addressed elsewhere, but that do not play a central role in the chapters written for this book. We list some additional references for project publications that discuss these additional topics, for those who wish to read further. These topics include (a) the next generation of assessments and testing of emergent bilingual students' science learning; (b) the role of families in science learning; and (c) attention to understanding student learning as well as teaching.

As John Dewey wrote in his 1922 book *Democracy and Education*, "The chief opportunity for science is the discovery of the relations of a man to his work – including his relations to others who take part – which will enlist his intelligent interest in what he is doing." (Dewey, 1922, n.p.) In other words, science can serve to connect the learner both to the world of work and to the world of others, and, as a result, serves not only to teach students intellectual skills, but also group and social skills as well. Among these social skills are the need to communicate one's ideas and understandings. Dewey integrated applied science projects, such as raising animals, gardening, cooking, and examining the workings of everyday machines, at the Laboratory School he started in 1892 at the University of Chicago. This represented one of the earliest attempts to integrate scientific knowledge with the lived experience of the student, unlike typical schooling at that time, which, according to Dewey, isolated science from lived experience, resulting in students learning that science was something disconnected from their world. As Dewey described it, the student "acquires a technical body of information without ability to trace its connections with the objects and operations with which he is familiar – often he acquires simply a peculiar vocabulary" (Dewey, 1922, n.p.).

While Dewey was not particularly focused on the language of science, this quote highlights a central theme of our book, namely that all students can succeed at learning and communicating about complex science concepts and practices if their learning experiences are adequately scaffolded. Such scaffolding should connect prior experiences in and beyond the classroom, new learning opportunities that engage students collaboratively in science investigations, and an explicit focus on the language of science and how this language can be applied in meaningful ways that don't simply result in students acquiring a "peculiar vocabulary."

There has been significant progress in the reform of science education over the past few decades, as we have transitioned from a focus on learning science as memorizing concepts to learning science as doing inquiry related to big ideas, to learning science as engaging in the three-dimensional model of disciplinary core ideas, crosscutting concepts, and science and engineering practices. Despite this progress, the roles of cultural and linguistic assets and competencies that all students bring to the science classroom, and to schooling more generally, have yet to receive the degree of attention that they require if all students, including emergent bilinguals, are to thrive in learning science.

Contributions and Recommendations for Classroom Practice Designed to Improve the Science Learning Experiences and Opportunities of Emergent Bilingual Learners

Research across the three long-term, multifaceted projects introduced in this book (P-SELL [Chapters 2–4], LISELL-B [Chapters 5–7], and ESTELL [Chapters 8–10]) has had an overarching goal of extending understanding of how to enhance elementary and secondary science teaching to support emergent bilinguals and English learners in robust science learning. This goal has gained urgency as both pre-service and in-service teachers across the nation encounter the challenges and opportunities offered by the increase in numbers of linguistically and ethnically diverse students in American classrooms that parallels a similar demographic change in classrooms across the globe. Educators in the P-SELL, LISELL-B, and ESTELL projects have developed pedagogical models to support emergent bilingual students with the thinking, communicating, and problem-solving skills and abilities needed to apply scientific understanding to everyday as well as more complex and abstract contexts that have been outlined in current reform documents in science education, such as the Next Generation Science Standards (NGSS

Lead States, 2013). These pedagogical models incorporate sets of recommended teaching practices and resources that are held in common across the three projects, but each project also offers some distinctive and complementary recommended teaching practices for helping emergent bilingual students draw on their home language and cultural knowledge as they make sense of unique aspects of the language of science and learn to communicate their scientific ideas in English in oral and written form.

The pedagogical models from all three of the projects, incorporating current understandings of how and where people learn science (National Research Council, 2007; Feder, Shouse, Lewenstein, & Bell, 2009), build on the idea that useful science knowledge includes a blend of practices, core conceptual ideas, and communication skills that are developed in a broad range of life-wide and life-long learning contexts. With the strengths and needs of emergent bilingual learners in mind, developers of the pedagogical models have drawn on insights from sociocultural and sociolinguistic research that highlight the challenges, resources, and support structures that must be considered so that all learners can be successful with science both in and beyond school (e.g., Buxton, Salinas, Mahotiere, Lee, & Secada, 2015; Rosebery & Warren, 2008). Emerging understanding of the unique academic needs and resources of bilingual learners (Lee, Quinn, & Valdés, 2013) has informed each of these three efforts to design pedagogy that addresses the expectation for engaging all students in robust science learning opportunities using the science and engineering practices outlined in the Next Generation Science Standards.

Educators in the P-SELL, LISELL-B, and ESTELL projects, aware that the language of the NGSS practices (e.g., planning and carrying out investigations; obtaining, evaluating and communicating information) is quite broad, address the concern that many students, but especially emergent bilingual learners, will require additional specificity and clarity if they are to take ownership of these practices. The teaching practices described in each project's pedagogical model assume that a basic ability to interpret and produce the language of science is prerequisite to the development of sustained scientific discourse, which, in turn, is needed to engage in the science and engineering practices advocated in the NGSS. This does not mean, however, that students should be excluded from engaging in science investigations until they have reached a certain level of English language proficiency, as has sometimes resulted from misguided school policies and practices. Thus, a second commonly held assumption is that all students can succeed at learning and communicating about complex science concepts and practices if teachers are prepared to design learning experiences and employ teaching practices that connect to students' prior experiences in and beyond the classroom. Such experiences should include an explicit focus on the language of science and how this language can be applied in meaningful ways. Recommended teaching practices scaffold students' opportunities to engage in productive science speaking, writing, and visually representing, at the same time as they support students in drawing on their linguistic resources and cultural funds of knowledge in making richer scientific meaning from their participation in science investigations. Below we provide a brief, integrated synopsis of the recommended teaching practices across the three projects, using the major components outlined in the ESTELL instructional framework, reordered and combined to reflect a comprehensive view of the common elements and unique features across the three projects.

Promoting Complex Thinking in the Context of Science Investigations

All three projects advocate teaching practices that provide guidelines and resource materials to support teachers in engaging students in scientific investigations where they can explore key science concepts linked to state standards and the NGSS. In the P-SELL project, this set of instructional practices is framed by educative curriculum materials for fifth grade, including student books with chapters organized around "Big Ideas" according to four bodies of knowledge – the nature of science, Earth and space science, life science, and physical science. The curriculum materials provide teachers with ways to engage students in the practices of science, as students are prompted to ask questions about natural phenomena, construct explanations, argue from evidence based on observations or data, and communicate findings using multiple forms of representation. A scaffolded inquiry framework that involves several processes such as questioning, planning, implementing, concluding, reporting, and applying guides student work. The student book is designed to move progressively from teacher-directed instruction to student-directed inquiry. With a more open-ended approach in later chapters, the curriculum is designed to encourage student initiative and exploration.

The LISELL-B project makes the language and practices of scientific investigation – those language skills and practices that are needed to engage in, make sense of, and communicate meaningfully before, during, and after participation in scientific investigations – central to its pedagogical model. Teachers and project staff have developed science investigation guides and kits, addressing science topics embedded in the state science standards for earth science, life science, physical science, biology, and physics across grades 6 to 10, that incorporate one or more of the science investigation practices highlighted in the LISELL-B project. Those science investigation practices are (1) coordinating hypothesis, observation, and evidence; (2) controlling variables to design a fair test; (3) explaining cause and effect relationships; and (4) using models to construct explanations and test designs.

In the ESTELL project, the teaching practice focused on Promoting Complex Thinking offers recommendations for how teachers can promote scientific reasoning and understanding and the development of science inquiry skills. In their science methods courses, teacher educators provide anchor lessons embedding

ESTELL practices and specific strategies for facilitating children's scientific reasoning and understanding, and then provide guidelines for assignments where pre-service students collaboratively develop lesson plans incorporating these strategies, followed by teaching and being observed using those plans in their kindergarten to grade 5 practicum placement classrooms.

Supporting Language in Science

The specialized ways in which language and literacy are integrated in science, including discourse practices that frame ways of talking, thinking, and writing about the natural world around us (Lemke, 1990), are explicit focuses of the recommended teaching practices in the three projects. In the projects' pedagogical models, learning the classroom discourse of science, with its own vocabulary (Bravo & Cervetti, 2008) and ways of presenting arguments in specific ways (Osborne & Patterson, 2011), is viewed as important for all students, and especially for emergent bilinguals, in order to engage in the robust science learning called for in reform documents (Lee, Quinn, and Valdés, 2013). The following selection of teaching practices illustrates ways of bring instructional attention to the specialized ways in which reading/writing (e.g., reading informational texts, writing observations, providing scientific explanations and arguments), talk (e.g., providing scientific explanations and arguments), and vocabulary (e.g., articulating inquiry terms and key concepts embedded in meaningful contexts orally and in writing) take place in the context of science. In addition, suggestions of material resources and strategies to support ELLs and other students in owning and utilizing these discourses of science as they speak, read, and write in the process of sense making in science investigations are outlined.

In the P-SELL project educative curriculum materials embed multiple examples of the language of science used in various contexts in hands-on and purposeful science investigation activities. A high level of classroom discourse (Lee et al., 2013) that integrates cognitively demanding science inquiry as scientists engage in the practices of science is modeled and supported for students as they are guided by teachers through science investigations and accompanying readings and prompts for talking and writing in the student books. In each chapter in the student books, in addition to focusing explicitly on making meaning in English of key science terms related to foundational science concepts, resources such as lists of focal vocabulary in Spanish and Haitian Creole to support student learning of the language of science are provided. Each chapter concludes with an expository text summarizing key science concepts, with Spanish and Haitian Creole translations available on the project website. Supplemental language development resources offered on the project website, such as Science Language for Beginning ELLs, Word Walls, and Semantic Maps, embed home languages. Monolingual teachers can use these resources to explore science terms in students' home language and identify cognates between English and the home language. Teachers can also use these resources to encourage bilingual peers to support emergent bilingual students in their home language.

In the LISELL-B pedagogical model, the two language of science investigation practices of *using general academic vocabulary in context* and *owning the language of science* were developed to address research findings asserting that in school science learning students are asked to contextualize and interpret their experiences of the natural world through a language that may often sound quite foreign (Halliday, 2004). These two aspects of the pedagogical model have been discussed in detail elsewhere (Buxton, Allexsaht-Snider, Hernandez, Aghasaleh, Cardozo-Gaibisso, & Kirmaci, 2016) so will only be highlighted here briefly. Research is just beginning to address how this language of science intersects with the unique academic needs and resources of bilingual learners in science classrooms (Lee, Quinn, & Valdés, 2013). Making sure students, especially emergent bilingual learners, have ample opportunity to talk about, think about, read about, or write about the content and science investigation practices they engage with during LISELL-B science investigation activities is a goal of the strategies and resources provided to teachers in the project. The prompts and scaffolds provided in project materials co-designed with teachers offer emergent bilingual learners a way to triangulate understanding across spoken and written texts and solidify communication skills and science understanding through practice in collaboration with peers. Teachers use materials such as bilingual general-purpose academic word cards to support general academic vocabulary development in meaningful context in science classrooms, embedding this vocabulary in science investigation lessons and building bilingual academic word walls. The LISELL-B practice of owning the language of science focuses explicitly on supporting students in adopting the specialized language and discourses of science to better understand and communicate scientific ideas, in addition to building credibility for their own scientific thinking. For example, students practice two-way rewriting, translating academic science language into everyday language and vice versa. Explicit deconstruction of the language of science can help all students, and especially bilingual learners, to better understand and communicate scientific ideas.

Research-based instructional approaches for leveraging linguistic knowledge in the service of ELLs' science learning and scaffolding content understanding (Goldenberg, 2008) are infused in the ESTELL instructional practice of *Scaffolding and Developing of Language in Science*. With this practice, by previewing and attending to vocabulary, teachers address two types of science-related vocabulary – process inquiry words (e.g., observe, predict) and focal science concepts (e.g., erosion, adaptation). In addition to offering definitions (e.g., word maps, bilingual glossaries, cognate lists in students' home languages), teachers provide multiple exposures and uses for key science terms and check for student accuracy and understanding in using these terms in their talk and writing. Teachers also incorporate explicit instruction on language structures common in science (e.g., metaphors, dual meaning words, nominalizations). Adapting to variation in their students' levels of English proficiency, prior schooling experiences, and native language fluency, among other factors (Bunch, Kibler, & Pimentel, 2010), teachers are coached to take these and other ELL student characteristics into account. They consider these characteristics when deciding which type of linguistic scaffold to enact (e.g., native language support, gestural, oral, pictorial, graphic, and textual modes of representation) and the intensity with which to implement these scaffolds (e.g., amount of time spent, number of repetitions) in order to provide individualized ELL instruction.

Promoting Science Talk/Facilitating Collaborative Inquiry and Shared Authority

In the ESTELL project, promoting science talk, facilitating collaborative inquiry, and shared authority are central features of the instructional practice framework. As in the LISELL-B and P-SELL projects, teachers guide students in analyzing and developing facility with the models and patterns of scientific discourse. In addition, however, the ESTELL project incorporates research about facilitating effective instructional conversations (Tharp, Estrada, Dalton, & Yamauchi, 2000) in supporting teachers to develop interactional, discursive modes in which they engage in more dialogic scientific talk with students. Teachers are taught ways to initiate talk in science learning activities and offer guiding questions while also following up on student responses. The particular attention paid in the ESTELL project to the uses of purposeful grouping structures, explicit communication of student tasks and roles in group work, and varied teaching structures as a means to both advance inquiry activities and ensure all students are involved in those activities is unique in its emphasis as compared to the other two projects. The LISELL-B project materials do include templates for guiding student roles and associated talk in group work, and build paired talking and writing activities into all science investigations. LISELL-B materials do not, however, use collaborative grouping structures to provide science-driven language feedback in the same way as is advocated in the ESTELL project. Another unique aspect of the ESTELL pedagogical model is the inclusion of strategies to support student voice in claiming a shared authority in the process of sense-making in science. Pre-service teachers learn how to present scientific knowledge as either one that is shared and challenged or as student-generated ideas.

Literacy in Science

Various literacy activities (making text-to-self connections in reading, writing science books with children, and semantic maps) are incorporated in the P-SELL project educative curriculum materials in student books. Embedded literacy components (e.g., literacy-based Post-its weaved throughout the teachers' guide version of the text, graphic representation throughout each inquiry) appear frequently to enable teachers to focus on key literacy strategies during pivotal points of science instruction. ESTELL instructional practices in the realm of literacy focus on an important meaning-making process available in science learning, i.e., authentic science literacy where students use reading and writing for conducting scientific investigations. Similarly, in the LISELL-B project teachers collaboratively design language boosters (short high-interest texts incorporating a science investigation practice and focused on relevant content concepts that include prompts for paired talk and writing) and lab templates that scaffold students' use of the academic language of science as well as everyday language to articulate their developing understandings of the science investigation process and science concepts they are exploring. The curriculum supports teachers in capitalizing on students' "funds of knowledge" (Moll, Amanti, Neff, & González, 1992) by incorporating students' cultural artifacts and community resources in ways that are both academically meaningful and culturally relevant. Home learning and practice activities are provided as optional resources for bridging from school to home in science learning.

Contextualizing Science Activity

Research has shown that student learning is enhanced when it occurs in contexts that are culturally, linguistically, and cognitively meaningful and relevant to students (e.g., Baquedano-López, Solís, & Kattan, 2005; Buxton, Salinas, Mahotiere, Lee, & Secada, 2013). All three of the projects incorporate instructional approaches for building on emergent bilingual students' cultural knowledge to advance science learning. In the P-SELL curriculum, the activities begin by engaging students with the world around them. Each chapter introduces key science concepts by relating them to students' prior knowledge or experiences in their home and community contexts. Students are asked, for example, to write out types of matter they observed that day; where they observed each one; which senses were used to observe each example of matter; whether each type was in solid, liquid, or gas form; and which properties were attributed to each type of matter. For the ESTELL practice of contextualization, pre-service teachers learn to probe what students already know related to their home and community as well as their local ecology in order to frame initial science lesson inquiries. Contextualizing instruction is seen as a way to elicit relevant prior knowledge but also as a way to expand on previous academic and cultural knowledge that students bring to the classroom. In the LISELL-B project, teachers have the opportunity to participate in science investigations with families during bilingual Steps to College through Science family workshops. These interactions help teachers to identify family funds of knowledge and experiences with science in out-of-school, work, and neighborhood contexts that can later be linked to classroom science learning.

Recommendations for Teacher Preparation and Teacher Professional Development to Improve the Science Learning Experiences and Opportunities of Emergent Bilinguals

As we have discussed in the previous section, one contribution that each of the three projects offers is a version of a pedagogical model for supporting the integration of science and language learning for all students, with a particular focus on the needs and the assets of emergent bilingual learners. Each project strives to provide teachers (whether pre-service or in-service) with a clear and systematic pedagogical model of instruction for supporting emergent bilingual learners in science, and then affords opportunities to practice applying that model with students. A second contribution that each project makes is the development of a framework for supporting teachers with the skills and experiences that will allow them to understand, practice, and eventually take ownership of the pedagogical model that is being promoted.

In the case of the ESTELL project, the primary focus is on the preparation of pre-service teachers. A secondary focus is on the professional learning of the mentor teachers who work with the pre-service teachers and on the professional learning of the teacher educators who teach the university science methods courses. In the P-SELL project, the primary focus is on the professional learning of the fifth-grade teachers who directly implement the pedagogical model. A secondary focus is on the professional learning of the school district liaisons who facilitate the teacher professional development workshops and other district personnel who need to understand and buy into the pedagogical model in order for a scale-up effort to be successful. In the case of the LISELL-B project, the primary focus is on the professional learning of the middle school and high school science and ESOL teachers who directly implement the pedagogical model. A secondary focus is on the professional learning of the veteran and next-generation teacher educators who facilitate the various teacher professional learning contexts. Below, we highlight three recommendations for teacher educators and others who engage in facilitating teacher professional development based on the work of these projects: (a) teachers must experience new pedagogical models in meaningful ways as learners before they can be expected to implement them as teachers; (b) teacher educators and teachers who are committed to inclusive and equity-oriented pedagogy that supports emergent bilinguals need to engage in collaborative self-study; and (c) the variety of experiences and skills needed for this work requires team effort and distributed expertise.

Teachers and Teacher Educators Must Experience New Pedagogical Models in Meaningful Ways as Learners before They Can Be Expected to Implement Them as Teachers

A common theme across each of the three projects is that in order for teachers (whether pre-service or experienced) to implement the relevant pedagogical practices in classrooms with students, they must first experience these practices as learners themselves and have time to systematically debrief those experiences. This understanding is at the heart of the ESTELL model as pre-service teachers in the ESTELL science methods course are systematically led through science investigations that model each of the six instructional practices. So, for example, they learn about the importance of high levels of persistent student interaction. They experience this practice as learners in the methods course and then attempt to facilitate the practice with elementary students in their field placements. As a second example, the pre-service teachers learn about the linguistic patterns and structures of scientific discourse and the importance of dialogic scientific talk (the notion of Instructional Conversation). Next, they experience what it is like to have a teacher (the methods instructor) facilitate a science lesson that both explicitly and implicitly makes use of language in these ways. Finally, the pre-service teachers are observed and evaluated as they attempt to use this practice with their own students in their field placements. Because they are observed using the ESTELL observation instrument, they receive targeted feedback that highlights their evolving efforts to enact the ESTELL instructional practices. A similar approach is taken for each of the practices.

From the earliest days of the P-SELL project, the project leadership team held the belief that if elementary grades teachers were to be expected to engage their students in science investigations as a way to promote scientific thinking and communicating, then the teachers would need to have the experience of participating in these investigations themselves as learners. Indeed, over the years of project implementation, the professional development time allocated to doing science investigations together only increased. Teachers routinely shared that they were hesitant to do any hands-on science investigations with their students that they had not already experienced in the P-SELL workshop settings. Teachers gained at least three advantages from this practice. First, at the process level, teachers gained comfort with the materials and supplies needed for an investigation, explored how to use the materials, and then got to practice the procedures themselves and think about where their students might encounter problems during the investigation. Second, at the conceptual level, teachers got to talk about the relevant science concepts with their peers and with the workshop facilitators, got to ask questions about the relevant science concepts in a safe space, got to consider how the concepts were demonstrated in the investigation, and again got to think about where their students might have problems understanding the concepts. Third, at the linguistic level, teachers got to plan for how they would scaffold the necessary language that their students would need to successfully engage in and make meaning of the investigation. Thus, as with the ESTELL project, the P-SELL project found it critical that teachers experience the project's pedagogical model in meaningful ways as learners before they could implement the practices as teachers.

In the LISELL-B project, the same basic premise about the need to experience the pedagogical model as a learner before doing so as a teacher held true.

While the LISELL-B project worked with secondary school teachers, who typically have more experience teaching science than do their elementary school counterparts, significant aspects of the LISELL-B pedagogical model were new for these teachers as well. Thus, significant portions of our teacher professional learning institute were dedicated to engaging in science investigations using the LISELL-B pedagogical model. Beyond this approach, we wish to highlight two additional aspects of the teacher institute work that are relevant to this topic. After engaging in several model lessons, teachers in the institute worked in content area groups with guidance from LISELL-B staff to develop additional science investigations using a highly scaffolded process we referred to as LISELLizing. This process had the double benefit of giving teachers additional practice familiarizing themselves with the components of our pedagogical model while simultaneously increasing teacher buy-in to use the investigation kits during the school year since they were involved themselves in developing the investigations to meet the needs of their students. Second, in addition to the teachers benefitting from the model lessons and kit creation process, the LISELL-B staff who served as school liaisons (and who had varied levels of science teaching backgrounds themselves) benefited from experiencing the pedagogical model within the professional learning framework as learners before they were expected to support teachers as facilitators of professional learning themselves.

As discussed in detail in the chapters focusing on each project, these models of teacher preparation all demonstrated that explicitly labeling and modeling the practices, and giving and receiving feedback on enactment of the practices, were important components of teacher learning models. This approach strengthened teachers' beliefs in the value of the pedagogies and practices and simultaneously strengthened teachers' abilities to enact the practices with students. Thus, one central recommendation that emerges from these projects is the need for facilitators of teacher learning to be very detailed and explicit both when discussing pedagogy that supports emergent bilinguals in more theoretical or conceptual terms and when crafting and facilitating experiences to model those practices. Further, as should be clear from the complexity of this work, teachers (novice and veteran alike) need repeated opportunities to engage in, reflect on, and revisit these practices in multiple contexts if they are to begin taking ownership.

Teacher Educators and Teachers Who Are Committed to Inclusive and Equity-Oriented Pedagogy That Supports Emergent Bilingual Learners Need to Engage in Collaborative Self-Study

A second contribution and corresponding recommendation that is explicit in the ESTELL and LISELL-B projects, and implicit in P-SELL, is the benefit of turning the research gaze inward to facilitate self-study by teacher educators who are committed to more inclusive and equity-oriented pedagogy. The ESTELL project found that because science teacher educators' own pedagogical orientations differed, this influenced the ways that each of the teacher educators implemented the ESTELL science course framework in his or her own methods course. The teacher educators needed to explore and reflect on these differences and they found, in the end, that while they each implemented the ESTELL pedagogy in somewhat different ways, each variation was still effective in meeting the goals of the project. This is a topic that deserves further exploration because it seems obvious that some possible pedagogical orientations would be less compatible with the goals of the ESTELL project. Thus, while the teacher educators in this case had differing orientations that resulted in differing practices, they clearly also shared common commitments around supporting emergent bilingual learners that allowed the model to succeed. Their teacher educator self-study served both to reinforce what was working in this aspect of the project and pointed to aspects of their pedagogical model that needed to be refined.

In the LISELL-B project, we found that science and ESOL teachers took advantage of a group session to examine summative teacher log data during a teacher summer institute for reflection on their own goals for implementing the LISELL-B language of science investigation practices over the past year. Teachers suggested that before examining their summarized log data, differences in patterns of instruction across the year were not always clear to them; many did not remember differences across the year in their enactment of LISELL-B practices. Having a large group of teachers with whom they could discuss gaps they saw in their own or in the group's practices was seen to be useful. Teachers felt it allowed them to share knowledge about how to integrate the LISELL-B practices into their teaching in the science classroom and to brainstorm new strategies for doing so. Engaging in conversations involving teachers from multiple schools and multiple districts, a rarity in most of the teachers' professional learning experiences, was seen as particularly productive. Combining teachers from different schools into the group ameliorated some of the political and interpersonal dynamics that could potentially disrupt constructive reflection. Teachers felt that this diversity expanded the breadth of experience from which the group could draw and learn. In large projects with multiple districts such as the P-SELL project, facilitators of professional learning serving different schools and districts might find documenting their practice with a teaching log and collaborative self-study of summative log data to be a dynamic catalyst for improving their pedagogy in professional learning contexts. Similarly, science teacher educators across institutions, and mentor teachers working in the field with pre-service teachers, such as in the ESTELL project, might design logs to document their work with pre-service teachers to foster the learning of the ESTELL instructional practices. The logs could serve as a useful tool for promoting collaborative self-study with a goal of improving teacher education practice.

While collaborative self-study on the part of the teacher educators was not explicit in the P-SELL model, and is not a topic addressed directly in the P-SELL chapters in this volume, the notion of ongoing reflection focused on how best to prepare and support project teachers to implement the P-SELL curriculum is a longstanding project practice. The P-SELL teacher professional development workshops have evolved over more than a decade of implementation and have been continuously adapted based on the changing needs of the teachers, new insights gained from the research, and the evolving nature of both the state science standards and the project research design. The project team itself has also evolved over time, as will inevitably be the case for projects of this duration. As new members joined the team over the years, more experienced team members oriented them not only to the research and development activities, but also to the need to explore one's own views about teaching science, teaching language through science, and teaching emergent bilinguals.

The Variety of Experiences and Skills Needed for This Work Requires Team Effort and Distributed Expertise

The question of how to ensure that teacher educators themselves are prepared to meet the goals of their projects relates to a final recommendation from the work of these three projects, namely that such an effort requires teamwork and distributed expertise. Much of the success of each of the projects stems from the teams that the projects were able to assemble. One of the ongoing challenges of supporting emergent bilingual learners in science is that, at a minimum, this requires expertise both in science teaching and in language teaching, and also in multicultural competence. While external funding is not a necessity to build this type of team effort, it is certainly a very helpful contributing factor. External funding allowed each of these projects to provide faculty and graduate students with financial support not only to do the work of conducting teacher education or professional development, but also to support bringing together diverse teams with varied expertise and a common interest in improving science learning experiences for teachers and for those teachers' students.

The ESTELL project model benefited from the collaborative work of teacher educators with backgrounds in science education, culturally responsive pedagogy, and second language acquisition. Further, the master elementary teachers who had experience successfully supporting emergent bilingual learners in their classrooms also received professional development from the ESTELL team and played a critical role. Without philosophically aligned and well-prepared mentor teachers in whose classrooms pre-service teachers can grow and develop, much of the good work done in the science methods course could have been undermined. True collaboration, where various team members bring unique skills and experiences, is needed to address the complexities of integrating language, literacy, culture, and science.

In the P-SELL project, there was a similar reliance on diverse team members with distributed expertise. The project leadership included science educators, English as a second language educators, and assessment experts, among others. The district liaisons who, in later iterations of the project, were responsible for conducting the teacher professional development, likewise had varied expertise and also met on a regular basis with the project leadership team to both plan and debrief the various professional development activities. The project team was also in frequent contact with school district leadership to solicit their input and ideas, which was especially important given the large size of the project. When taken together, the distributed expertise of the group that was involved directly or indirectly with P-SELL teacher professional development helped make certain that project teachers were well prepared to meet the science learning needs and build on the assets of their emergent bilingual students.

As with the other two projects, in LISELL-B there was a clear understanding that no one member of the project team possessed the variety of experiences and skills needed to carry out the teacher professional learning component of the project. Rather, from the outset, the leadership team engaged other faculty members, a highly international group of doctoral research assistants, and our teacher participants in open questions about how best to carry out our work together. The project embraced the idea of distributed expertise in all its aspects, including the teacher professional learning component. For example, as we planned the project, we formed a teacher advisory board in addition to a more traditional advisory board of expert scholars because we were aware that teachers' experiences would eventually shape the degree of success we had with the project. We also organized meetings with families who had worked with us on a previous project to get advice and suggestions directly from emergent bilingual students and their parents. When taken together, the experiences of the three projects point to the clear need for a team approach to the challenge of preparing teachers to excel at teaching science to emergent bilingual learners.

Recommendations for Further Research Related to Supporting Teachers in Meeting the Needs and Building on the Assets of Emergent Bilingual Learners

Each project in this book can be seen as a research and development effort in which the research team strives to develop resources that help in-service and pre-service teachers of science to better meet the needs and build on the resources of their emergent bilingual leaners. These development efforts, focused on the integration of language and science teaching practices to support science learning for emergent bilingual learners, become the context for the research components of each project. These research efforts differ in significant ways across projects, but also include common features. For example, each project considers the overlaps and intersections among the teaching of science concepts, the teaching of the language of science used to explore those concepts, and the awareness and integration of the students' local contexts and cultural resources that can help facilitate access to both the science and language learning.

Research Recommendations Grounded in the ESTELL Project

The research component of the ESTELL project tested the effectiveness of a model for integrating language, literacy, culture, and science in ways that simultaneously facilitate students' science understandings and English language development. To accomplish this, the research team needed to develop a new observation instrument that could disentangle these different aspects of science learning for research purposes, while also showing how they worked together to support student learning in practice. The resulting ESTELL Dialogic Activity in Science Instruction (EDAISI) observation instrument allowed the team to study the degree to which the ESTELL practices were being implemented by teacher candidates who had received the ESTELL training as they planned and delivered science instruction in classrooms with emergent bilinguals.

One key recommendation from this work relates to the value of an observation instrument that combines numerical rating of a clear and bounded set of subscales reflecting the valued practices of the model, with semi-structured fieldnotes and observation debriefs (qualitative) that document how teachers adapted the practices based on the specifics of the lesson and their knowledge of their students. Using this approach, the ESTELL team was able to provide clear research-based recommendations to teacher candidates, such as effective ways to integrate students' home language through the use of bilingual glossaries and cognate lists, and ways to identify language choices that might prove problematic for emergent bilinguals, such as dual meaning words.

The mentor teachers who worked with the ESTELL teacher candidates likewise were able to benefit from the use of the EDAISI observation instrument. They found that using this instrument helped them to guide the debrief and reflection sessions they held with the teacher candidates in more productive ways that distinguished between good teaching generally, and teaching approaches that explicitly supported emergent bilinguals. Further, as the ESTELL team has noted, their observation instrument and the process for using it provides an alternative to the value added models (VAM) that have been embraced in many states and school districts for evaluating teacher performance. While VAM approaches have been critiqued for having poor validity and reliability for assessing teacher practices and student learning (AERA, 2015), the EDAISI research approach uses a more formative process of assessment to guide science instruction for all students while addressing the special considerations of emergent bilinguals and providing productive opportunities for teachers to reflect on and incorporate recommendations for modifications in future lessons.

As described in the third chapter of the ESTELL project section, the research team extended their activities to study their own practices as teacher educators teaching the science methods courses that prepared teacher candidates in the use of the ESTELL framework. By turning the research gaze upon themselves through the use of their EDAISI observation instrument to study their own teaching, the researchers showed how university faculty can apply the practices they advocate for teacher candidates in their own teaching and how they might further improve the integration of language, culture, and science teaching in their own classrooms. Additional research by this team or by others could examine the relationships between the implementation of instructional practices for supporting emergent bilinguals in university methods courses and the ways in which teacher candidates apply these practices during their student teaching experience and their first year in their own classroom. Again, the mix of scored quantitative components and descriptive qualitative components in the observation instrument can support richer debriefing discussions and more targeted adaptations to teaching practices.

A final salient point from this research is the question of how instructors in university methods courses can simulate the inclusion of emergent bilingual learners in their teaching. Much of the university coursework on learning to teach is disconnected from the linguistic, behavioral, and other contextual features that teacher candidates then face in field experiences and student teaching. This disconnect is readily apparent and often commented on by teacher candidates as well as by external critics of university-based teacher education. We see research efforts such as the ESTELL project as providing insights that may help address such limitations and respond to the critics.

For additional information about the research on pre-service science teacher education in ESTELL, please see:

Shaw, J., Lyon, E. G., Stoddart, T., Mosqueda, E., & Menon, P. (2014). Improving science and literacy learning for English language learners: Evidence from a pre-service teacher preparation intervention. *Journal of Science Teacher Education, 25*, 621–643.

Stoddart, T., Bravo, M. A., Mosqueda, E., & Solís, J. L. (2013). Restructuring pre-service teacher education to respond to increasing student diversity. *Research in Higher Education Journal, 19*, 1–19.

Research Recommendations Based on the P-SELL Project

The P-SELL project provides research recommendations that move in a somewhat different direction from that of the other two projects, as both the research and development efforts of the project have focused on pushing the intervention to a larger scale using an experimental design that has rarely been attempted in science education research. However, one aspect of the research that is shared across the projects is the desire to establish clearer relationships between teacher change and student outcomes within the context of the interventions. The design and the scale of the P-SELL research are both assets in addressing this challenge.

A common tension that often must be negotiated between researchers who wish to implement intervention research in schools and the leadership in those schools and districts is the question of the time it may take for interventions to show a positive outcome. The P-SELL research has shown that for many teachers it takes multiple years to learn how to effectively implement a new approach that results in positive student outcomes. Teachers need time and support to adopt and adapt new approaches and researchers need time working with those teachers to determine how best to support this process. By studying the mechanisms that facilitate implementation or adaptation over time, researchers may eventually be able to speed up this process. The eventual student gains seen in the P-SELL research should serve as a reminder for practitioners and school leaders that although everyone desires immediate results, intervention programs almost always require time to take root and demonstrate an impact.

A second recommendation based on more than a decade of P-SELL research is the need to continue to develop and improve measures of teacher knowledge and practice in science education. There are numerous challenges to developing useful measures for this work. For example, such measures must be valid and reliable not just in a particular setting, but across the range of settings in which the intervention occurs. Such measures must be sensitive enough to detect changes that address an array of science topics over time in order to make valid causal claims about effectiveness. The EDAISI observation instrument in the ESTELL project, the teacher task log and constructed response assessments in the LISELL-B project, and the science content knowledge assessment for teachers in the P-SELL project are all attempts at using research to show that tracking changes in science teacher knowledge and practice can be difficult but is possible. Additional research should use these and other approaches to measure teacher change and then look to connect that change with students' science learning outcomes.

When considering the evaluation of science interventions on a large scale, more research is needed on the logistical challenges that scale up along with other aspects of the research. While intervention research at any scale typically faces logistical challenges, these challenges are exacerbated by questions of scale. So, for example, the P-SELL efficacy and effectiveness studies both required data collection at the beginning and end of the school year. However, teacher assignments, student rosters, teacher and student mobility across schools, and many other logistical aspects of school structure are unstable and subject to change at the start of the school year, making such data collection problematic. The LISELL-B project encountered this challenge working in only 10 schools with approximately 50 teachers. Such issues were greatly magnified in the P-SELL project working across 66 schools and approximately 450 teachers.

While we have highlighted the ESTELL project's EDAISI observation instrument as a fruitful model for future research, the question of scaled-up interventions in the P-SELL project points to challenges in the use of such observation instruments as well. In the P-SELL efficacy study, classroom observations were included in the research design but were found to be one of the most challenging aspects due to the amount of training required of the research observers and the human and financial resources needed to conduct this component of the study. Further, the limited number of observations that could be conducted in each classroom meant that the observations were of limited use. For this reason, in the subsequent P-SELL effectiveness study the researchers decided that it was not a worthwhile research investment to conduct classroom observations. Similar reasoning led the LISELL-B research team to develop the teacher task logs as a way to supplement the limited number of classroom observations that could be conducted.

Another research recommendation that emerged from the long-term and large-scale nature of the P-SELL research was the critical importance of earning and maintaining the trust and support of participating schools and school districts. Time must be taken to build relationships, to negotiate shared commitments, and to establish a reputation as trustworthy collaborators who have the best interest of students, teachers, and schools in mind at all times. As educational researchers, we do care deeply about students, teachers, and schools, but we do not have exactly the same agenda and goals as the school and district leadership. For example, school leaders often look at yearly changes in student performance on standardized tests as the most critical measure of effectiveness of an intervention, while as researchers we may have more complex or nuanced ways of thinking about the effectiveness of our projects. If stakeholders fail to agree on what counts as success or what supports growth, then researchers may be restricted in terms of what portions of their intervention they are allowed to implement. Thus, the P-SELL project was not able to utilize its project-developed student assessments during the efficacy study because the school district did not see enough value in the assessment to warrant asking the students to complete an additional assessment.

To support collaboration with school and district leaders, the P-SELL project invested in a number of efforts to strengthen relationships. These included conducting research team meetings with the district team every two months, hiring a full-time district liaison for each district (a school district staff member funded temporarily by the research project), having these district liaisons facilitate the P-SELL professional development workshops to demonstrate district buy-in to school leaders and teachers, and having district personnel work with research team members to organize logistics of data collection. The research team also learned to be more flexible both in terms of the implementation component (e.g., adapting to various district needs and policies) and in terms of the research component (e.g., scheduling make-up sessions for teachers who could not attend the main sessions where data collection activities took place).

A final research recommendation related to building trust and collaboration involves the value of positive testimonials from teachers and school leaders who have previous experience as participants in the research and who had a positive experience. Teachers are more likely to trust other teachers and school administrators are likely to trust their administrative peers when it comes to doing a cost-benefit analysis regarding participation in a project that will take a substantial commitment of time and energy. Researchers looking to recruit new teacher participants to continue or expand an existing project should solicit positive past (or current) participants to help identify and/or speak with potential future participants.

For further information about teacher change in P-SELL, please see:

Diamond, B. S., Maerten-Rivera, J., Rohrer, R. E., & Lee, O. (2014). Effectiveness of curricular and professional development intervention on elementary teachers' science content knowledge and student achievement outcomes: Year 1 results. *Journal of Research in Science Teaching, 51*, 635–658. *(P-SELL efficacy study)*

Lee, O., Llosa, L., Jiang, F., Haas, A., O'Connor, C., & Van Booven, C. (in press). Teachers' science knowledge and practices with English language learners. *Journal of Research in Science Teaching.* *(P-SELL effectiveness study)*

For further information about research measures in P-SELL, please see:

Maerten-Rivera, J., Huggins, A. C., Adamson, K., Lee, O., & Llosa, L. (2015). Development and validation of a measure for elementary teachers' science content knowledge in two multiyear teacher professional development intervention projects. *Journal of Research in Science Teaching, 52*(3), 371–396. *(both P-SELL efficacy study and effectiveness study)*

Research Recommendations Based on the LISELL-B Project

In our initial LISELL exploratory project, we developed a classroom observation instrument with some similarities to the ESTELL (EDAISI) observation instrument as one of our primary research instruments. We used this observation instrument in what we referred to as a Grand Rounds approach, modeled loosely after medical grand rounds. A LISELL project teacher would volunteer to host an observation, and in addition to members of the research team attending, other teachers from the school who were participating in the project would come to observe the focal lesson as well. The group would then meet (usually after school) for a debrief session and mini-workshop in which we would all share ways in which we saw the LISELL project practices being implemented in the lesson and make suggestions for continuing to build on student assets and to address areas of challenge.

While there were many positive aspects of this model, and while we have retained it in a limited degree in the LISELL-B project, we encountered several limitations to this aspect of our research. First, as mentioned in the discussion of the P-SELL project, as projects scale up it becomes more difficult to conduct adequate numbers of observations and, from a research perspective, it becomes more challenging to compare observation data across different contexts with different policies, different school expectations, and other differences. Second, and more unexpectedly, we found that as high stakes teacher evaluation systems have become prominent in our context (and in many other parts of the country), teachers are increasingly resistant to being observed in their classrooms. While intellectually they may make a distinction between observations by their school or district administrators that have significant professional consequences and observations by our project team and their colleagues that have no such consequences, we nonetheless got the clear message that any sort of classroom observation had become much more stressful to teachers.

For these reasons, we decided to develop a new teacher log instrument for the LISELL-B project that allowed teachers to self-report their enactment of the LISELL-B practices and their use of project resources. We have just completed our second year of using the teacher log and have gained several insights that may be useful to other researchers considering the development of instruments for tracking participant implementation of project practices. As we alluded to in the chapter about the teacher log, we have a philosophical resistance to the notion of fidelity of implementation in educational research and prefer to think in terms of the concept of multiplicities of enactment.

Teacher log data, while fairly simple data, do seem to provide valuable information, both for research purposes and for teacher professional learning purposes. Because we view teachers as active agents who know their students better than members of the research team do, and are, therefore, better positioned to adapt project practices and resources to their needs rather than implementing practices with prescribed fidelity, we see the log data as a powerful reflective tool for engaging teachers in self-reflection and self-critique as they participate in the ongoing refinement of the intervention. Teachers are able to use their own log data, and compare it to the data of other teachers who teach their same grade level and content in other schools, to get a picture of their own ongoing and evolving practice over a prolonged period of time. While this is useful to the teachers, these data are equally useful to the researchers who can discern and discuss patterns of enactment, and then connect these patterns to other data sources. The log data thus spark a variety of generative conversations about the contextual factors that encourage the enactment of certain practices in some contexts and hinder the enactment of others. Such conversations also support and sustain our philosophical commitment to multiplicities of enactment rather than traditional views of fidelity of implementation.

As we noted in the teacher log chapter, there is also a practical research advantage of relatively low cost to collect the teacher log data as compared to conducting classroom observations with the same or similar regularity. The project does pay teachers a modest stipend each semester for completing the logs once every two weeks, and because the logs are less stressful for teachers than observations, our response rates are acceptably high (a mean of roughly 80 percent of possible logs completed over the course of the school year). Teachers also feel a greater sense of buy-in with the logs because a number of teachers in the project were involved in the piloting and refinement of the research instrument. This is an important recommendation in that our initial iteration of the log was too time-consuming, and without teacher testing and feedback that resulted in a simplified version, we would likely have suffered from a lower response rate.

The log data serve multiple purposes and have proven to be useful for program improvement as well as for effectiveness research. Fundamental to the LISELL-B research effort is our attempt to understand the relationships between teachers' engagement in the range of professional learning experiences that constitute our LISELL-B professional learning framework, teachers' enactment of the project practices that constitute our pedagogical model, and the abilities of the emergent bilingual students in these teachers' classrooms to engage in and communicate about language-rich science investigations. Researchers and the teachers we work with can all benefit from opportunities to reflect together on our practices. The teacher logs our project team developed in collaboration with project participants have provided us with a valuable research tool for helping to trace the complex relationships between teacher professional learning, teachers' classroom practices, and students' science and language learning.

For further information about the LISELL-B pedagogical model and professional learning framework, please see:

Buxton, C., Allexsaht-Snider, M., Hernandez, Y., Aghasaleh, R., Cardozo-Gaibisso, L., & Kirmaci, M. (in press, 2016). A design-based model of science teacher professional learning in the LISELL-B project. In A. Oliveira & M. Weinburgh (Eds.), *Science Teacher Preparation in Content-Based Second Language Acquisition*. New York, NY: Springer.

Buxton, C. Allexsaht-Snider, M., Kayumova, S., Aghasaleh, R., Choi, Y., & Cohen, A. (2015). Teacher agency and professional learning: Rethinking fidelity of implementation as multiplicities of enactment. *Journal of Research in Science Teaching*, 52(4), 489–502.

Other Important Topics for Improving the Science Learning Experiences and Opportunities of Emergent Bilingual Learners

As we have described in several places, the three projects described in this book are each multifaceted and strive to address many aspects of the teaching and learning process for English learners in science. In selecting topics for the chapters to submit for this volume, each project needed to decide on which aspects of the work to highlight and which to pass over in this context. In this section we wish to briefly mention a few of the other areas that the P-SELL, LISELL-B, and ESTELL projects engage in relevant to the overarching topic of improving science and language teaching and learning with emergent bilinguals.

Family Engagement

The role of family engagement is well known to play a central role in students' long-term academic success (Fan & Chen, 2001). Teachers' feelings about their students' parents, and the nature of those interactions, have also long shown an effect on student success in school (Epstein & Dauber, 1991). Each of the three projects in this book value connections between school, family, and community. The LISELL-B project includes the strengthening of family connections as an explicit piece of the project, while this aspect is more implicit in the work of the other two projects. Since 2009, LISELL-B has offered an annual series of bilingual family science workshops for emergent bilingual students, their families, and their science and ESOL teachers. These four-hour workshops held on Saturday mornings take place at various universities, technical colleges, and school district career academies, and routinely attract roughly a hundred participants.

During each workshop the students, families, and teachers circulate together through three experiences: (a) a bilingual family conversation session in which the group talks about planning for post-secondary education; (b) a science investigation session in which participants work together on bilingual language-rich science experiments; and (c) a career pathways session in which participants visit science labs and discuss educational and occupational pathways with current students and faculty at the host institution. Each workshop ends with a shared meal to encourage informal dialogue among teachers, families, college students, and researchers.

We have found that when families, students, and teachers participate in science together, parents become better aware of the academic expectations that are being placed upon their children in school. Students benefit from seeing their parents as co-learners who possess resources, interests, and funds of knowledge related to science and other academic topics. For their part, teachers get to see their students' parents in a new light, as committed to their children's academic success and as willing to overcome hurdles such as language barriers in order to support their children's education. In such learning environments all participants come to see that they have something to learn and something to teach.

For further information about the LISELL-B family engagement work, please see:

Allexsaht-Snider, M. (in press, 2016). Families and science education. In L. Bryan & K. Tobin (Eds.), *13 questions: Reframing education's conversation: Science*. New York, NY: Peter Lang.

Buxton, C., Allexsaht-Snider, M., & Rivera, C. (2012). Science, language and families: Constructing a model of language-rich science inquiry. In J. Bianchini, V. Atkerson, A. Calebrese Barton, O. Lee, & A. Rodriguez (Eds.), *Moving the equity agenda forward: Equity research, practice and policy in science education* (pp. 241–259). New York, NY: Springer.

Kayumova, S., Karsli, E., Allexsaht-Snider, M., & Buxton, C. (2015). Latina mothers and daughters: Ways of knowing, being, and becoming in the context of bilingual family science workshops. *Anthropology and Education Quarterly, 46*(3), 260–276.

Understanding Student Learning

The focus of this book has been primarily on the work of teachers and how our research and development projects have supported teachers in their efforts to better meet the needs of all their students, and particularly their emergent bilingual students. Each of these projects has also focused in other ways on how to understand emergent bilingual students' science learning.

A focus on student learning is important from an equity perspective in that while teachers tend to believe that their students are capable of learning grade-appropriate material (Klassen & Chiu, 2010), many teachers are increasingly worried that the next generation of standards and assessments are setting expectations out of reach for many of their students (Haager & Vaughn, 2013). Although some students may demonstrate only limited proficiency in English language use, such limitations should not diminish teachers' perceptions of these students' competence in content area understanding or problem solving. Each of the three projects takes explicit steps to help teachers in not underestimating the abilities of their emergent bilingual learners, seeing them instead as capable science thinkers and communicators.

As one way to address this concern, the P-SELL project developed a research component to explore the prior knowledge relevant to school science concepts that emergent bilingual elementary students brought to the classroom from home and play contexts. Students were engaged individually or in pairs in a science investigation that had explicit connections to home and play contexts (various measurement tasks for third grade; force and motion of rolling balls for fourth grade; and the changing seasons for fifth grade) and were asked to "think aloud" as they engaged in the tasks. Video recordings of the students were then shared with their teachers and the teachers were interviewed about how they saw their students making connections between academic topics and experiences from home and play. The project found that teachers gained a better understanding of the connections that emergent bilingual learners made between in-school and out-of-school experiences and this, in turn, led to increased teacher awareness of the academic resources that students brought to their classroom and improved the teachers' strategies for enhancing emergent bilingual learners' academic success.

Similarly, the LISELL-B project focuses on students' science and language learning both through the use of a bilingual constructed response assessment and by collecting student work samples from science investigations that take place in the classroom using language-rich science investigation kits that have been developed by project teachers and research staff. By trying to understand the linguistic choices that emergent bilinguals make when given the opportunity to read and write in the language(s) of their choice, the researchers are helping teachers and the students themselves think about the intersections of science and language learning. We have found that exploring their students' constructed responses helps teachers to see their students' academic assets more clearly.

The ESTELL project focuses on student learning more indirectly by supporting teachers in better understanding the scientific and linguistic resources that emergent bilinguals bring to the science classroom. For example, the project helps teachers see the value of focusing on Spanish and English cognates that Spanish-speaking students can use to make sense of complex science concepts.

For more information about students' science learning in P-SELL please see:
Buxton, C., Salinas, A., Mahotiere, M., Lee, O., & Secada, W. G. (2015). Fourth grade English learners' scientific reasoning complexity, inquiry practices, and content knowledge in home, school and play contexts. *Teachers College Record, 117*(2), 1–36. (*P-SELL development study*)

Llosa, L., Lee, O., Jiang, F., Haas, A., O'Connor, Van Booven, C. D., & Kieffer, M. (2016). Science achievement of English language learners. *American Educational Research Journal*, 53(2), 395–424. *(P-SELL effectiveness study)*

Maerten-Rivera, J., Ahn, S., Lanier, K., Diaz, J., & Lee, O. (in press). Science achievement over a three-year curricular and professional development intervention with English language learners in urban elementary schools. *The Elementary School Journal*. *(P-SELL efficacy study)*

For more information about students' science and language learning in LISELL-B, please see:

Buxton, C., Allexsaht-Snider, M., Kim, S., & Cohen, A. (2014). Potential benefits of bilingual constructed responses science assessments for emergent bilingual learners. *Double Helix*, 2(1), 1–21.

Buxton, C., Allexsaht-Snider, M., Suriel, R., Kayumova, S., Choi, Y., Bouton, B., & Land, M. (2013). Using educative assessments to support science teaching for middle school English language learners. *Journal of Science Teacher Education*, 24(2), 347–366.

For more information about integrating science and language learning in ESTELL, please see:

Bravo, M. (2011). Leveraging Spanish-speaking ELs' native language to access science. *AccELLerate!*, 3(4), 21–23.

Stoddart, T., Solís, J., Tolbert, S., & Bravo, M. (2010). A framework for the effective science teaching of English language learners in elementary schools. In D. Senal, C. Senal, & E. Wright (Eds.), *Teaching science with Hispanic ELLs in K–16 classrooms* (pp. 151–181). Charlotte, NC: Information Age Publishing.

Assessment Issues in Research with Emergent Bilinguals

With the arrival of the Next Generation Science Standards, which followed on the footsteps of the Common Core State Standards, a new generation of science education curriculum materials, instructional strategies, teacher professional development frameworks, and assessments are currently being developed. As we have noted throughout this book, all of these other changes to our educational system are occurring concurrently with substantial changes to the student demographics in our public schools, including large increases in numbers of emergent bilingual learners in nearly every state and region of the country. Thus, schools are raising the bar for academic rigor and intensive use of academic language while simultaneously welcoming increased numbers of students who will need different kinds of instructional and linguistic supports if they are to thrive in this environment. Assessments, which are often blamed as part of the problem with America's schooling today, are actually just one more tool that can be used to guide and improve teaching and learning, or can be misused in ways that are at best a waste of time and resources, and at worst, abusive to students and to teachers.

Both the P-SELL project and the LISELL-B project have attempted to link evaluation of a professional learning intervention, appraisal of desired changes in teachers' classroom pedagogy, and development of an assessment to measure growth in student learning of science concepts and practices. The development of assessments of students' science and language learning that are not only valid and reliable for a wide range of students, including emergent bilinguals, but also worthwhile and potentially educative for students and for teachers is quite a tall order for assessment design.

In this section, we describe a number of challenges and issues that arise when assessing emergent bilinguals or when conducting assessments of implementation research more broadly. The list is not exhaustive, but rather focuses on significant issues that have arisen in work such as that undertaken by the P-SELL and LISELL-B project teams. We note that in the following discussion we use the term test in a broad sense that can include a wide range of assessment formats and is not meant to be limited to a traditional exam.

Longitudinal Research

The design of the research and development projects that have been described in this book are each conducive to longitudinal research questions examining hoped-for changes in teaching and learning over time. Investigation of the effects of such project implementation requires comparing performance from the beginning of an intervention to the end. This sounds relatively simple and straightforward, but it is not necessarily so. One concern is making sure to measure the appropriate content in a way that is accessible to the learners. Unless a test is designed to fit the level of achievement of the learners in the study, then the results will not be sufficiently informative about changes that are due to the intervention.

Another issue with respect to measuring change over the course of an intervention is to collect data before the intervention starts and after the intervention has finished. Again, this sounds simple, but may be more complicated than it first appears. For example, students, of course, are not blank slates waiting to be filled, and so they will start an intervention with a wide range of prior knowledge (and misunderstandings) that are relevant to what they will be learning. As a rather extreme example of this, in the LISELL-B project, two of our schools had also been involved in one of our previous related research projects, meaning that some teachers and even some students had prior exposure to similar materials, thus problematizing what it meant to take a pre-test.

A third issue has to do with the existence (or not) of a comparison or control group to be compared with the implementation condition. While a true experimental design with random assignment to either a treatment or a control group is a methodologically powerful way to consider whether differences seen after an intervention are possibly due to that intervention, in the case of school-based research, such an approach is often not feasible. Thus, in the P-SELL efficacy and effectiveness studies, the project was able to get permission to assign schools randomly to the treatment and control conditions. By contrast, in LISELL-B, the project team did not receive school district permission to conduct randomized assignment. The school district told the project team which schools could participate in the intervention and which school could be used for comparison purposes. Such non-random assignment clearly has the potential to influence the detection of intervention effects.

There are other kinds of designs that have the potential to accomplish some of the same goals as a random pre/post-assessment design. One of these approaches is embedding tests over the course of instruction, an approach that can help monitor learning over the course of an intervention (Cohen, Bottge, & Wells, 2001). Embedded tests are typically short and take up relatively little time but provide useful information about the change over time in students' learning. One concern with this kind of design is that the short tests need to be placed on the same scale so that change can be measured and compared. This can be done by first administering all the items to a separate sample of students who had already had the instruction included in the treatment. Using an item response theory model (IRT; Lord & Novick, 1968), the responses to the items can then be placed onto the same scale. The LISELL-B project team is proposing to use this approach in the next iteration of their project.

Missing Data

Missing data are a continuing problem of longitudinal research. Participants drop out of a study or move to a different school or miss the day on which assessments are given, resulting in missing information. In order to estimate the model parameters with missing data, maximum likelihood, multiple imputation, and Bayesian approaches are the three must common estimation methods. For the maximum likelihood model, the covariance matrix of all available data is used to estimate the missing parameters (Yuan & Lu, 2008). For the multiple imputation model, imputed data are drawn from distributions and then parameters estimated from imputed data are combined (Ong, Lu, Lee, & Cohen, 2014). For the Bayesian approach, model parameters and imputed values are drawn from their corresponding posterior distributions and then the statistical inference of parameter estimates is calculated from the converged Markov chains (Lu, Zhang, & Lubke, 2011).

Regarding missingness mechanisms, an important concern with missing data is why the data are missing. If data are missing at random, then it can be assumed that the missingness is not related to the intervention. If data are missing but not at random, then the reason for the missingness needs to be determined so that it can be accounted for in the analysis (Lu & Zhang, 2014). Latent variables, such as a student's attitude, can sometimes be the source of missingness (Lu, Zhang, & Lubke, 2011). Thus, in projects such as P-SELL or LISELL-B, it is important to try to understand the nature of missing data. In the LISELL-B project we wondered if emergent bilingual students would be more or less likely to have missing data than native English speakers. We found that during two of the four administrations of the assessment emergent bilinguals were more likely to have missing data than native English speakers, but that this was not true for the other two administrations.

Outliers

Most longitudinal research makes an assumption of a normal distribution in the data. Data from educational interventions, however, are often contaminated with numerous outliers. This is problematic because regular statistical models can be highly sensitive to outlying cases and can result in biased parameter estimates, unreliable standard errors, and misleading statistical inferences, which can affect the conclusions. To deal with outliers and correct parameter biases, new methods have been proposed, such as applying t-distributions to growth curve models for heavy-tailed or contaminated data (Lu & Zhang, 2014; Zhang, Lai, Lu, & Tong, 2013).

To use the example of the LISELL-B data, box plots, histogram plots, and QQ plots indicated that there were outliers for each wave of data collection, so robust growth curve models based on t-distribution were used in place of normal growth curve models. Also, because some degree of attrition in longitudinal data is inevitable, a series of (12) robust growth curve models with missingness were fitted to the data.

Comparing Performance over the Course of the Study

In order to measure growth, we need to be able to compare the performance of participants over the course of the study. This requires some means of placing assessments on the same scale so we can compare them, either by equating scores from pre-test to post-test or by some form of linking test items to a base scale. Equating refers to placing the scores from different forms of a test onto the same scale (Kolen & Brenan, 2004). Linking requires placing the items from different forms of a test onto the same scale (e.g., Cohen & Kim, 1998; Kim & Cohen, 1995). Both of these methods are complex and require care in implementing and maintaining the scale. The type of equating method often depends on the sample size and on the statistical models used to score and analyze the test. If the sample is very small (e.g., samples of less than 100), then neither linking or equating can be done using more complex statistical methods, such as those contained in IRT, and simpler methods, such as simple linear equating, need to be implemented. Because fairly large sample sizes are needed for many of the approaches we are discussing here, it is clear why most research and development projects for supporting the teaching of science to emergent bilingual learners have not addressed these types of assessment issues; they were not working at a large enough scale to generate the required sample size.

New Types of Test Items and New Testing Technologies

New types of test items and new testing technologies require either adaptation of existing psychometric models or development of new models. For example, in the LISELL-B research we looked at the reliability issue in the context of the constructed response and multiple-choice items that we use on our assessments (Kim, Lu &, Cohen, under review). Tests with constructed response items are typically shorter than multiple-choice tests and are scored by hand. Quite often, each item is scored by awarding partial credit for answers that are not completely correct. Current psychometric methods will often underestimate the reliability of short tests (e.g., tests with 5 or 10 items) or tests scored with items that are scored with different numbers of points. To determine reliabilities for tests like this, we extended an existing psychometric model so that it can account for reliabilities of very short tests and for tests with items that are scored with different numbers of points.

Speededness occurs when people do not feel they have sufficient time to complete a test. This most often occurs in tests with time limits. For example, on the LISELL-B assessment students have one class period to complete the assessment. In such a case, the added effect of speededness is not something that is desired and needs to be accounted for in the test design. One approach is to shorten the test so it fits more easily into the available time. In our research, we have found speededness effects in the constructed response items that we have used to measure student achievement in the LISELL-B intervention. This issue may be particularly important when assessing emergent bilingual learners and other students who may need more time to process the language demands of the test.

Different Ways of Measuring Growth and Change

There are also different ways of measuring what examinees know than scoring their items as correct, incorrect, or partial credit. In particular, we can look at the actual answers that students use in responding to constructed response items to see if there is information about cognitive changes in performance. Current research on student assessments in the LISELL-B project suggests that this may be a fruitful means of looking at treatment effects even though the test scores do not show much change (Kim, Kwak, & Cohen, 2016). Our results suggest that the kinds of word choices that students use in their written responses change from the pre-test to the post-test. On the pre-test, students used very few terms that reflected understanding of scientific practices such as cause and effect, hypothesis testing, or independent variables. Most terms on the pre-test were effectively everyday language. Post-test results appeared to be quite different. Students' use of language to construct answers to our assessments consisted of more academic language and appropriate use of terms about these same scientific practices. The number of words students use changed only minimally but the quality of the words used was clearly in the direction of the intervention.

While student assessments have frequently been critiqued for providing too narrow a measure of what students actually know and can do, constructed response assessments provide the potential to give researchers and teachers valuable information about student learning and about the effectiveness of at least some aspects of research and development projects. To use assessments in meaningful ways, we must become more sophisticated both in terms of how we measure science learning and how we disentangle the role of language from other aspects of science reasoning and learning (Solano-Flores, 2008; Solano-Flores & Trumbull, 2003). In other words, linguistic challenges for emergent bilingual learners may unfairly underrepresent their true understanding of science concepts when measured by assessments that are also unintentionally measuring English language proficiency, creating testing gaps that are not truly indicative of science abilities or of intervention effects. Projects such as P-SELL, ESTELL, and LISELL-B have the potential to help the research field get smarter about how to use constructed-response science assessments to support teachers and emergent bilingual learners in documenting their science and their language learning.

Final Thoughts

To return to Dewey, at the end of his life, he continued to lament the disconnect between school and society, and the missed opportunities that resulted.

> From the standpoint of the child, the great waste in the school comes from his inability to utilize the experiences he gets outside the school in any complete and free way within the school itself; while on the other hand, he is unable to apply in daily life what he is learning in school. That is the isolation of the school – its isolation from life. When the child gets into the schoolroom he has to put out of his mind a large part of the ideas, interests and activities that predominate in his home and neighborhood. So the school being unable to utilize this everyday experience, sets painfully to work on another tack and by a variety of artificial means, to arouse in the child an interest in school studies. ... [As a result there is a] gap existing between the everyday experiences of the child and the isolated material supplied in such large measure in the school. (1956, pp. 75–76)

One can only hypothesize that if he were writing today, Dewey would similarly advocate for schools making robust attempts to build cultural and linguistic connections to students' home and community experiences as well. We believe that Dewey would see the projects that are described in this book as positive steps in that direction. All of the project teams engaged in this work are aware that these projects are outliers in the sense that most emergent bilinguals in the U.S. (or in most other nations) are not receiving science learning opportunities that are in line with the effective practices described in this volume.

Developing more nuanced frameworks for studying teaching and learning seems especially important at the present historical juncture of increasing cultural and linguistic diversity in the student population, new cognitively and linguistically demanding standards and assessments in all content areas, and major shifts in fruitful academic and occupational pathways. Existing research has highlighted both challenges and assets for emergent bilingual learners that are language-based, culture-based, and content-based. It is our hope that increasing numbers of researchers, educators, schools, communities, families, and students will come together to connect science, language, and lived experience in ways that help all of us see the necessity of a scientifically literate and equitable society.

References

AERA. (2015). AERA Statement on use of Value-Added Models (VAM) for the evaluation of educators and educator preparation programs. *Educational Researcher, 44*(8), 448–452.

Baquedano-López, P., Solís, J. L., & Kattan, S. (2005). Adaptation: The language of classroom learning. *Linguistics and Education, 16*(1), 1–26.

Bravo, M. A., & Cervetti, G. N. (2008). Teaching vocabulary through text and experience in content areas. In A. E. Farstrup & S. J. Samuels (Eds.), *What research has to say about vocabulary instruction* (pp. 130–149). Newark, DE: International Reading Association.

Bunch, G. C., Kibler, A., & Pimentel, S. (2012). *Realizing opportunities for English learners in the Common Core English Language Arts and Disciplinary Literacy Standards.* Paper presented at the Understanding Language Conference at Stanford University. Stanford, CA.

Buxton, C., Allexsaht-Snider, M., Hernandez, Y., Aghasaleh, R., Cardozo-Gaibisso, L., & Kirmaci, M. (2016). A design-based model of science teacher professional learning in the LISELL-B project. In A. Oliveira & M. Weinburgh (Eds.), *Science teacher preparation in content-based second language acquisition* (pp. 179–196). New York, NY: Springer.

Buxton, C., Salinas, A., Mahotiere, M., Lee, O., & Secada, W. G. (2015). Fourth grade English learners' scientific reasoning complexity, inquiry practices, and content knowledge in home, school and play contexts. *Teachers College Record, 117*(2), 1–36.

Cohen, A. S., Bottge, B. A., & Wells, C. S. (2001). Using item response theory to assess effects of mathematics instruction in special populations. *Exceptional Children, 68,* 23–44.

Cohen, A. S., & Kim, S. -H. (1998). An investigation of linking methods under the graded response model. *Applied Psychological Measurement, 22,* 116–130.

Dewey, J. (1922). *Democracy and education: An introduction to the philosophy of education.* New York, NY: Macmillan. Retrieved April 27, 2016 from www.gutenberg.org/etext/852.

Dewey, J. (1956). *The child and the curriculum and the school and society.* Chicago, IL: University of Chicago Press.

Epstein, J. L., & Dauber, S. L. (1991). School programs and teacher practices of parent involvement in inner-city elementary and middle schools. *Elementary School Journal, 91*(3), 269–305.

Fan, X., & Chen, M. (2001). Parental involvement and students' academic achievement: A meta-analysis. *Educational Psychology Review, 13*(1), 1–22.

Feder, M. A., Shouse, A. W., Lewenstein, B., & Bell, P. (Eds.). (2009). *Learning science in informal environments: People, places, and pursuits.* Washington, DC: National Academies Press.

Goldenberg, C. (2008). Teaching English language learners: What the research does – and does not – say. *American Educator, 2*, 8–23.

Haager, D., & Vaughn, S. (2013). The common core state standards and reading: Interpretations and implications for elementary students with learning disabilities. *Learning Disabilities Research & Practice, 28*(1), 5–16.

Halliday, M. A. K. (2004). *The language of science.* London, UK: Continuum.

Kim, S., Kwak, M., & Cohen, A. S. (2016, April). *A mixture generalized partial credit model analysis using language-based covariates.* Poster presented at the 2016 annual meeting of the American Educational Research Association, Research in Progress section, Washington, DC.

Kim, S., Lu, Z., & Cohen A. (under review). *A nonlinear internal consistency reliability for tests with items having different numbers of ordered categories.*

Kim, S. -H., & Cohen, A. S. (1995). A minimum $\chi 2$ method for equating tests under the graded response model. *Applied Psychological Measurement, 19*(2), 167–176.

Klassen, R. M., & Chiu, M. M. (2010). Effects on teachers' self-efficacy and job satisfaction: Teacher gender, years of experience, and job stress. *Journal of Educational Psychology, 102*(3), 741.

Kolen, M. J., & Brennan, R. L. (2004). *Test equating, scaling, and linking: Methods and practices* (2nd ed.). New York, NY: Springer-Verlag.

Lee, O., Quinn, H., & Valdés, G. (2013). Science and language for English language learners in relation to Next Generation Science Standards and with implications for Common Core State Standards for English language arts and mathematics. *Educational Researcher, 42*(4), 223–233.

Lemke, J. (1990). *Talking science: Language, learning, and values.* Norwood, NJ: Ablex Publishing.

Lord, F. M., & Novick, M. R. (1968). *Statistical theories of mental test scores.* Reading, MA: Addison-Wesley.

Lu, Z., & Zhang, Z. (2014). Robust growth mixture models with non-ignorable missingness: Models, estimation, selection, and application. *Computational Statistics and Data Analysis, 71*, 220–240.

Lu, Z., Zhang, Z., & Lubke, G. (2011). Bayesian inference for growth mixture models with latent class dependent missing data. *Multivariate Behavioral Research, 46*(4), 567–597.

Moll, L. C., Amanti, C., Neff, D., & González, N. (1992). Funds of knowledge for teaching: Using a qualitative approach to connect homes and classrooms. *Theory into Practice, 31*(2), 132–141.

National Research Council. (2007). *Taking science to school.* Washington, DC: National Academies Press.

Next Generation Science Standards Lead States. (2013). *Next Generation Science Standards: For states, by states.* Washington, DC: National Academies Press.

Ong, M., Lu, L., Lee, S., & Cohen, A. (2014). A comparison of the hierarchical generalized linear model, multiple-indicators multiple-causes, and the item response theory-likelihood ratio test for detecting differential item functioning. In R. E. Millsap, D. M. Bolt, L. A. van der Ark, & W. C. Wang (Eds.), *Quantitative psychology research.* Springer series in Mathematics & Statistics, 89 (pp. 343–357). New York, NY: Springer.

Osborne, J. F., & Patterson, A. (2011). Scientific argument and explanation: A necessary distinction? *Science Education, 95*, 627–638.

Rosebery, A. S., & Warren, B. (2008). *Teaching science to English language learners*. Alexandria, VA: National Science Teachers Association.

Solano-Flores, G. (2008). Who is given tests in what language by whom, when, and where? The need for probabilistic views of language in the testing of English language learners. *Educational Researcher, 37*(4), 189–199.

Solano-Flores, G., & Trumbull, E. (2003). Examining language in context: The need for new research and practice paradigms in the testing of English-language learners. *Educational Researcher, 32*(2), 3–13.

Tharp, R. G., Estrada, P., Dalton, S. S., & Yamauchi, L. A. (2000). *Teaching transformed: Achieving excellence, fairness, inclusion and harmony*. Boulder, CO: Westview Press.

Yuan, K.-H., & Lu, L. (2008). SEM with missing data and unknown population using two-stage ML: Theory and its application. *Multivariate Behavioral Research, 43*(4), 621–652.

Zhang, Z., Lai, K., Lu, Z., & Tong, X. (2013). Bayesian inference and application of robust growth curve models using students' t distribution. *Structural Equation Modeling, 20*(1), 47–78.

CONTRIBUTORS

Rouhollah Aghasaleh, University of Georgia
Martha Allexsaht-Snider, University of Georgia
Marco A. Bravo, Santa Clara University
Cory A. Buxton, University of Georgia
Lourdes Cardozo-Gaibisso, University of Georgia
Linda Caswell, Abt Associates
Allan Cohen, University of Georgia
Alison Haas, New York University
Yainitza Hernández Rodríguez, University of Georgia
Elif Karsli, TED University, Turkey
Shakhnoza Kayumova, University of Massachusetts at Dartmouth
Okhee Lee, New York University
Lorena Llosa, New York University
Zhenqiu Lu, University of Georgia
Jaime Maerten-Rivera, University of Buffalo
Daphne Minner, Daphne Minner Consulting
Eduardo Mosqueda, University of California, Santa Cruz
Corey O'Connor, New York University
Gabe Schwartz, Abt Associates
Jorge L. Solís, University of Texas at San Antonio
Trish Stoddart, University of California, Santa Cruz
Regina Suriel, Valdosta State University
Christopher D. Van Booven, New York University
Max Vazquez Dominguez, University of North Georgia

INDEX

academic standards 4–5, 16, 17, 20–1, 25, 27, 71, 149, 212–13, 234
accountability 17, 18, 21, 25, 33, 52, 62, 63
achievement gaps, in science 16, 17
Actor Network Theory (ANT) 72–8, 88–91
agency 122, 123, 129
aging population 3
ANT see Actor Network Theory (ANT)
assemblages/assemblage theory 119, 120, 122–3, 129–35
assessments: as assemblages 129–30; close 36; distal 36; with emergent bilinguals 234–9; math 37; science 16–17, 33, 34, 36–40, 61–3
authority 143, 144, 157, 159–60, 183, 217

Barad, Karen 122
Bennett, Jane 120, 129
"Big Ideas" 20–1, 43, 214
bilingual students 25; see also emergent bilingual learners; English language learners (ELLs)
bodily-affective practices 119, 122–3
Brookings Institution 2
Butler, Judith 120

Callon, M. 73–5, 87, 88
Caspio 98–9
Center for Research on Education, Diversity, and Excellence (CREDE) 158

CFSEP see CREDE Five Standards for Effective Pedagogy (CFSEP)
classroom environment 133
Classroom Observation Protocol (COP) 158
classroom observations 60–1, 229
close assessments 36
cognitive theories 135
collaboration 143, 144, 159–60, 182–3, 223–4
collaborative inquiry 157, 159–60, 182–6, 217
collaborative self-study, by teacher educators 221–3
college degrees 2
Common Core 5, 234
Common Guidelines for Education Research and Development 17
complex thinking 145, 214–15
comprehensive curriculum 18
computers 121, 122–3
content knowledge 18–19, 24, 26, 41–6, 62, 122, 130, 147, 206, 227
content scaffolding 143, 144, 162, 164–5, 174, 178
context: national 16–17; research 17–19
contextualization 149, 150, 182, 184, 218
contextualizing science activity 143, 144, 157, 165–7, 176–7, 184, 189–90, 218
COP see Classroom Observation Protocol (COP)
co-teachers 4

Council of Chief State School Officers 5
CREDE *see* Center for Research on Education, Diversity, and Excellence (CREDE)
CREDE Five Standards for Effective Pedagogy (CFSEP) 142, 158–9
cultural diversity 147
cultural practices 132, 133–4
curriculum: comprehensive 18; educative curriculum materials 22–4; P-SELL 20–2, 215–16; science 17–18, 26–7, 34

data: log 93–118, 229–31; missing 236–7; observational 96, 103
data analysis 62–3
data collection 58–9; common approaches to 96; in qualitative research 124; teacher logs for 96–118
DeLanda, Manuel 130, 131
Deleuze, G. 73, 119, 129, 131, 135
demographic trends 2–4, 17
Derrida, J. 124
deterritorialization 131–2
development study 17–18, 54; characteristics of 32–3; overview of 34; student measures and outcomes 37; teacher measures and outcomes 41
Dewey, John 211–12, 239
Didakis, S. 133
distal assessments 36
distribute expertise 223–4
district coordinators 54–7, 60–1
district leadership 55–6, 228

educative curriculum materials 22–4
effectiveness study 17–19, 52–3, 227–8; characteristics of 32–3; classroom observations 60–1; data analysis 63; logistics and data collection 58–9; overview of 35–6; school districts and 55–7; student measures and outcomes 39–40; teacher measures and outcomes 43–5
Effective Science Teaching for English Language Learners (ESTELL) 180–207, 212–14; contextualization and 218; instructional exemplars 145–7; instructional practices 158–9, 182, 216–17; introduction to 141–2; language support in 216–17; limitations of 177–8; literacy activities 218; overview of 10; pedagogy 142–7, 151–2, 156–7; practices 143–5, 214–15;

pre-service teacher preparation program 10, 147–51; professional development 150–1; research recommendations based on 225–6; science methods course 149–50, 180–200, 214–15; scientific practices and 182; student learning and 233; theoretical framework 142–3
efficacy study 17, 18, 52–4, 227; characteristics of 32–3; classroom observations 60; data analysis 62–3; logistics and data collection 58–9; overview of 34–5; school districts and 54–5; student measures and outcomes 37–9; teacher measures and outcomes 42–3
ELLs *see* English language learners (ELLs)
embodiment 119
emergent bilingual learners 2–6, 120–1; *see also* English language learners (ELLs)
employment trends 2–4
energy sector 3
English as a Second Language (ESL) programs 16
English as a Second Language (ESL) teachers 121
English for speakers of other languages (ESOL) programs 16
English for speakers of other languages (ESOL) teachers 4
English language learners (ELLs) 15; amplified science instruction for 156–79; assessment of 33; assets and resources of 2; challenges for 2; classroom practices to improve learning experiences of 212–18; cultural contexts for 132; differentiated instruction for 4; diversity of 156; growth in number of 141; learning needs of 22; as percentage of U.S. students 16; resources to support 133–4; science achievement of 40; science standards for 16; teaching science to 1–11; underachievement by 141
English monolingualism 3
enrollment 74, 79, 81, 82, 83
equity-oriented pedagogy 221–3
ESTELL *see* Effective Science Teaching for English Language Learners (ESTELL)
ESTELL Dialogic Activity in Science Instruction (EDAISI) 157–79, 186, 187, 225–6; demographics 171; development of 158–9; ethnographic fieldnotes 169–70; exemplifying

scores 171–7; limitations of 177–8; overview of 157–8; post-observation debriefs 170; psychometric properties 168–9; qualitative dimensions 169–71; reliability analysis 168–9; results 171–7; subscale dimensions 159–68
ethnographic fieldnotes 169–70
evaluation: challenges in large-scale 58–63; data analysis 62–3; data collection 58–9; logistics 58–9; measures 60–2; of P-SELL intervention 52, 58–63
Exploring Students' Science Writing workshops 77, 79, 82–5

Facilitating Collaborative Inquiry (FCI) 143–4, 157, 159, 182–6, 188, 196, 217
faculty epistemological stances 188–98
family engagement 231–2
Florida Comprehensive Assessment Test (FCAT) 20–1
Foucault, M. 124
Framework for K–12 Science Education 4, 8, 17
"funds of knowledge" 25

grand rounds classroom observations 76, 77
Guattari, F. 73, 119, 129, 131, 135

Halliday, M. A. K. 5
Handbook of Research on Teacher Education 69
hands-on activities 21, 23–5, 27, 206
health care sector 3
high-stakes testing 16–17, 20–1, 33, 52
home language 135
homogenization 132–3
humanism 123–4

implementation: challenges, in P-SELL project 52–8; fidelity 93–5; of interventions 93–4; prevention program 93–4; science methods course 186–98; of teacher logs in LISELL-B project 101–2
incentives, for schools 57
inclusive pedagogy 221–3
information, skills 1
inquiry-oriented approach 21, 23–5, 27; see also scientific inquiry
instructional practices 158–9; ESTELL 143–5, 214–15; LISELL-B 214; P-SELL 214
instructional technology 121–3

Integrating Science and Diversity Education (ISDE) 158
interactive white boards 121, 122–3
interessement 74, 79, 81, 84–8, 90
international context 7–8
inter-rater reliability 159
interventions: evaluation of 52, 58–9, 226–8; implementation of 52–8, 93–4; scaling 52; school districts and 54–7; teachers as facilitators of 94–5; testing effectiveness of 109–10; see also specific interventions
interviews 124

knowledge, generation of 123–4

Laboratory School 211–12
language: acquisition 6–7; culture and 132; development 23–5, 27, 61, 157, 162, 164–5, 173–4, 184–6, 189–90, 216–17; home 135; scaffolding 143, 144, 156, 157, 162, 164–5, 173–4, 178, 184–6, 216–17; of science 5–7, 76, 143–5, 212–17; skills 5–7; support 215–17
language-based policies 4
language cards 133
Language-rich Inquiry Science with English Language Learners (LISELL) 9, 71
Language-rich Inquiry Science with English Language Learners through Biotechnology (LISELL-B) 9, 212–14; context 75–6; contextualization and 218; data sources for analysis 77–8; family engagement and 231–2; introduction to 69–72; language support in 216; literacy activities 218; pedagogical model 71, 76; Practice Theory and 95; professional learning framework 76–87; research recommendations based on 229–31; results 78–87; science talk promotion and 217; student learning and 233; teacher professional learning and 88–9; teachers' role in 95; theoretical framework 72–5, 78, 90–1; use of teacher logs in 93–118, 229–31; value of theory and practice in 119–37
large-scale interventions: evaluation challenges 58–63; evaluation of 52; implementation challenges 52–8; school districts and 54–7; schools and 57; teachers and 58
Latour, B. 72, 73, 78

Law, J. 88
learning: environment 133; traditional 1
Lee, Okhee 54
limited English proficiency 16
linear theories 135
linguistic blindspots 177
LISELL *see* Language-rich Inquiry Science with English Language Learners (LISELL)
literacy in science 143, 157, 162, 163, 173, 184–6, 217–18
log data *see* teacher logs, in LISELL-B project
logistics, for evaluation 58–9
longitudinal research 235–6
low-income families 3

manufacturing jobs 3
materiality 119, 120
math assessment 37
measures and outcomes: students 36–41; teachers 41–5
merit pay 69
method 119
minority students 3, 141
missing data 236–7
mobilization 74–5, 84

National Assessment of Educational Progress (NAEP) 16, 37, 42, 44
National Center for Education Statistics (NCES) 16
national context, for P-SELL 16–17
National Council on Teacher Quality (NCTQ) 69
National Science Education Standards 17
new empiricism 123–4
new materialism 119, 122–4
Next Generation Science Standards (NGSS) 4–6, 15, 27, 71, 212–13, 234
NGSS *see* Next Generation Science Standards (NGSS)
No Child Left Behind 1

obligatory passage points 75
observational data 96, 103
occupational trends 2–4
ontology 123–4
open-ended questions 61
outliers 237

parent engagement 132
pedagogical content knowledge 46, 62, 122, 147

pedagogy/pedagogical models 212–14, 219–21; ESTELL 142–7, 151–2, 156–7; inclusive and equity-oriented 221–3; LISELL-B 71, 76
Phillips, M. 133
phonocentrism 124
plug-ins 119–35
post-humanism 123
post-observation debriefs 170
post-qualitative research 123, 124
"post" theories 119, 123
poverty 3
Practice Theory 95
pre-service teacher education *see* teacher education
pre-service teachers: enactment of amplified science instruction by 156–79; preparing, to work with ELL students 141–55; recommendations for preparation of 219–24
prevention program implementation studies 93–4
principals 57
problematization 74, 79, 81, 83–8
professional development 31; ESTELL project and 150–1; evaluation of 31, 46; recommendations for 219–24; student achievement and 31, 46; of teacher educators 70, 78–87, 89–90; workshops 24–6, 56–9; *see also* teacher education
professional learning 4, 9, 10, 11, 88–9, 219–24; *see also* professional development
proficiency levels 62–3
project website 24
Promoting Science among English Language Learners (P-SELL) 15–27, 31, 212–14; characteristics of 32–3; contextualization and 218; curriculum 20–2, 215–16; development study 17–18, 32–4, 37, 41, 54; effectiveness study 17–19, 32–3, 35–6, 52–3, 55–61, 63, 227; efficacy study 17, 18, 32–5, 52–5, 58–63, 227; evaluation of 52, 58–63; impact of 45–6; implementation challenges 52–8; implications of 26–7; literacy activities 217–18; measures and outcomes 31–46; national context 16–17; overview of 8–9, 15–16, 33–6; research context 17–19; research recommendations based on 226–9; school districts and 54–7; schools and 57; student components of 19–22; student measures and outcomes

36–41, 233; teacher components 22–6, 58; teacher measures and outcomes 41–5; theory of change 15, 19–26, 31
proximal assessments 36
P-SELL *see* Promoting Science among English Language Learners (P-SELL)

qualitative research 124

Race to the Top 1
randomized controlled trials 57
research context, for P-SELL 17–19
research recommendations 224–31; based on ESTELL project 225–6; based on LISELL-B project 229–31; based on P-SELL project 226–9

scaffolded inquiry framework 21
scaffolding 81, 132, 143, 144, 156, 157, 162, 164–5, 173–4, 177–8, 183–6, 189–90, 212, 216–17
school districts 54–7
schools: accountability for 17, 18, 21, 33; annual evaluations of 16–17; large-scale interventions and 57; trust of 228–9
science: achievement gaps in 16, 17; acquiring and using language in 5–7; field of 132; language of 5–7, 143–5, 212–17; literacy in 143, 157, 162, 163, 173, 184–6, 217–18; nature of 182–6
science assessment 16–17, 33–4, 36–40, 61–3
science curriculum 17–18, 26–7, 34
science instruction: amplified, for ELLs 156–79; changes in 1–2; classroom environment and 133; to English language learners 1–11; ESTELL project and 10, 135–7, 158–9, 182, 216–17; evaluation of 52; language development and 23–5, 27; LISELL-B 214; P-SELL 214; recommendations for 212–18
Science Instruction for All (SIFA) 158
science interventions: evaluation of 58–9, 226–8; implementation challenges 52–8; scaling 52; *see also specific interventions*
science knowledge, of teachers 41–6, 61–2
Science Language for Beginning ELLs 25
science methods course 149–50, 180–200, 214–15; areas of convergence 182; facilitating collaborative inquiry in 182–6; faculty epistemological stances and 188–98; implementation 186–98;

model of integration planning 181–6; observations of 188–98; suggested lesson plan format 206–7; syllabus excerpt and assignments 203–5
science standards 4–5, 16, 20–1, 25, 27, 71, 149, 212–13, 234
science supplies 22
science talk 27, 143, 144, 145, 157, 160–2, 171–2, 190, 193, 196, 199, 217
science vocabulary 162, 163
scientifically based research 85–7
scientific discourse 143, 184–5
scientific inquiry 21, 23, 27, 76, 144, 167–8, 182–6, 212
scientific investigations 214–15
scientific reasoning/thinking 144, 145, 157, 167–8, 184
scientific understanding 19–20
second language pedagogies 25
Semantic Maps 25
soccer, as cultural resource 134
social networks 72–5
sociocultural theory 142–3
Spivak, G. C. 124
standardized tests 20–1, 36, 62
Stanford University 5
STEM skills 2–4
steps to college through science bilingual family workshops 76, 77
student achievement 31, 36–41, 46, 200, 238
student book 20–2
student components, of P-SELL intervention 19–22
student engagement 19–20
students: bilingual 25; demographics of 2–4, 17; with disabilities 33; diversity of 16, 141, 156; interaction 143; learning by 232–4; measures and outcomes 36–41, 226–7; minority 3, 141; mobility of 52; non-mainstream 132; resources of 2; *see also* English language learners (ELLs)
student science academy 76, 77
Study of Instructional Improvement 96
subjectivity 119
supplementary teacher resources 24
symmetry principle 73, 82–5

teacher components, of P-SELL intervention 22–6
teacher education 69; coherence across 148; ESTELL 147–51, 180–207;

ESTELL model of 10, 141–55; lack of ELL preparation in 141–2, 147, 151; recommendations for 219–24; research on 142; in university setting 91; *see also* professional development
teacher educators: experience and skills needed by 223–4; experience of, with new pedagogical models 219–21; preparation of 69–72; principles for supporting professional learning of 89–90; professional development of 70, 78–87; self-study by 221–3
teacher guide 22–4
teacher knowledge test 41–6, 49–51
teacher logs, in LISELL-B project 93–118, 229–31; advantages of 103; development of 96–100; implementation of 101–2; implications of 110–11; parts of 97–8; piloting of 99–100; screenshots of 114–16; teacher self-reflection and 105–9; testing of intervention effectiveness using 109–10; uses of 103–10
teacher preparation programs *see* teacher education
teacher professional learning 88–9, 219–24
teacher professional learning institute 76, 77
teachers: ESOL 4, 121; experience of, with new pedagogical models 219–21; as facilitators of interventions 94–5; further research on supporting 224–31;

measures and outcomes 41–5; mobility of 52, 59; P-SELL project and 58; quality of 69; reflection by, on own practice 105–9; role of 27
teacher science test 61–2
teacher workshops: for exploring student writing 77, 79, 82–5; professional development 24–6, 56–9
teamwork 223–4
technology 1, 121–3
technology jobs 3
territorialization 131–2
testing technologies 238
test items 238
theory of change 15, 31; for P-SELL model 19–26; student components 19–22; teacher components 22–6
thing power 120, 129–30
translation, ANT framework of 73–5
Trends in International Mathematics and Science Study (TIMSS) 37, 42, 44
Turkish National Science Foundation 8

Understanding Language Initiative 5
University Institutional Review Board 38
urban schools 52
U.S. Department of Labor 2

value-added models (VAMs) 178, 225
Vygotsky, L. S. 132

Word Walls 25